the End of the Revolution

Mexico, the End of the Revolution

DONALD C. HODGES AND ROSS GANDY

Westport, Connecticut
London

Library of Congress Cataloging-in-Publication Data

Hodges, Donald Clark, 1923–
    Mexico, the end of the revolution / Donald C. Hodges and Ross Gandy.
        p. cm.
    Includes bibliographical references and index.
    ISBN 0–275–97330–1 (alk. paper)—ISBN 0–275–97333–6 (pbk. : alk. paper)
    1. Mexico—Politics and government—20th century.   2. Mexico—History—Revolution,
1910–1920.   3. Partido Revolucionario Institucional.   I. Gandy, Daniel Ross, 1935–.
II. Title,
    F1234 .H7975   2002
    972.08′2—dc21   2001034623

British Library Cataloguing in Publication Data is available.

Library of Congress Catalog Card Number: 2001034623
ISBN: 0–275–97330–1
        0–275–97333–6 (pbk.)

First published in 2002

Praeger Publishers, 88 Post Road West, Westport, CT 06881
An imprint of Greenwood Publishing Group, Inc.
www.praeger.com

Printed in the United States of America

The paper used in this book complies with the
Permanent Paper Standard issued by the National
Information Standards Organization (Z39.48–1984).

10 9 8 7 6 5 4 3 2 1

By the nature of their geographical location, wealth, population, and character, I expect that the Mexicans . . . intend to establish a representative republic in which the executive will have great powers. These will be concentrated in one person, who, if he discharges his duties with wisdom and justice, should almost certainly maintain authority for life.

Simón Bolívar, "The Jamaica Letter,"
Kingston, September 6, 1815

The President of the Republic in our Constitution becomes the sun fixed in its orbit, imparting life to the universe. This supreme authority must be perpetual, for in nonhierarchical systems more than in others a fixed point is needed about which leaders and citizens, men and affairs can revolve. . . . For Bolivia this point is the life-term President. . . . For Bolivia, I have borrowed the executive system of the most democratic republic of the world. The island of Haiti . . . was in a state of perpetual insurrection. Having experimented with an empire, a kingdom, and a republic, in fact every known type of government and more besides, the people were compelled to call upon the illustrious Pétion to save them. After they had put their trust in him, Haiti's destinies pursued a steady course. Pétion was made President for life, with the right to choose his successor. . . . There you have conclusive proof that *a life-term president, with the power to choose his successor* is the most sublime inspiration amongst republican regimes. . . . By means of this device we shall avoid elections, which result in that great scourge of republics—anarchy, which is the handmaiden of tyranny. Compare the tremendous crises in republics when a change of rulers takes place with the equivalent situation in legitimate monarchies.

Simón Bolívar, "Message to the Congress of Bolivia,"
Lima, May 25, 1826

Contents

Introduction

The twentieth century opened with Asia and Africa in the coils of European imperialism and Latin America in the economic net of the United States. With guns and trade the center ruled the world periphery. In the periphery two social explosions lit up the coming century: the lightning of the Russian Revolution flashed through the shadows of colonialism; and sparks from the Mexican Revolution soon ignited struggles in tropical countries.

From 1917 to 1921, through revolution and civil war the idealistic Leninists nailed down their political power; then fanatical Stalinists took over to make a social revolution and win a world war. By the 1950s true believer Nikita Khrushchev, promising to bury the West, was shaking up his post-revolutionary *nomenklatura* with economic reforms. In 1964 aging Leonid Brezhnev initiated a period of growing corruption and stagnation that would finally issue in Mikhail Gorbachev's desperate efforts at renovation. Perestroika attempted to revive the floundering state enterprises by connecting them to the scientific institutes, and glasnost let a flood of light into the darkness of the political system. In 1991 perestroika and glasnost resulted in collapse of the regime. Throughout the century the Russian Revolution had spawned children in Poland, Czechoslovakia, Hungary, Yugoslavia, Bulgaria, Albania, China, North Korea, Vietnam, Laos, Cambodia, and Cuba, and cousins in Ethiopia, Angola, Mozambique, Namibia, and Zimbabwe.

In Mexico, through revolution and civil war from 1910 to 1920, populists struggled for political power. Then the new revolutionary regime built a state economic sector, carried out land reform, and defended the self-determination of peoples. In the 1930s puritanical President Lázaro Cárdenas armed the masses with rifles and walked among them without bodyguards. He favored striking workers, put socialist education into the schools, seized Tampico from the Rockefellers, and faced down the "seven sisters" of world oil. The Bible-reading Cárdenas discovered that Jesus was a friend of the poor, and persecuted that friend of the rich, the Church. The triumph of the Mexican Revolution was personified in his Jacobin idealism.

After 1940 the regime entered a period of state-led economic growth. This was a time of politicians lining their pockets and workers with empty pockets, but nationalist rhetoric and economic growth continued until 1970. After 1970 growth slowed, as the newly powerful business class invested its capital in San Antonio real estate and New York securities.

From 1970 to 1982 populist Presidents Luis Echeverría and José "Pepe" López Portillo imitated Khrushchev's attempt to stir up revolutionary ideals. This irritated the Mexican bourgeoisie, which sent its capital to greener pastures in other countries. So from foreign banks the populists borrowed huge sums to finance development. But after 1982 the industrialization drive collapsed under the debt burden, and the overprotected economy stagnated: Mexico could not sell its shoddy goods abroad; at home the underpaid workers could not buy them.

Down to 1994 Presidents Miguel de la Madrid and Carlos Salinas tried to stimulate their flagging industries with market reforms that led to the crisis of 1995: the bottom dropped out of the economy and Uncle Sam could save it only through a $50 billion bailout.

President Ernesto Zedillo, an economist trained at Yale, took over the ship of state. Professor Zedillo was a sincere believer in liberal democracy and neoliberal economics. For the first time since liberal President Francisco Madero (1911–1913), Zedillo permitted real freedom of the press. Educated Mexico found its voice, and a flood of criticism lashed everyone from *el Presidente* to the untouchable military. (Television, the poetry of the masses, remained firmly under censorship.)

Zedillo was attacked for his sexual behavior, the generals were accused of narcotraffic, and even the Virgin of Guadalupe had her clothes ripped off. Vanguard painter Manuel Ahumada exhibited a picture revealing the Virgin as a naked Marilyn Monroe—the last taboo had fallen!

In Zedillo, Mexico had found its Gorbachev. Like Gorbachev, Zedillo did not know how to solve the nation's economic problems. He continued to "reform" the economy, but for 90 percent of the population, life grew worse. By the turn of the century, one out of three Mexican children was suffering from anemia due to malnutrition.

Just as Gorbachev lifted the heavy hand of state authoritarianism in the Soviet Union and released centrifugal forces that spun out of control, so Zedillo liberalized the Mexican political system. What kind of system? For decades Mexican presidents had named the governors of states, the senators in Congress, and the winners in disputes between elites. At the helm of the ruling Institutional Revolutionary Party (PRI), presidents steered with a grip of iron. Helmsman Zedillo, a technocrat with no political experience, simply withdrew from the bridge and waved the flag of laissez-faire at the stormy political sea. As so often happens to overcentralized governments when controls are dropped, the system slowly went to pieces. Zedillo did not intend to sink the PRI, but this nerd in the National Palace was unable to stem the rising storm of opposition to the oldest continuously ruling political machine on earth.

In the year 2000 the PRI lost the presidential election. The winner was Vicente Fox, the charismatic leader of the conservative National Action Party (PAN). Fox hails from the state of Guanajuato, where as a manager for Coca-Cola he had become a millionaire and a PAN governor. Guanajuato is the stronghold of the Cristeros, who in the 1920s tried to overthrow the Mexican Revolution with guerrilla warfare supported by the Church. With Fox's victory, for the first time since Benito Juárez's anticlerical Constitution of 1857 and the Revolutionary Constitution of 1917 modeled on it, a friend of clericalism became president. The day after Fox's triumph in the presidential election, the state of Guanajuato passed a law declaring that any raped woman who had an abortion would be prosecuted as a criminal. The Mexican Revolution had given up the ghost.

During the twentieth century the Revolution's attempt to find a Third Way between capitalism and communism had many imitators. In 1924 the Peruvian revolutionary Victor Raúl Haya de la Torre wrote his seminal work *El antimperialismo y el APRA* in Mexico City. He then founded the American Popular Revolutionary Alliance (APRA), an international of revolutionary populist parties trying to realize the Mexican Revolution's ideals of political sovereignty, economic independence, and social justice. Augusto César Sandino's struggle in Nicaragua (1927–1933) was inspired by the Mexican Revolution and was secretly aided with arms shipments from the regime in Mexico City.

From 1944 to 1954 the land reform and literacy campaigns of Guatemala's Revolutionary Party (PR) were modeled on the Mexican experience. Fidel Castro trained his guerrillas in Mexico, seized power in Cuba, and mentioned Benito Juárez as a forerunner—before his Cuban revolutionary nationalists were driven by Washington to pull Uncle Sam's beard. (When they pulled it, he kicked them into the arms of Khrushchev.) Juan Domingo Perón, the Argentine philanderer who led a national revolution to free his country from British economic domination, was a student of Mexican President Alvaro Obregón's writings and an advocate of the Third Way. The Mexican Revolution has many cousins, such as Kemal Ataturk's modernizing revolution in Turkey and the Nasserite regimes in the Middle East. A number of African states have imitated articles in Mexico's Revolutionary Constitution.

The Mexican Revolution mirrored the European tradition of class struggle. In 1789 a revolution began in Paris, and for a generation shook the foundations of European society. Napoleon was the real executor of the antifeudal Revolution; everywhere he went, he carried his law book and put the old order to shame. He was soon suppressed by the Holy Alliance, but revolutions broke out in 1820, in 1830, in 1848, and in the Paris Commune of 1871. The International Working Men's Association was founded in 1864, and the Socialist International in 1889. In the New World, revolutions in Latin America and the English colonies accompanied this wave of political violence. But the nineteenth century was dull compared to the twentieth. Our time has been an electric age of world wars, ideological terror, ethnic conflicts, and social upheavals. From 1889 to 1989 the motor of history was the struggle to achieve socialism.

Poking about in the laboratory of history, political scientists often classify revolutions by their class content. For example, during the antifeudal transformation of France, the fireworks in the political sky— 1789, 1792, 1793, 1830, 1848, 1871—reflected the struggles of the Paris proletariat that did most of the fighting and dying. But the gradual transfer of the bulk of the surplus product from landowners to capitalists, completed by the 1860s, was the secret history of the process. In the end it turned out to be a bourgeois revolution.

What were the social forces driving the Mexican Revolution? From 1910 to 1920 an armed struggle finished off rule by the landed oligarchy, a struggle on four fronts. The Constitutionalist Army seemingly led by the entrepreneurial millionaire Francisco Madero, then by the liberal Venustiano Carranza—both ideologically representing interests in the business community—rallied the northern masses against the dictators in Mexico City. But the Constitutionalist Army was in fact led by generals Alvaro Obregón and Plutarco Calles, spokesmen for rising military stars and bureaucrat-professionals—men looking for a place in the sun. Pancho Villa's Division of the North, made up of "los de abajo" (underdogs), of miserable and forsaken peons and proletarians—the wretched of the earth—stormed down the northern railroad line in a series of suicidal charges toward Mexico City. Meanwhile, in the south, Emiliano Zapata's poor peasants carried on a guerrilla war against the great landed estates in a bloody struggle to retrieve their stolen corn patches. The 1917 Constitution, shaped by the victors in the civil war, contained a social pact among these four parties.

If the Mexican Revolution was a multiclass struggle, it was also a national revolution. Once the landed oligarchy had bitten the dust, its lands slated for seizure and distribution among the peasants, the surviving social classes identified the Revolution with the national interest. The social pact embraced the nation.

In this work we try to solve the puzzle of "What happened to the Revolution?" What happened to the social pact that was supposed to benefit the business community, the bureaucrat-professionals, the proletarian workers, and the landless peasants? Since 1989 we know what happened to the Russian Revolution, but the outcome of the Mexican Revolution is still a mystery.

In February 1917 the Russian Revolution began with the overthrow of the czar and a social pact between business interests, bureaucrat-professionals, landless peasants, and proletarian workers. Six months later, leaders of the business community and the intelligentsia of bureaucrat-professionals happily perceived the revolution as slowing down. However, among the rural landless and the wage earners one could hear talk of "the land to the peasants and the factories to the workers!" Was the Revolution really speeding up?

In *Ten Days That Shook the World* (1919), Harvard graduate John Reed explained what had happened. The national revolution of February was slowing down: the social pact was eroding to the benefit of the business community and the bureaucrat-professionals, at the expense of peasants and workers. At the same time the underclasses thirsted for a second revolution that would go beyond the February Revolution. This second revolution would target the monied interests and the landowning class. This new revolution exploded in October under Bolshevik leadership, and the result was a so-called dictatorship of the proletariat. The momentous historical process that shook the world proceeded at a furious pace, compressed into a period of seven months.

In Mexico a comparable process took place in historical slow motion—not seven months but seventy years—jerking along so slowly that its new revolution never took off. The social pact formalized in the Revolutionary Constitution of 1917 was enacted into law over the next two decades. But around 1940 the revolutionary process began to slow down. It was soon arrested and reversed.

As in Russia during the seven months of 1917 before October, months in which the social pact was collapsing into a one-sided arrangement favoring the business community and its bureaucrat-professional allies in the provisional government, so also in Mexico we can understand the erosion of the social pact as the slowing down of land distribution to the peasants and the end of giving in to factory workers. The rash of wage hikes, self-management in state industries, and the cooperativization of the economy ended in 1940.

By then the moderate socialists in the Mexican government had decided that the revolutionary drama had proceeded through two acts: the destruction of the old regime and the construction of a new one. The first act had dragged on through ten years of bloody civil war, from 1910 to 1920—a population of 15 million had dropped to 13 million. The first act—the greatest social explosion in the history of the Western Hemisphere—had left 2 million cadavers and the birth of a new regime. The second act, from 1920 to 1940, was a desperate attempt by the revolutionary regime to hammer down the De la Huerta military coup, the Cristero rebellion, the coups of Francisco Serrano and José Escobar, the second Cristero uprising, the world boycot of Mexico's nationalized oil, and the coup by the fat, illiterate, Catholic, Indian general Saturnino Cedillo. The second act had distributed land to communal villages, nationalized the railways, doubled wages, and proclaimed socialism to be the goal of the ruling party in the distant future. By 1940 the triumphant but exhausted government decided that the revolutionary process had gone far enough—the time had come to "institutionalize" the Revolution.

The bureaucrat-professionals at the helm of state were former generals vomited up by the armed struggle, upstart intellectuals, lawyers, and populist politicians paying themselves privileged salaries. They feared that in the balancing act required by the social pact—the balancing of business and professional interests against those of peasants and workers—the regime had leaned too far to the left. So it was time to restore the balance by swinging rightward toward the business community.

A big difference between the Russian and Mexican revolutions is that in the Mexican government, the moderate socialists held their own against the social revolution threatening from below. There was to be no second revolution, no Mexican "October."

So after 1940 the pendulum of Mexican politics swung to the right as the regime favored industrial elites with government subsidies, high tariffs, easy credit, and low taxes. Enraged peasants immediately stabbed at the government from the left. Rubén Jaramillo, an old Zapatista commander, rose in guerrilla warfare against the regime, once again demanding land and freedom. He played cat-and-mouse with the Mexican army for a year before he accepted an amnesty. In 1952 he returned to armed struggle in order to protest a stolen election in the state of Morelos. The Mexican army—the last cavalry on earth—chased him around the mountains of eastern Morelos until his amnesty in 1958. In 1962 Jaramillo was sharpening his guerrilla knife for still another thrust when the army dragged him and his family to the ancient site of human sacrifice at Xochicalco. There the soldiers applied the *Ley Fuga*, allowing the Jaramillos to run for their lives down the rocky slopes. A hail of bullets slaughtered them under the pitiless eyes of the ancient gods.

In 1965 radical guerrilla warfare flared up in Pancho Villa's old haunts in the state of Chihuahua as Arturo Gámiz attacked the military barracks at Madera City; the survivors fled into the sierras with the army in pursuit. They were hunted down one by one and dispatched. A wounded survivor hid in a monastery in the mountains.

In 1968 a student rebellion ripped through Mexico City with street fighting, burned buses, and barricades. It ended in a terrifying massacre of innocents at Tlatelolco.

As 1970 opened, guerrilla actions were popping in the state of Guerrero like corn on a hot plate.

Worried about destabilization, the bureaucrat balancers in the government and their socialist allies responded to the new insurgency by urging a swing to the left in defense of the dead-letter Constitution of 1917. They wanted to revive the social pact eroded by the renewed guerrilla warfare answering government repression. Urban guerrillas of the September 23 Communist League were assassinating police in Mexico City as casually as peasants butcher chickens. So from 1970 to 1982 the populist elements in the government tried to restore the political balance by reviving the Mexican Revolution and its ideology. They failed. From 1982 to the end of the millennium, the Revolution was betrayed by the bureaucrat-professionals. They had ceased being socialists.

As early as 1940 the government had chosen the capitalist road of development, and by 1970 Mexico could boast of a flourishing capitalist economy. Capitalism was producing a growing economic surplus, but it was not being shared with workers and peasants. Up to 1970 the business community was taking the lion's share of the surplus as profit, interest, and dividends. But the statistical evidence shows that the 1970s were the threshold to a new economic order: by then the knowledge revolution had so increased the number of professional workers that collectively they were outstripping the business community in their share of the economic surplus. Through high salaries, expense accounts, bonuses, and perks, the share of professionals had edged above that of propertied interests. The business community slipped into the role of junior partner in a new government coalition that shut out peasants and workers altogether.

The revolution had not only been betrayed; an invisible hand had also remodeled the business corporation. Professionals had not only seized the reins; they had become the corporations' chief beneficiaries.

In Russia a different process had comparable results: the Revolution also ended with the victory of the professional *nomenklatura*. Thus, in Mexico political scientists are now using the term *nomenklatura* for their new governing class.

Mexico is the largest Spanish-speaking country in the world, and within a decade its emigrants will make up the number one minority in the United States. The Mexican giant has passed Brazil as an export platform. Mexico is the gateway to the Latin South.

As Mexico goes, so goes the continent.

1

The People in Arms

Mexico is the land of the shaking earth. A fault line stretching through the capital and twenty active volcanoes make this seismic zone dangerous for its inhabitants. Throughout history Mexican society has resembled the country's geological makeup: the crater of revolution has often erupted to shake the nation to its foundations. During the Spanish colonial period there were scattered uprisings against the aristocratic class. In the first century after Mexico gained its independence from Spain in 1821, there were 1,000 armed attacks on the State. The Mexican Revolution which began in 1910, vented subterranean pressures and long-hidden changes. It was the blast of a social volcano formed centuries earlier by the impact of Spanish imperialism on an ancient civilization.

The Spanish did not come to Mexico to develop the economy; they came to loot it. In 1520 what impressed the conquering Hernán Cortez was not the gigantic market at Tlatelolco with some 50,000 Aztecs selling their wares, but the gold and silver jewelry worn by the nobles. "We Spaniards," he told them, "are troubled by a disease of the heart for which the specific remedy is gold."[1] He did not subjugate 25 million indigenous Mexicans to improve their lot. Mexico was a huge vein of silver, and the Spanish opened it to pump its contents to Europe. The "Indians," as the Spanish called the Aztecs, were enslaved in the silver mines; they caught European diseases and almost vanished as a race. The Mayas, who had a sophisticated mathematics and a calendar more exact than ours, met a similar fate. By the 17th century only a million of the original "Mexicans" remained.[2]

Centuries of Spanish colonialism weakened the native crafts of Mexico and made it a land of plantations and mines sending food and minerals—sugar, tobacco, wheat, chocolate, and shiploads of silver—to Europe. The colonial system created a country of Indians and mestizos (mixed bloods) crushed by racist whites. Some of the conquistadors who came from Andalusía had yellow hair, and for centuries they taught the brown Mexicans that blonde and white is beautiful and bright, whereas color is inferior. Then Spain made most Mexicans inferior by excluding people of color from education.[3]

Worked from dawn to dark in fields and mines, the underclasses died of hunger and disease; on the great landed estates the overseers lashed them without mercy. The mestizos begged and starved in the cities; usually at least one of them was hanging from the gibbet in the plaza. As bandits they infested the countryside, and the police nailed them to roadside crosses for a slow death. Over this colonial barbarism floated *Te Deums* sung by the Church while the white elite concealed its thoughts under the watchful eyes of the Spanish Inquisition.

The social volcano rumbled and spluttered: there were Indian uprisings on the land and *tumultos* in the cities. On June 8, 1692, the numerous slum dwellers in Mexico City broke loose, burned down the gibbet and the jail, along with some buildings, and looted the shops. Ten thousand Indians and mestizos rioted all day, and troops could restore order only by firing on the crowds in the evening. In the *tumultos* the social order cracked open to reveal lava below.

INDEPENDENCE AND REFORM

The first eruption of the volcano was the Independence War of 1810 to 1821. With the cry "Death to the Spaniards!," Father Miguel Hidalgo detonated a social revolution: at the head of 100,000 Indians he stormed from city to city setting the Mexican North in flames. Hidalgo demanded land for the Indians and lower taxes. His capture passed the leadership to the mestizo José María Morelos, once a peon, then a priest who discovered a revolutionary mission. Through guerrilla warfare Morelos freed southern Mexico and raided to the outskirts of the capital. But all whites united against his social program: republican government, the crippling of Church power, and land reform. Morelos planned to break up the great landed estates and to give every poor Mexican a farm. The whites pounded down his revolution with Spanish cannon, and by 1820 they had capped the revolutionary lava. Then suddenly, in 1820, the government of Spain itself was seized by—liberals.

In Mexico the white landowners declared independence from Spain—these conservatives wanted Mexico for themselves. This new Mexican elite formed a rigid social crust over the colored masses. Independent Mexico had fertile lands, rich mines, many laborers—and a static society. The Mexican whites did not know how to run a government, for imperialist Spain had always excluded them from administration. Nor could they operate the mines which the Spanish had abandoned. Nor could they develop manufacturing: the imperialists had fled with the liquid capital.

English interests rushed in to pump away the wealth of the mines, and the white landowners continued exporting raw materials to Europe. The new administration failed to finance Mexico's government, and the army and the bureaucracy bankrupted it. Stable government vanished in exhausting civil wars.

During half a century of anarchy, emerging liberals struggled to smash the Church, ally of the landowners and generals. The anticlerical liberals were admirers of Adam Smith and Thomas Jefferson, of free enterprise and democracy. The Church owned half of the land;[4] the priests controlled education and drained off money to Rome. But the liberal elite feared to mobilize the masses of suffering Indians and mestizos. The volcano smoked and rumbled. In Yucatán, Mayan villagers fought the white landowners in the caste wars of the nineteenth century, sometimes supported by the landlords' Mayan serfs. The white liberals, with no social force behind them, shot their brilliant ideas into a void.

Spain had so misshaped Mexico that it emerged from the colonial period economically stagnant, without an independent middle class but with masses of ignorant mestizos, with millions of Indians who spoke no Spanish, without the leadership to free themselves and the nation. As the misery of the masses deepened, a man of the people emerged to lead the liberal reformers—Benito Juárez.

In 1857 the volcano erupted again. For ten years, from 1857 to 1867, fratricidal passions split Mexico open and gushed over the land; churches were looted and prisoners shot; guerrillas roamed the country; massacres of civilians followed great battles; liberals and conservatives captured the government from one another; and civil war seemed perpetual. France intervened on the side of the conservatives, but its puppet ruler Maximilian died before a liberal firing squad. Supported by some mestizos, the Indian President Benito Juárez and his liberals finally came out on top. They delivered powerful blows to the

Church but failed to carry through land reform, and their 1857 Constitution brought democracy only on paper. As they died off, Mexico slid toward the shadows of the Porfiriato. (Mexico's historical periods are named after dictators and presidents: the "Age of Santa Anna," the "Age of Juárez," the "Age of Díaz.")

PORFIRIO DÍAZ: TERROR AND PROGRESS

Porfirio Díaz reigned from 1876 to 1911, Mexico's Age of Iron.[5] He applied the liberals' plan to break up the Indians' communal lands; and new laws on land registration encouraged hacendados (big landowners) and speculators to seize the plots of peasants everywhere. Without land most Mexicans became serfs, migrants, and beggars; some found work in mines and mills—at pitiful wages. The 1910 census reported 836 hacendados and approximately 400,000 rancheros (landowning farmers, typically owners of family-size farms). Half of Mexico's land was owned by the hacendados, and most rural family heads had no land at all.[6]

On the semifeudal haciendas in central Mexico, the peon sweated from dawn to dark, forever in debt to the company store. He slept on a straw mat in a filthy two-room hut with his family. When he fathered a child, he knew it would probably die: the infant mortality rate was higher than in Asia. The water was bad, and horrible diseases crept about. The peon's diet was the eternal tortilla and the bean, and he was lucky to have it: thousands starved to death every year. If he ran away, the mounted police hunted him down and dragged him back. If he stole a peso, he had to endure the lashes of the foreman. Not every peon had access to the hacendado. He might be away in the capital, or even in Paris, enjoying the opera. He was like a feudal lord drawing rent. The hacienda produced its work animals and tools, furnished candles for its church, doled out food to peons from the company store. In central Mexico 5 million peons rarely handled money.[7] A peon might kill his boss and flee to the mountains: there social bandits like Pancho Villa robbed the rich and gave the proceeds to the poor.[8] Sometimes the poor revolted against their masters, but these revolts were quickly crushed.

In the tropical areas farther south there were modern (capitalist) forms of production, as in Morelos, where brown men worked under a glaring sun on sugar farms or in distilleries, or loaded boxcars. But often enough in the valleys of Oaxaca and Chiapas or on the plantations of Yucatán, the coffee and tobacco and hemp were cultivated by slaves bought and sold in Yucatán at $40 a head. It is estimated that there were about 750,000 slaves in the tropical south.[9] Slavery had been abolished for the first time in 1814, and for the second time in 1835; and the Constitution of 1857 was one of the most progressive in the world—but it was honored more in the breach than in the observance. Overseers armed with whips walked the fields, driving the slaves on. At night the foreman locked them in stockades guarded by men with rifles. On a meager diet the slaves were worked to death under the tropical sun. Who were these slaves? Men and women convicted of petty theft, contract laborers tricked into slavery, captured Yaquis and Mayas, and political suspects from every class of society. Conditions were worse than in czarist Russia. Russia's Siberia is hell frozen over, people used to say, but Yucatán is hell aflame.[10]

Foreigners helped Díaz administer the country. The minister of finance was of French origin, and his *científico* friends advised the government. Most of the *científicos* (scientists) were Mexicans who decided that they could develop the country with foreign capital. These Mexican businessmen linked Díaz to overseas investors, enriching themselves through financial maneuvers, land speculation, and the arrangement of concessions for foreign capital. The government handed over the country to foreign capitalists for plunder: they grabbed a fifth of Mexico's land, including the mineral veins and oil deposits.[11] More gold and silver were lugged out of Mexico's mines than in the previous 400 years; the oil fields were the richest on the planet. On railways built by Americans this loot rolled north into the United States, along with lead, copper and iron; or it floated away in the imperialists' ships to Germany, France, and England. The British planned to run their navy on Tampico's oil.

Porfirio Díaz was trying to modernize his medieval nation, but at a tremendous cost in human suffering. In the copper mines, textile mills, oil fields, and railways—owned by foreigners—the proletariat slaved thirteen hours a day for centavos. The owners threw injured workers out to starve; unions brought on the wrath of the *patrón*; old age meant job loss and beggary. The foreign capitalists held down wages while profits soared—out of the country. Could radicals fail to labor in this vineyard? Anarchists went to work, teaching sabotage and the strike. Between 1906 and 1909 strike waves rolled back and forth over the nation, but Díaz halted them with gunfire. He answered rebelling Yaquis and Mayas with the bullet and the lash. Standing on a volcano, he thought he could still the shaking earth with a whip.

The dictator had forged his instruments of power: the army, the *rurales*, the police, and the death squad. The regular army garrisoned the towns and could reach most of the country in hours. The *rurales*

were hitmen who could ride like Satan, formed into mounted state police to terrorize the countryside. Secret police lurked in the capital; uniformed gendarmes infested the cities. For agitators the government
death squad came, usually at night, leaving its victims in an alley or
gutter.

Díaz appointed state governors and political bosses from the top
down; Congress and the Supreme Court used rubber stamps. While
his *científico* ministers bought landed property, many generals acquired
large estates. The landowning oligarchy was the ruling class of Mexico.

Governors chosen from the hacendados gave orders to the army, the
rurales, and the death squad; they kept the sweating masses down,
though peasant revolts flashed here and there, strikes steadily
increased, and Yaquis fought on in the mountains. Planters and
hacendados, foreigners and *científicos* all worked with Díaz to guaran-
tee their labor force: the Mexican people groaned and cursed, but
slaved twelve to sixteen hours a day to escape punishment. There was
no way out. The profits squeezed from their toil were among the highest in the world.

Order and Progress was the watchword of the Díaz era. And there
was certainly progress, as injections of foreign capital into the economy
brought spurts of uneven development. In 1880 there were only 1,000
kilometers of railroad in the vast extent of Mexico, but by 1900 the
nation had 25,000 kilometers of track. Huge locomotives chugged
across one of the largest railway grids on earth. The telegraph network
stretched out to remote areas—a sevenfold increase in size. The number of post offices tripled. The earth vomited up coal; there was a flood
of oil at Tampico. Díaz was building the framework of an industrial
economy: transportation, communication, energy.[12]

Mexico was still "El Dorado," and the silver miners at Guanajuato
continued their 400-year-old quest for the mother lode. But at last
Mexico diversified her exports. Copper, lead, and iron ore came out
of the sierras; the tropics yielded rubber, hemp, tobacco, vanilla, coffee,
sugar; the northern lands threw cattle and goat leather onto the world
market.

Alongside luxury imports for the aristocrats' use, shiploads of steel
and machinery docked at Veracruz. These usually went to mining
camps, railroads, and oil fields; but foreigners and Mexicans were also
building textile factories in the center of the country.

During the Porfiriato, Mexico awoke from its age-old slumber: the
cities began to grow; most of the state capitals doubled in size. Migrant
laborers followed the harvests across the country, and tens of thousands streamed into urban centers. Though foreigners owned most of

the industry and sucked profits abroad, Díaz and his *científicos* said they were building a nation.

Some scholars argue that during the Porfiriato, Mexico was a capitalist society, that the volcanic upheaval of 1910 to 1920 was only "a great rebellion" against capitalism, and that capitalism continued after 1920—there was no social revolution. But in Mexico the capitalist banks, oil fields, factories, mines, and railways were foreign enclaves nailed into the larger semifeudal economic system. Consider the railroad grid at the service of foreign powers: the American- and British-owned railways led north into the United States or to Veracruz (toward Europe); on the trains U.S. conductors, firemen, and engineers worked; American managers pumped the profits out of the country and spent their own exceptional salaries back home; the official language of the railway, spoken on trains and in offices, was English. The foreign enclaves were capitalist but not Mexican. Under Díaz, Mexico had a semifeudal economy, and the Revolution of 1910 to 1940 issued in a capitalist society.[13]

Germs of Mexican capitalism did indeed proliferate in the thickening soup of the feudal Porfiriato. In northern towns like Monterrey and Saltillo there emerged a new class of Mexican industrialists led by the charismatic Francisco I. Madero. The enterprising Madero was an idealist: on his hacienda there were schools and doctors for the peons. The Maderos set up textile mills on their haciendas to turn their cotton into cloth; they transformed cattle hides into leather; and for their vineyards they built a wine bottling plant. Discovering copper on their lands, they constructed foundries to transform the mineral into metal. This brought them into conflict with a rival, the American Refining and Smelting Company, owned by the Guggenheim family. Porfirio Díaz favored foreign business interests: the Guggenheims and the Rockefellers, McCormick and Hearst, Anaconda and U.S. Steel. The growing Mexican business community hated him. The Mexican enterpreneurs were liberals in the tradition of Benito Juárez: they wanted free enterprise and a free election. (In those days "liberalism" had nothing to do with social democracy and the welfare state.)

Another middle social layer appeared in Mexico: government employees like the idealistic military officer Felipe Angeles, the state intellectual Justo Sierra, and the schoolteacher Otilio Montaño; independent professionals like the anarchist lawyer Antonio Díaz Soto y Gama, the radical journalist Ricardo Flores Magón, and the dedicated doctor Mariano Azuela, a physician working with the poor for little pay; and in the emerging industries, executive managers, salaried administrators, technical personnel, supervisors, and underpaid engineers. Their income did not come from owning land, factories, and banks; it flowed in as pay for what they knew how to do. This bureaucrat-professional class was angered by moderate salaries, limited opportunities, and partial unemployment.

In the southern state of Morelos lay the sugar bowl—a gigantic valley filled with cane fields ringed by moutains. The hacendados were doubling sugar production to meet the rising world market demand for "white gold." They needed a workforce during the sugar harvest, but the peasants would rather till their corn patches than cut cane under the tropical sun. So by force and fraud the hacendados robbed the villages of their lands and drove the peasants onto the sugar es- tates during harvest time. The peasants ran to the courts, waving title deeds to their property, only to discover that in Morelos the Constitu- tion of 1857, guaranteeing property, was considered a scrap of paper. The expropriation of peasant land placed a social time bomb in the sugar bowl. Within the memory of living men most of the poor had eaten their corn and tomatos in peace, and these peasants wanted their lands back.

Throughout Mexico, Porfirio Díaz had a policy of encouraging hacendados and foreign surveying companies to legally "denounce" untitled land and seize it. Thus he drove millions away from their corn patches to become a rural proletariat moving from harvest to harvest, or an industrial proletariat in the new oil fields, mines, railways and factories.

When the dictator reached his 80th birthday, the hacendados cel- ebrated at fashionable parties; in Chapultepec Castle twenty carloads of champagne were downed in toasting the "Hero of Modern Mexico" as well as Hidalgo's mestizo and Indian army. The year was 1910.

MADERO MAKES A REVOLUTION, 1910–1911

In 1910 the volcano erupted against the old order in Mexico, and continued to explode for a decade of great battles, the bloodiest in Mexican history. French advisers, Church power, regular army, secret police, *rurales*, serfdom, and slavery disappeared in the fiery lava of the Revolution. This time the lava changed the political landscape for- ever. How did this breakout happen?

Since 1700 serious revolutions in Europe had often been preceded by an economic and financial crisis.[14] The Mexican Revolution fits this pattern. In the center of Mexico the traditional haciendas could not grow the grain to feed the country, and as food grew scarce, prices rose. Expensive food caused people to starve. Agricultural Mexico exported minerals and imported food. From 1900 on, the world market prices of Mexico's exports curved downward, and mines began to lay off workers. In 1907 a recession in the United States deepened the depression in Mexico's export economy. The government, borrowing more and more abroad, slipped toward financial crisis in 1910.

In the same decade the Díaz regime drifted toward a political crisis. In 1904, at the age of 74, the dictator prepared to run for President again. But what would happen to the government when he died in office? Díaz *was* the State. Would his disappearance bring chaos, take the lid off the volcano? The ruling class urged him to pick a Vice President—the brilliant *científico* José Limantour or the competent mestizo General Bernardo Reyes. Reyes's faction saw him as a new and enlightened edition of Díaz, while the white *científicos* hoped to advance Mexico with Limantour. Instead, Díaz chose Ramón Corral, the race murderer of the Yaqui Indians, a man feared by both factions. Could he rule after Díaz's death? The dictator grew older, and the nation drifted.

As the 1910 "election" approached, the Mexican business community clamored for a share in government. Business families like the Maderos—active in banking, mining, manufacturing, and agriculture—resented a government favoring American capitalists over Mexicans. Francisco Madero, the leader of the local industrialists, asked the 80-year-old Díaz to give up the presidency. Díaz stuck to his original choice. Madero writhed on the horns of a dilemma: he foresaw chaos if Díaz was not removed in time, yet feared that removal by force would unplug the crater. "Porfirio is not an imposing leader," said Madero. "Nevertheless, to topple him will require a revolution. But who will it topple after that?"[15] Liberal friends of Madero, such as the lawyer-philosopher José Vasconcelos, founded clubs to support Madero's struggle for democracy. When Díaz blocked Madero, Vasconcelos urged revolt.

The upper classes could not go on in the old way, and Madero called for revolution. His call came from Texas, for the United States offered him sanctuary. This was a change in American policy: for years the U.S. government had deported Mexican revolutionaries across the Rio Grande; the *rurales* galloped away with their prey into the desert; shots rang out, and the prisoner died while "attempting to escape." Madero avoided this fate, for Washington encouraged him against Díaz, who had angered American business interests. As U.S. capital embraced the nation like a boa constrictor, Díaz shook off the coils of Standard Oil. The black gold now gushed from his wells into British tanks. American oilmen said that the old dictator had turned senile. They plotted to retire him.

From Texas, Madero's *Plan de San Luis Potosí* promised democracy and a bit of agrarian reform—the land stolen from the peasants of Morelos would be returned to them. The program called upon Mexico to rise in revolution against the dictator. Democracy fired the imagination of the native business elite; Latin businessmen dreamed of Mexican capitalists in the National Palace. And the promised land reform burned through the rural masses to strike powder: explosions occurred in Chihuahua and Morelos. Guerrilla warfare flamed up in Mexico's North and South. The Villista guerrillas were a motley crew of peons, frontiersmen, cowboys, beggars, bandits, rancheros, servants, mechanics, and adventurous youth; the Zapatistas were "free" villagers who had been stripped of their lands as the big growers in Morelos doubled sugar production between 1905 and 1910. The huge, lumbering mass that does the fighting in most revolutions began to move.

In the opening months of 1911 riders thundered across the wilderness of Chihuahua, raiding mining camps in the sierra, haciendas on the plain, and isolated federal garrisons. These mounted guerrillas flashed out of nowhere and disappeared like shooting stars. One of the brighter lights was the former peon Pancho Villa, the Robin Hood of the North.[16] Another was Pascual Orozco, whose guerrillas ambushed a federal force chasing them and sent the uniforms of the dead soldiers to Díaz with the jibe, "Here are the wrappers, send us some more tamales."[17]

In the South, riding through the mountains below Mexico City, the peasant Emiliano Zapata led peons in attacking the haciendas and towns of Morelos. Out of thousand-year-old villages these men, communing in Nahuatl, began to mount horses and grasp rifles. They wanted their village lands back.

Uprisings exploded here and there across the nation like firecrackers in a raucous religious celebration. "It is an evident fact," a political historian once remarked, "that collapse of discipline in the Army has been a condition of every victorious revolution."[18] This collapse usually occurs (says modern sociology) through defeat of the regular army in war. But not always: for decades Díaz was victorious in the only war he fought—the one against his people. In that war he crushed uprisings in the towns, where he threw in 30 men for every rebel; his regulars machine-gunned Yaqui warriors armed with bows and arrows; his soldiers hunted Mayas for farm slaves. Troops fired on striking workers with deadly aim. But now guerrillas began to spread across Mexico: raging in and out of the forested sierras, concentrating to slay a column of regulars, then vanishing like demons. Díaz ordered his army against them, but some generals were as old as he, and their lieutenants had white hair. They acted too slowly or too late. History is the graveyard of aristocracies that have grown too weak to rule.

The handwriting was on the wall. Dynamite explosions lit up the letters as Pancho Villa blasted his way into Ciudad Juárez. Foreseeing defeat, Limantour persuaded Díaz to resign in May 1911. Spring passed into summer, and the dictator passed out of history. "Madero has unleashed a tiger," said Díaz, sailing for France. "Let's see if he can control it."[19]

THE TIGER DEVOURS MADERO, 1911–1913

In the fall of 1911 an election made Madero president. His friends and family moved to grab the booty of political office. Venustiano Carranza, a liberal hacendado in Madero's home state of Coahuila, got what he had craved for years—the governorship. President Madero's uncle, brother, and cousin trooped down to the National Palace to take high posts; Mexican businessmen had captured executive power. But did they control the State? The Díaz army lay coiled at the president's rear, waiting for a false move. Would the army strike?

The native business community flexed weak muscles as the President threatened foreign capital. For years this tiny liberal group had struggled to grow while Díaz's policies kept it a dwarf. How could it build heavy industry without the raw materials that the imperialists carted off with Díaz's blessing? How could it build light industry without a market? In foreigners' factories worked wage slaves; on the haciendas debt slaves; in the tropics, chattel slaves—they lacked money to buy any goods produced. How could Mexican business compete with American know-how? Díaz laughed at its plea for protection. American capitalists owned more of Mexico's industry than Mexicans did, and the gringos had twice as many investments as the British, the French, and the Germans together.[20] A third of U.S. overseas investment had taken root in Mexico. Even conservative historians admit that by 1900 Mexico was an economic colony of the United States.

Díaz was gone, and native business had a champion in Madero. What was this man like, and the clan he brought to govern? Madero was a political liberal: he believed in free speech and a really democratic republic. He also believed in the economic "liberalism" of his time: free enterprise and a free market. The Maderos, one of the richest families in Mexico, were hacendados getting into manufacturing and finance. They drew sap from rubber trees and processed it; they raised mountains of grapes and squeezed out the juice for wine; they founded the first Mexican bank in the North. We have seen that on their lands they discovered copper. They mined it and set up smelters, which became an important Mexican industry. The American Refining and Smelting Company, owned by the Guggenheims, sullenly stared at this new rival. The Guggenheim interests hated the Maderos. And the Maderos, like the class they led, despised foreign capital.

This entrepreneurial class, a new creature in the sea of hacendados and foreigners, thrived in the North. On the national scale a minnow, but in the states along the Rio Grande a whopper, this new bourgeoisie breathed life into northern politics. The states of the North were growing strong. They gave the young business community clout in the nation.

Madero became the political leader of the democrats. A revolutionary democratic wave swept him into the presidency, and he turned to his first task—taming the tiger loose in Mexico. He ordered Zapata to disarm revolutionaries in the South. Zapata asked Madero if the Díaz officers still commanding the Federal Army would tolerate the Revolution after it had surrendered its weapons. Also, Zapata demanded land reform in exchange for rifles. "Look, Señor Madero," said Zapata (rifle in hand), "suppose I relieve you of your gold watch. Suppose that the next time we meet, you're armed: Wouldn't you demand your watch back?" The hacendados, Zapata went on, had robbed his villagers of their land; now his men had rifles—and demanded their lands back. Why should they lay down their weapons?[21]

Armed revolutionaries urged President Madero to go forward with reforms; hacendados and foreigners insisted he stand fast. Madero and his class were in a cold sweat. Janus-faced, the liberals stared at the masses behind and the reaction before. Madero again ordered Zapata to disarm, and slapped a tax on foreign oil companies. He looked for a compromise. But the agrarian revolt flared up in the Zapatista South; and the American ambassador, an agent of the Guggenheims, began to dream of a coup from the right. In 1912 several conservative revolts occurred; Madero snuffed them out. He allowed the urban workers to organize anarchist trade unions in a labor central, the House of the World's Worker; he sent troops against Zapata's agrarian radicals; he made speeches against foreign capital. He veered back and forth, riding a tiger.

The Zapatistas fought on in the South. They wanted land. Madero's commander took a leaf from the Americans' book: in the Comanche and Philippine wars they had shown how to wipe out guerrillas.[22] General Juvencio Robles now went to work with gusto. He burned villages, herded peons into concentration camps, and hunted down peasants. They fled to lengthen Zapata's columns. Madero tried another general, Felipe Angeles. This new general burned Zapatista villages and massacred prisoners, but wrung his hands over it. The guerrilla war deepened and spread while the hacendados fretted in Mexico City. Madero rejoiced that the "dark vandalism" of the peasants did not overflow to the North, and his generals continued their bloody work.[23]

In Mexico City the foreigners fumed and plotted. The Americans wondered if dollar diplomacy could help Mexico find a better president. Early in 1913 Madero, the idealistic defender of the business community, waved the national flag from the balcony while ranking army officers lured his hard-nosed brother into a trap and tortured him to death. The American ambassador, Henry Lane Wilson, was privy to the plot that planned the President's removal. General Victoriano Huerta seized the presidency and assassinated Madero; the hacendados cheered him as the savior of Mexico.[24]

All the great powers but one rushed to recognize him. In the United States a new president, Woodrow Wilson, was taking office, and he wanted to know more about Huerta. He sent John Lind to find out. Lind suggested that the United States withhold recognition. Alarming reports reached Wilson from other sources. As more and more oil thundered to the surface, Huerta favored the British companies—against Americans. The Protestant Wilson and his Bible-quoting aides began to speak of righteousness and justice, of Huerta's wickedness, of constitutionalism and democracy, of the usurper's dictatorship, of the need for a legal Mexican president. Weighed in the balance, Huerta was found wanting.

What kind of man was Huerta? Amid applause of hacendados and foreigners he calmly murdered the liberals. The anarchist workers resisted, and he drove them underground. He moved from one saloon to another, holding cabinet meetings in barrooms, greeting ambassadors with glass in hand. He strengthened the army. In 1913 he planned to take up where Díaz had left off. He would plug the sputtering volcano with balls of iron.

SMASHING THE OLD REGIME, 1913–1914

For a hundred years the volcano had built up its cone: periodic eruptions released pressure from below but did not blow off the archaic social structure. In 1913 this structure trembled and cracked. Huerta would hold it together, and he went savagely to work. The Church sang his praises. His officers followed orders. The hacendados voiced support through their press. And the English, French, German, Spanish, and Japanese ambassadors shored up his government.

Throughout 1913 the magma of revolution was working toward an explosion that would change Mexico. The Zapatista South erupted in a People's War against the dictator; loud noises came from the North as Coahuila, Chihuahua, and Sonora smoked with revolt. Huerta felt the crater shaking beneath him.

In the northern states three men symbolized the social movements emerging there: Álvaro Obregón of Sonora, Pancho Villa of Chihuahua, and Venustiano Carranza of Coahuila. United at first, these men (and their movements) would end up fighting one another. "This is the fate of all revolutions," remarks one student of the subject: "No sooner is the victory gained against the common enemy than the victors become divided among themselves into different camps and turn their weapons against one another."[25] But in 1913 Zapata, Obregón, Villa, and Carranza had a common enemy—the new dictator, Huerta.

Venustiano Carranza, the middle-aged governor of Coahuila, rose against Huerta first. A liberal hacendado with a law degree, Carranza had served Porfirio Díaz during three terms in the Senate ("the herd of tame horses").[26] In 1909 he frowned on Madero and swore loyalty to Díaz, then asked for the governorship of Coahuila. Díaz refused him, and Carranza decided that the 80-year-old dictator was too feeble to rule. So this Juarista landowner backed Madero's thrust for power, joined his cabinet, and received the governorship of his state. Carranza was content until Huerta seized the presidency and had Madero shot. Then the liberal governor called the Mexicans to arms and proclaimed himself "First Chief" of all the rebels.

In his proclamation Carranza concentrated on political reforms and the struggle for free elections. Once in power, he was of a different mind. The historical evidence is overwhelming: he opposed the growing social revolution and did everything he could to prevent it from happening.

This was not clear to Pancho Villa in Chihuahua, where guerrillas buzzed about the state stinging the Federal Army. Villa accepted the leadership of the First Chief, but he thirsted for social change: first a peon, next a roving Robin Hood, and then a revolutionary chieftain, he knew how Mexico's masses suffered, and he shared their longing for land. Slowly he built a guerrilla army. In the fall of 1913 he captured a federal train, hid troops on board, and chugged into Ciudad Juárez. The Villistas poured out of their Trojan horse to capture this border town. Modern weapons flowed to Villa across the American border, paid for with rustled cattle. He turned south and took Chihuahua City. There, in the spring of 1914, he formed his Division of the North. From every fissure in the old order people streamed into his army: migrant laborers, rootless Indians, mule drivers, deserting soldiers, bandits, beggars, rustlers, cowboys, smugglers, prostitutes, servants, drifters, railwaymen, miners, runaway peons, landless peasants, and *soldaderas* (poor women who joined Villa to form battalions with their own officers). Some of his recruits were put to work on construction projects. He lowered the price of meat and distributed clothes to the poor. He promised 62 acres to every male in Chihuahua. His army's morale rose steadily; the Villistas were marching into a new age. A wave of hope swept over the ragged foot soldiers as they tasted the first fruits of social revolution. They would fight to the death.

Álvaro Obregón who had seized control of Sonora early in 1913, also recognized Carranza as First Chief. A former employee on a chickpea hacienda and then a ranchero, Obregón mirrored his class: he supported land and labor reforms. Most observers agree that he was no radical. Nevertheless, this able organizer believed that social change was inevitable, and recruited into his army foot soldiers from the rural proletariat: miners, peons, migrant laborers, railway workers, and hundreds of Yaquis armed with bows and arrows. He made them salute and drill. Carranza came to Sonora, and for many years Obregón took orders from the First Chief.

In Sonora, Carranza made windy speeches while Obregón organized his Army of the Northwest; in Chihuahua the Division of the North sharpened its teeth under Pancho Villa. Throughout 1913 these revolutionary storm centers sucked youth toward them. Many who could find no place in the old society fled from the southern cities to the storm gathering over Mexico. There were trained engineers without work: in the factories and railways run by foreigners, jobs went to French and American personnel. Men with diplomas could not always get jobs in the government bureaucracy, for there weren't enough to go around. New ideas danced in their heads; some joined the revolution to find a place in the sun. Such elements of the new bureaucrat-professional class were becoming a revolutionary force. Teenagers brought the hope of youth with them. These gusts out of the South accelerated the tornadoes whirling over Sonora and Chihuahua.

In the North, 1913 was a year of guerrillas forming armies: weapons crossed the border into Chihuahua, Obregón put uniforms on his ragged men in Sonora. Carranza, the Porfirian landowner wearing a liberal hat, firmly took command; his program was simple—to remove Huerta and hold "elections." Obregón, who would turn into one of the skilled generals of the Revolution, sensed that only social reforms could bring peace. Villa, the wild man of the sierras, dreamed of transforming Mexico into a free society of peasants, ranchers, artisans, and small producers. Everyone followed the First Chief. (In the South, Zapata's peasant guerrillas rose like a cloud of mosquitoes from the bloody sugar bowl to sting the Federals beyond the state of Morelos.)

Victoriano Huerta, the new President, ordered the northern Federal Army to fall back on Torreón. This desert city on the railroad leading south blocked the way to the capital. There the Federals built fortifications and assured Huerta that Torreón was impregnable. They had Villa trapped in the North. Could they crush him? They were too busy in the South, where the war was spreading over six states. In the mountains of Morelos, the Zapatista guerrillas galloped near Mexico City.

In March 1914 Villa hurled his Division of the North upon Torreón. The fortifications held, and desperate fighting began. From the Villista trenches John Reed wrote reports of battle: "From behind us came running feet, and men in sandals, with blankets over their shoulders, came falling and slipping down the ditch, and scrambling up the other side. . . . Between running legs we could see the soldiers in the trench leap their barricade like a breaking wave. And then the impenetrable dust shut down and the fierce stabbing needle of the machine gun sewed the mighty jumble of sound together."[27] The battles raged for 12 days, as the Villistas fought from trench to trench, from house to house, from grave to grave. Torreón fell, and the federal trains retreated. The Federals fortified Zacatecas in the South, still blocking the rails to Mexico City.

Obregón's army crept down the Pacific coast, urged on by Carranza—he must beat Villa to the capital. In June 1914 Villa's ragged troops stormed the mountain citadels of Zacatecas, smashing the Federal Army and scattering it in all directions. The road to Mexico City was open—a path to glory. This was Villa's greatest contribution to the Revolution: at Zacatecas his fanatical soldiers and *soldaderas* destroyed the power of the old dictatorship.

That posed the question of revolutionary power. Power is the ability to make others do what you want them to, whether they want to or not. In Latin America power grows out of the barrel of a gun: the essence of political power is command of a loyal army. But where was the power? In the South, Zapata directed 70,000 guerrillas practicing hit-and-run tactics with little ammunition; in Zacatecas, Villa commanded 40,000 devoted troops; First Chief Carranza and the (so far) obedient Obregón were shuffling down the western railway line with 20,000 soldiers.

Carranza made the same mistake Madero had made before him. As First Chief with the formal power, Carranza decided that he must seat himself in the Presidential Chair in the National Palace—that would be final. So he ordered his men in the North to cut off Villa's coal supply in order to halt the trains in Zacatecas. Villa cursed while Carranza and the faithful Obregón marched toward the captial. (Carranza correctly saw that the formal power lay in the Presidential Chair, but where was the *real* power?)

The United States had slowly pressed Huerta to the wall. From the beginning he had favored the British imperialists. Britain grew stronger in Mexico. As the Revolution frightened American investors, Huerta stretched out his hand to the British oil companies. Over the diplomats' meetings hung the ugly smell of petroleum. The fumes fueled ideological engines in the White House, and phrases about "democracy" floated south toward the Mexican dictator—a menacing cloud. President Woodrow Wilson and his Secretary of State, William Jennings Bryan, beat their breasts over Huerta's dictatorship. Bryan, a frequent visitor to Mexico for many years, had publicly said in 1907 that everyone should thank Porfirio Díaz for "his great work."[28] But Huerta's work with the British enraged Bryan, and he remembered democracy. The democratic phrases were followed by American actions. The United States refused the dictator recognition, watched arms flow to Villa, and warned off the British. In April 1914, U.S. marines killed hundreds of Mexicans to seize Veracruz, cutting off Huerta from the customs revenues. His government's financial artery was severed; it rapidly bled to death.

In the South, Huerta's government rested on a foundation that was honeycombed, ready to collapse. From Guerrero to Veracruz, Zapata's guerrilla bands had tunneled through it like termites. The guerrilla war had spread to meet Huerta's attacks. In the spring of 1913, Huerta sent Robles to deport 20,000 peasants for slave labor in Quintana Roo. If the guerrillas swam through a peasant sea, Robles would drain that sea. "How wonderful it will be when we are rid of the people of Morelos," he said. "If they resist me, I'll hang them from the trees like earrings."[29] In May he deported 1,000 peasants in boxcars. Soon the hoofbeats of approaching troops sent villagers into the ravines, only to return after the soldiers left. In July, Robles herded families into concentration camps and deported 2,000 people. The officers who reinforced him were even more brutal and destructive. The ruthless Colonel Luis G. Cartón murdered peasants, burned fields, and looted villages. The villages emptied, as the women and children fled to Zapatista camps in the mountains. Children wandered homeless, and women seized weapons to form roving bands. The men swelled Zapatas's guerrilla army.

A People's War exploded in Morelos. The cry *Constitución y Reforma!* grew louder, and the war overflowed to the neighboring states: Guerrero, México, Oaxaca, Puebla, Tlaxcala, Hidalgo, Veracruz. In

Morelos the people seized the hacendados' lands. In September 1913 Huerta gave up, and sent troops north to fight Villa; in the South his generals retreated into the cities while the rebels held the countryside. Zapatistas raided to the limits of Mexico City. To guard the capital, Huerta used troops needed in the North.

Zapata could not take the cities to end the war, for he lacked cannon and bullets. But Chilpancingo fell to him in March 1914. There he captured Cartón and his mass murderers. These officers faced a People's Court, then a firing squad. (In Morelos 20 percent of the people had died.) In April, Zapata encircled Cuernavaca. In the summer his army campaigned on the outskirts of Mexico City and ran out of bullets. He strengthened his *Plan de Ayala*: the hacendados would lose their lands to the people without compensation.

Pressured by the victories of the Constitutionalist armies in the North and harassed by Zapata's forces in the South, in July 1914 Huerta packed his bags full of brandy and fled into exile to drink himself to death in peace.

THE SPLIT IN THE REVOLUTIONARY FORCES, 1914–1915

Obregón liberated the capital in August. In Mexico City he reopened the House of the World's Worker, headquarters for the anarchist laborers, and urged them to join Carranza's movement. The workers turned a deaf ear. Carranza, they said, was no friend of working people. Obregón, promising labor reforms, continued to woo them. He felt more and more uneasy: the urban workers rebuffed Carranza; Villa roared "Treachery" and threatened to march on the capital from Zacatecas; in vain Zapata urged Carranza to accept the South's *Plan de Ayala*, legalizing land seizures across the nation.

Carranza's speeches made these radicals suspicious. For him the Revolution was not a matter of distributing land, of opening schools, of sharing the nation's wealth; it was a matter of constitutional government. Carranza's deeds—before and after 1914—spoke even louder. When his populist generals carried through reforms, he quashed them. Lucio Blanco divided a hacendado's lands among peons; Salvador Alvarado swept out Yucatán's slavery through labor reforms; Francisco Múgica ordered empty churches turned into schools. Carranza tried to annul the reforms. Surrounded by fawning lawyers, the old landowner argued that reforms should wait until he became president.

With Huerta gone, Villa and Zapata slowly turned against Carranza. Their suspicion fractured the Revolution. As the split widened, Obregón suggested calling a convention to smooth things over. Villa and Zapata sent intellectuals and revolutionary generals; Carranza sent generals and lawyers. In the fall of 1914 they gathered in Aguascalientes to decide the fate of the Revolution. "In periods of revolutionary crisis," Karl Marx observed, "people conjure up the spirits of the past and borrow from them battle cries and costumes in order to present the new scene of world history in time-honored disguise."[30] The radicals in the Revolutionary Convention claimed the French Jacobins of 1793 as a model. They declared the Convention sovereign in the land, and talked of revolutionary decrees, laws, and programs that would remake the nation. From afar, Carranza washed his hands of them.

In the Convention, Obregón came forward, hiding his ambition. He urged the mulish Carranza and the radical Villa to step from the stage to permit a compromise. They refused, and Obregón's center group had to choose between them. They chose Carranza, and left the Convention to the radicals and their flaming oratory. In November 1914, Obregón again asked the Mexico City workers to join Carranza, but they had eyes only for the radical Convention. Obregón and Carranza, weaker than Villa, withdrew their army to the port of Veracruz, and the Convention marched on the capital. The Revolution had split open.

In Mexico City the Convention "ruled" for two months; many anarchist leaders worked closely with it. But the powers behind the Convention—Villa and Zapata—could not answer the question What is to be done? Zapata had only his *Plan de Ayala*, granting land to ancient village communities in the South; Villa had only vague notions about land reform. They were two rural chieftains pacing up and down in the big city like lions in a cage, and they hated it. Villa felt at home in Chihuahua; Zapata, in Morelos. Zapata left some intellectual lieutenants in the capital and rode away to the South. Both leaders preferred the saddle to the chair of *el Presidente*. Neither was educated enough to run the government: during the Revolution they read books for the first time. Both were men of the people, and yet the people they knew were in a rural region. How well did the two chieftains know the nation?

The Mexican nation was a kaleidoscope of classes and regions: Mayan slaves in Yucatán, mestizos in the mine pits of Sonora, enserfed peons on Durango haciendas, Yaquis in the sierra, textile workers in Puebla, cowboys on the Chihuahua plains, waiters in Mexico City restaurants, roughnecks in Tampico, laborers in the shoe factories of the capital, metal workers in northern smelters, peasants in Zapatista villages, rural school teachers, hordes of servants in the cities, bandits in the countryside, migrant laborers in the North, and Zapotec Indians in the South—such were the "little people" of Mexico. As this kalei-doscope of races, classes, and regions whirled in revolution, Villa and Zapata went color blind. Each could see only one region—Chihuahua or Morelos, the *patria chica*. They strained to glimpse the whole through the lens of Zapata's agrarian program. Zapata focused his *Plan de Ayala* on the nation, announced that it could work; Villa promised support. With his *Plan de Ayala*, Zapata thought to transform Mexico from the Texas border to Yucatán. The vision of the two men was national but the content was utopian: a republic of small peasants.

In December 1914, in Mexico City, Villa's soldiers looted to celebrate victory. The soldiers obeyed only Villa; the Convention and its President Eulalio Gutiérrez, became a shadow government. For trivial reasons the leader of the Zapatistas in the Convention, Paulino Martínez, was murdered by Villista soldiers. Other smoldering differences between the two groups created a breach in the agrarian revolution.

In the capital the Convention talked and debated, but no dramatic laws were enacted. Across the land, workers and peasants sweated from sunup to sundown. Where was the decree promising land to the tiller? The President was busy calling rioting troops to order. Where was the law guaranteeing every worker a minimum wage? The Convention was occupying itself with colorful speeches. Disorder spread, and the flow of food into the capital slowed to a trickle.

From December 1914 to January 1915 the armies of Villa and Zapata patrolled the nation; they had Carranza trapped on the coastal strip running from Tampico to Yucatán. Would they drive him into the sea? They let the weeks fly past. While the Villistas enjoyed the fleshpots of the capital, the Zapatistas tilled the fields of Morelos. In Veracruz the Carrancistas built up their army. In December 1914 Obregón finally had his way: Carranza announced to the nation that he would carry out political, legal, labor, and land reforms during his struggle against Villa.

CARRANZA TURNS POPULIST, 1915–1916

Carranza's promises of December 1914 were a shout of despair. With his back to the sea, he faced a nation dominated by radicals. To survive, he had to steal their thunder. Thus he appealed to miners, peons, clerks, Indians, mechanics, storekeepers, peasants, migrants, slaves, teachers, the unemployed, and workers—to all the "little people" of Mexico. He forgot no class or region in his new populism. He talked to the whole nation.

In January 1915 his populist politics gathered momentum with a new Agrarian Law. From Veracruz he promised land to the Indians, peons, villagers, and peasants of Mexico. How many noticed that Article 10 provided compensation to big landowners whom the courts had decided had been damaged by redistribution? Or that the Agrarian Law placed land reform in the hands of authorized generals and the governors of each state? (In Zapatista country the haciendas were seized by the people themselves.) These details escaped most Mexicans.

Obregón led Carranza's strengthened army out of Veracruz toward Mexico City; Villa withdrew toward Querétaro to prepare for the last battle. Obregón, the scriptwriter of the new populist rhetoric, marched into the capital.

In February 1915 he found the capital paralyzed: worthless paper money littered the streets; shops were boarded up; factories stood idle; water was in short supply; food no longer rolled into the city; and the workers were starving. Obregón set up aid posts, executed food speculators, and struggled to organize the capital. He began to woo the anarchist workers again. To the House of the World's Worker, the trade-union center or house of labor, he gave buildings and printing presses. His agents handed the union leaders money for desperate workers. He invited the anarchist House to join Carranza's movement, but the retreating Convention drew the workers like a magnet—they did not trust Obregón. When the electricians' union struck against the telephone company, Obregón settled the dispute quickly: he turned over the company to the strikers. He pressed his suit of the anarchist House harder. An open assembly attended by rank-and-file workers refused him, but a secret meeting of leaders finally accepted an alliance with Obregón.

In a pact with Carranza the leaders promised to organize union members into battalions for the army. The leaders agreed to spread Carrancista propaganda among the workers throughout Mexico. With bad grace Carranza consented to labor reforms. In February 1915 these labor leaders tried to recruit soldiers for Carranza. The rank-and-file workers, more radical than their leaders, had no love for the "First Chief," but thousands faced starvation in the hapless capital. To get food and money, they joined Obregón's army: carpenters, masons, waiters, tailors, cobblers, bakers, mechanics, printers, metallurgists, conductors, and textile workers. They formed six "Red Battalions" of 9,000 workers to fight against Villa.

The name "Red" was not Obregón's idea; the petty bureacracy of the House of the World's Worker forced it on him in an effort to win over the rank and file. Obregón accepted it and cleverly maneuvered the industrial workers into forming battalions, but the pact between the Constitutionalists and the House showed his movement's weakness. If the two Constitutionalist elites—Carranza's liberal interests and Obregón's bureaucrat-professional interests—were to defeat Villa's horde of have-nots, the Constitutionalists needed the industrial workers to tilt the balance.

Obregón's army with its Red Battalions marched north. During his advance he spread revolutionary propaganda about Carranza's program of land and labor reforms. Students and generals called meetings to discuss the revolutionary ideology. They explained the Agrarian Law to the people. As Obregón sped toward Villa, he left the House's labor agitators in his wake; they organized unions and spread Carrancista promises.

In the spring of 1915 Obregón and Villa clashed in a series of great battles, first at Celaya and then at León and Aguascalientes. Obregón's advisers had learned trench warfare in Europe: they laid rolls of barbed wire between machine-gun nests. In battle after battle the Villistas, against professional advice, charged Obregóns trenches, only to hang up on the wire under roaring machine guns.

They repeated mistakes and failed to learn. Had their will to win weakened? In war, Napoleon once said, moral factors are to material factors as three to one. The Villistas' morale was slowly fading: in the capital they muffed their chance to govern; next they lost contact with Zapata's guerrilla armies; then they watched the urban workers desert to Obregón; and finally they let him steal the agrarian revolution with populist promises.

Obregón's populism flared brighter than ever. In the midst of the great battles, he decreed a minimum wage for all areas under Carranza's control. Domestic servants, debt peons, factory hands, migrant laborers, copper miners, plantation slaves, textile workers, restaurant waiters, foot soldiers, northern cowboys, southern serfs, urban proletarians, rural day laborers—to all these he appealed for support. Under his machine guns Villa's army broke up, and Obregón pursued the remnants toward Chihuahua. To secure the cities in his rear, the House's labor agitators organized unions.

In October 1915 the American government finally grasped the class lines separating the radicals from the Carrancistas: the old hacendado, in spite of his demagogic populism, was more conservative than either Zapata or Villa. Carranza, winning the civil war, promised law and order; and American business interests wanted an end to chaos. Only then would the profits again freely flow north to the United States. Washington recognized Carranza, sent him aid, and laid down an arms embargo against Villa. This was the death blow: without modern weapons Villa slid back into guerrilla warfare. For years, hundreds of Villistas held out in the mountains of Chihuahua.

CARRANZA DROPS HIS POPULIST MASK, 1916–1920

With the armies of the northern radicals crushed, Carranza dropped his populist mask to reveal the calculating "liberal" hacendado who thirsted for the presidency. He betrayed his promises to the people. This turn to the right worried his populist commanders: Antonio Villarreal, Francisco Múgica, Salvador Alvarado, and Álvaro Obregón.

The Red Battalions were dissolved. In the opening months of 1916, Carranza ordered his generals to arrest militants of the House of the World's Worker. He closed their Mexico City headquarters. In July the House paralyzed the capital with a general strike; Carranza jailed the leaders and broke the strike with death threats. Obregón met leaders in hiding to suggest that they dissolve the House until things calmed down. Posing as a friend of labor, Obregón had his way: the anarchist confederation of unions quietly vanished.

In 1916 Carranza sent his most reactionary general, Pablo González, to attack the Zapatistas in Morelos. There in the South the agrarian revolution was complete. The villagers had divided up the hacendados' lands: some sugar fields and distilleries were owned in common; and a people in arms defended the new order. Generals in Zapata's people's army wore sandals; its soldiers were little more than a popular militia, ready to exchange plows for rifles.

González began a scorched-earth campaign in Morelos. He robbed, burned, sacked, raped, and massacred. He deported prisoners to slave labor in Yucatán. And the old pattern recurred: a People's War surged up against him. Driven back into the cities, his shattered army caught the virus of revolution. It grumbled against the policy of murdering peasants.

The social volcano rumbled under the nation. Villa's guerrillas fought on in the North—this time against the United States intervention under "Black Jack" Pershing; a People's War raged in the South against Carranza's reign of terror; a general strike paralyzed Mexico City.

Carranza's turn to the right alarmed the populist generals and ideologues, military men like Obregón, and professionals such as the intellectual Luis Cabrera. The vanguard of the Revolution wanted to stay in power, and it saw that power required at least the people's passive consent.

The military-professionals made Carranza call a convention to write a constitution for the nation. In December 1916 these leaders met in Querétaro to cast their populism in legal form, and by January they had forged the law of the land. The Constitution of 1917 was—in that year—the most radical in the world.

The Constitution of 1917 contained a promise of social revolution, a program for leveling the social volcano. It was the work of military commanders and populist professionals backed by Obregón. The President decided to ignore the Constitution; Carranza would sign but not enforce it.

In 1917 he launched his second scorched-earth campaign against the Zapatistas, and in 1918, a third. By 1919 Morelos suffered from famine; two-fifths of the original population was missing. High above the Valley of Morelos towered the gigantic mountain Tepozteco, where the Aztecs had fed the wind god human hearts. At its base nestled the Zapatista village of Tepoztlán. In 1910 Tepoztlán contained 12,000 people; by 1919, it had only 3,000. The ancient gods leaned down to slake their thirst, as the sugar bowl filled with bubbling blood.

There was talk of an American intervention. In 1919 Zapata was betrayed and killed in an ambush. His movement broke up, but villagers kept lands seized during the Revolution. In 1920 Pancho Villa laid down his arms in the North.

The military phase of the Revolution drew to a close. The last act in this drama, an armed struggle over the presidency, took place in 1920. As Carranza's term ended, the nation looked for the old "liberal" to allow the election of Obregón. But Carranza betrayed his promise of democracy; he prepared the "election" of a stooge he could control. Obregón revolted, the army rallied to him, and the nation backed his march to the capital. Carranza fled with government gold, but was betrayed and killed in the mountains. The road to the presidency opened before Obregón. He brought his populist style of politics to the government, and Mexico was surprised by—peace.

POPULIST OBREGÓN AND THE CONSTITUTION OF 1917

Obregón had survived them all—Díaz, Huerta, Madero, Villa, Zapata, Carranza—and he controlled Mexico. How did he manage this *tour de force*?

In the torrent sweeping Mexico toward a new order, Obregón had the advantage of the centrist position. In the French Revolution the centrist Robespierre joined with Danton's right to destroy the left; then Robespierre sent the right to the guillotine, and the center emerged triumphant. The process was repeated in the Russian Revolution. Joseph Stalin played Robespierre to Nikolai Bukharin's Danton and crushed the left; then Stalin purged the right opposition and the Stalinist center came out on top. In Mexico the Revolutionary Convention was the first act in the same drama, unfolding scene after scene, from Obregón's split with Villa in 1914 to Carranza's death in the mountains in 1920. Obregón's centrists worked under the rightist Carranza to destroy Villa and Zapata, then Obregón eliminated Carranza, and the populist center became the government of Mexico.

The key to Obregón's victory from beginning to end was his populism. He promised something to everyone: guarantees to businessmen, the spoils of power to the bureaucrats, land reform to the peasants, labor reform to the workers, and defense against imperialism to all classes. To the army he offered plunder and promotion; to the professionals, equal pay with foreigners; and to the intellectuals, government posts.

His rivals helped by limiting their appeals. Madero's and Carranza's 19th-century liberalism aimed to reestablish the constitutional regime, but did not take "the social question" seriously. Villa never got beyond a mild agrarian law, and this came late in the struggle. Zapata's *Plan de Ayala*, promising the return of stolen lands to villages, captured the hearts of southern peasants—there were free villages in the South. But what could Zapata's program mean to workers in Puebla's textile mills, to enserfed peons on haciendas in Guanajuato, to laborers on Yucatán's hemp plantations, to miners in Sonora? The Zapatistas finally published a program of reforms aimed at these groups, but the program forgot to mention the minimum wage and came too late to do any good—the radicals were broken. The labor unions preached a class-oriented anarchism to their workers and ignored everyone else. This anarchist ideology was beyond many proletarians; they could not read, they came from rural areas, they lacked a nationwide union to lead them.

By contrast, Obregón wooed the Mexican masses with simple appeals and popular slogans. He talked the language of many classes and races—he could speak some Yaqui and Maya. To everyone he made promises. His vision was national; he craved power, and he knew it lay in Mexico City. He would use it to manage the masses. He gave the land distribution agency to Antonio Díaz Soto's peasant leaders, money to Luis Morones's unions, and government posts to intellectuals like José Vasconcelos.

Were the Mexican revolutionaries thus betrayed? No. They were co-opted in a social pact that would be enacted into laws in the coming decades. The Constitution of 1917, written in Querétaro under the battle-aged eyes of Obregón, embodied the social pact aimed at satisfying all classes.

By 1917 the nucleus of a new political and military bureaucracy had formed in Mexico. Emerging from the Constitutionalist Army, it had spread over the nation to penetrate the people's life like mold on bread. In its core lurked the army's generals (there were many generals, one for every 200 soldiers). Government careerists near Carranza formed part of the core. Army officers and civil servants made up expanding layers of this new and influential group. And ambitious professionals were climbing the political ladder to pelf and place.

In Querétaro the writers of the Constitution were not brokers, bankers, merchants, rentiers, investors, or factory owners living off profits—they were not capitalists. They were men drawing a salary: schoolteachers, journalists, engineers, intellectuals, government offi-cials, and numerous generals. These delegates to the Constitutional Convention belonged not to the liberal bourgeoisie but to an emerg-ing civilian bureaucracy of professionals. Generals and colonels are also professionals, but in Querétaro "military men constituted only 30 percent of the delegates," Mexicanist scholars assure us. Most of the delegates were young and hungry civilian professionals. "The large majority were young and middle class; because they had been denied meaningful participation during the Porfiriato, many were politically ambitious." The Constitution writers "constituted a new social elite."[31]

This bureaucracy, clutching an unsteady throne, saw that social re-forms might close the jaws of the Revolution yawning below. As 1917 opened, the nation wavered over the abyss: almost 2 million people had died; paper money choked the economy; the mine pits were empty; haciendas lay in ruins; in outlying states, generals ruled by whim. People went about their labors armed. Columns of guerrillas snaked through Chihuahua and Morelos, while American regulars hunted Villa in the Mexican sierra and threatened to roll across the nation to restore order. A Mexican nationalist might urge reforms to keep the nation from going under; an idealist might demand reforms from love of the people. Such motives drove a few of the Constitution writers, but most of the Obregonista generals, political bureaucrats, and populist professionals backed reforms out of an instinct for sur-vival. To retain power, they needed peace.

In 1917 Mexico cried out for reform: the army pushed civilians around at gunpoint; the Church, though weakened, spread ignorance; and a few big owners still held most of the land. Workers and peas-ants, slaving long hours for poor fare, could not read and write. At Tampico foreigners still sucked up the nation's oil and shipped it home.

The Constitution of 1917 outlawed the old Mexico and declared a new society. Yet the old society lingered on. Did the Constitution's authors think to abolish militarism, clericalism, and landlordism with their clattering typewriters? No. The Constitution was a program for social change, a program made into the law of the land. The Constitution promised the Mexican people that in their struggle for a new order, they could count on the government for help. This promise aimed to quiet the masses.

The constitutional program was a social pact among four revolutionary currents: the liberal business community, the bureaucrat-professional elite, the rural masses demanding land, and the radical industrial workers—a pact that would hold for decades to come. The Constitution fired a volley of promises at each social group.

To businessmen the Constitution seemed reassuring, for private property was guaranteed. Through it ran the themes of 19th-century liberalism—everyone has a right to property. Private property, individual enterprise, and free competition promised to become a liberal pillar of the new economic system.

But the bureaucrat-professional elite added to the Constitution several paragraphs with a socialist tendency, guarding the interests of the nation and their own interest against the greed of businessmen. The nation has the eternal right, declared Article 27, to give private property the forms dictated by the public interest, thus opening the door to the nationalization of industries, the formation of cooperatives, and collectivist inroads on capitalist production. The State could limit the size of farms, said the Constitution (and, by inference, the size of corporations and incomes). The State could break up monopolies and, for the public good, curb individual pursuit of wealth. All lakes and rivers belonged to the State, and also the diamonds, copper, gold, and iron in the mountains, along with the oil in the earth. Individuals could own only the land's surface, and they could freely develop their property only if they furthered the interests of all.

To the peasants the Constitution promised land reform: village communities would get back the fields and waters stolen from them by great owners, and the rest of the population would receive land. The big owners would have compensation—someday. (This convenient mañana frightened rich Mexicans.) Their haciendas would be broken up into smaller plots, each state fixing the maximum size for farms. And so the Constitution appealed to the "little people" who might want land: rancheros, peons, villagers, Indians, migrants, and peasants.

To the workers the Constitution guaranteed a better life. Accident compensation, a share of employers' profits, the right to unions and to strike—these appealed to men working in railways, factories, and mines. There were also measures aimed at women: no more child labor, an end to night work for women, and equal pay for equal work regardless of sex. The Constitution, turning toward the peon, ordered a day of rest once a week, the end of debt peonage, and the closing of company stores. For all workers there would be social security, the eight-hour day, and a minimum wage.

The Constitution contradicts itself: it is both *capitalizante* and *socializante*. It springs from 19th-century liberalism, yet contains a sharp attack on this tradition. That did not disturb its authors, for populist ideologues are rarely consistent. They become, like St. Paul, "all things to all men."[32] They try to bring people together, to make the social system work. Far from preventing capitalism in Mexico, the Constitution temporarily strengthened its development. In the 20th century, ruling classes in many countries copied the Constitution's famous Article 27.

This article gave great power to the State. The government bureaucracy, growing ever larger, would use it to build up its power over other classes—through the presidency. The republican constitution, providing for a Congress and a Supreme Court, would become a fig leaf covering the nakedness of the president's power (and he was the bureaucracy's man). For decades he was to make all law for the nation, while the Congress and the Court used rubber stamps.

In Article 123 the Constitution allowed the State elite to step into conflicts between employers and workers. Strikes were legal only if they aimed to restore social equilibrium, to harmonize the relationship between labor and capital. In such conflicts, arbitration committees, with equal numbers of unionists, employers, and State bureaucrats had the final decision. This gave the State the decisive voice, for it could side with either labor or business. The State became the great dictator, the brain making the body's members work in harmony.

The Constitution set the stage for the State to co-opt and control workers, peasants and businessmen. And the Constitution gave the bureaucratic State weapons against those ancient enemies of the Mexican people—the army, the Church, and the oligarchy.

The army was boxed in with rules: in peacetime no requisitioning, no quartering of troops in private homes, no internal police actions; all town garrisons under federal control—to avoid future coups. The Church faced a battery of regulations: foreign priests were to leave Mexico, religious schools were to close, and the State was to take all Church lands—and buildings. As for the landed oligarchy, big haciendas were to break up into small plots, and every state government was to limit the land a person could own.

THE OUTCOME

Historical sociology has discovered that almost every society is governed by an elite that finally closes its ranks to new blood from the social layers below and degenerates into an idle and harsh ruling stratum. When this happens, middle social layers mobilize the underclasses to overthrow the ancient order, and a new elite takes the place of the old. The lot of the underclasses may improve for a time, but they are never the winners in the circulation of elites. History is the graveyard of ruling elites that are murdered one after another in colorful and exciting social crises.[33]

Between 1910 and 1920 the old Porfirian landowners, the liberal business community, the bureaucrat-professional class, the landless peasants, and the exploited workers struggled for political power in Mexico. Madero and his businessmen started the struggle by mobilizing the underclasses, but it ended with the bureaucrat-professional class occupying the National Palace under Obregón. Some Marxists, misled by the liberal ideology of Madero and Carranza, have interpreted the Mexican Revolution as a bourgeois revolution. But its outcome under Obregón was a bureaucratic political revolution with a populist, *socializante* ideology.

Between 1920 and 1940 a social revolution followed. In the next chapter we shall see that by 1940 a complete land reform had smashed the semifeudal landowning class and issued in a capitalist society. While the bureaucracy became the leading class in the Revolution, the capitalists would become its economic beneficiaries. And in the settling-down period from 1940 to 1982, we shall trace a silent evolution in the depths of the economy—a bureaucratic social revolution in slow motion—in conjunction with the abortive efforts of the native business class to acquire political power through a government of its own.

For Marxian sociology, workers and peasants are the driving forces of the 20th-century social revolution,[34] and this holds for Mexico in that these classes did the fighting and dying. (They did not lead the Revolution.)

Functionalist sociology teaches that the conditions for revolution are an unstable society and an inflexible elite.[35] This also holds for Mexico. Porfirio Díaz's inflexible elite violated its own Constitution by stealing peasant lands in Morelos, and Madero attacked Díaz with a program specifically promising to return the stolen lands to the villages. So with the cry *Constitución y Reforma!* Zapata's peasant guerrillas supported Madero's uprising, but the Maderistas betrayed their promise and repressed the Zapatistas. The law-abiding, legalistic, religious, unlettered, traditional, conservative peasants merely wanted their property back. Zapata's original *Plan de Ayala* proclaimed that once the stolen lands had been returned and constitutionality restored, there would be a moderate land reform distributing a third of the haciendas to still landless peasants—with full compensation for the landowners. This timid, legalistic program, typical of the conservative peasant class, was met with implacable rage by the Morelos landowning elite. The peasants only wanted to live, they only wanted to till a corn patch, but the moderate reform was resisted to the death by the voracious ruling class. Thus in Morelos the rulers provoked a gigantic People's War that would finally expropriate the haciendas and deliver a social revolution.

2

The Great Transformation

From 1910 to 1920 the social volcano blew away huge pieces of its cone, but the crater remained. Many of the Revolutionary army's generals began to behave like officers of the nineteenth century: they enriched themselves and shot protesting civilians. In doing so, military men followed an old tradition. Since the War of Independence against Spain, a thousand attacks on the Mexican government had taken place. In 1920 many generals mouthed the old threats and demanded high salaries: a starving nation dug into its pockets to pay.

In 1920 the Church towered over Mexico, cast shadows of superstition across the country, and preached disobedience to Álvaro Obregón's new government. The Church was the inheritor of the tradition of the Spanish Inquisition, of the fanatical War against Reform, and of the landowning bishops.

In 1920 foreigners and hacendados clung to much of Mexico's land, though there were fresh faces among the landowners—the brown faces of mestizos. These were revolutionaries-turned-rich. Mexico still needed a land reform.

The old crater remained—the army, the Church, and the oligarchy. In 1920 the volcano stopped erupting, but had it gone dead? There were rumblings down below. Everyone knew its power: for ten years the nation had suffered chaos; more than 2 million Mexicans had died; and a ruling class had lost the government. In the National Palace, Mexico's new bureaucrat-professionals wanted to avoid a similar fate.

From 1910 to 1940 they slowly leveled the crater as successive presidents—first Obregón, then Plutarco Calles, and finally Lázaro Cárdenas—provided populist leadership for the people's struggles against the old order. The people struggling were industrial workers, rural peasants, liberal businessmen, and bureaucrat-professionals—the four participants in the social pact of the Revolution.

The great transformation did not turn Mexico into a democracy, nor did it raise the underclasses out of their misery, nor did it shake off the chains of economic imperialism. But it brought a political stability unknown in Latin America. The political current that emerged in 1915, and seized the State in 1920, held continuous power for the rest of the 20th century. It allowed opposition parties to run but not to reign. As a coalition of views and parties that finally formed as the ruling party, it was to change its name several times. It was to become the oldest continuously ruling party on the planet. The Mexican party, father of firm government, did not free the masses—it managed them. With their help it broke the traditional blocks to Mexico's development (army, Church, oligarchy) and released powerful economic forces. These forces drove the nation ever deeper into the maelstrom of world capitalism. While Mexico's capitalist development brought wealth to a few, the lot of the "little people" improved only temporarily. Yet the State continued to manage them. For eighty years it applied its tested formula—violence plus co-optation—with unequaled success.

Mexico's great transformation followed roughly the same lines as Russia's great transformation. According to the historical sociologist Karl Polanyi, what we call the Russian Revolution "really consisted of two separate revolutions, the first of which embodied traditional Western ideals, while the second formed part of the utterly new development of the thirties." While the 1917 Revolution was the last of the political upheavals in Europe following the path of the French Revolution, the revolution that started with farm collectivization around 1930 was the first of the great social changes that transformed our world. In Europe, Polanyi should have said, because the 1917 Mexican Constitution had already written finis to the incipient market system in the tropical republic. "To take labor out of the market [Article 123] means a transformation as radical as was the establishment of a competitive labor market. . . . To remove land from the market [Article 27] is synonymous with the incorporation of land with definite institutions such as the homestead, the cooperative [*ejido*]."[1]

Even before capitalism had a chance to develop and become the dominant sector of the economy, it was threatened with controls and restrictions. That was not what Madero and Carranza wanted; thus they were hostile to organized labor and land reform. The 1917 Constitution was not to Carranza's liking; thus he refused to implement it.

After the years of political overturn, Obregón, Calles, and Cárdenas embraced the social pact and enforced the Constitution—that was the great transformation. How did this change come about and what concrete forms did it take?

SLAYING THE MILITARY DRAGON

Mexico tamed the beast that devours governments in Latin America—the army. In Latin countries the politicians often wake up in jail or exile; each country is occupied by its army. This makes for unstable regimes: in 150 years Bolivia has had 180 governments. In 1920 Mexico wallowed in this violent tradition, for the previous hundred years had seen a thousand calls for armed uprisings in this unhappy country, a record in Latin America.

To Mexico the army meant crime and corruption, and by 1920 the monster had swelled to twice its normal size. It staggered under the weight of its huge head—thousands of officers, a general for every 200 soldiers. There were generals 19 years old. The Revolution had thrown up these officers overnight, along with roving bands of armed men, and the nation was at their mercy. They lacked discipline and uniforms, and though some were idealists, many were little better than bandits. Their salaries gobbled up the federal budget while the nation shivered in poverty. How could Mexico get rid of them?

Obregón Disciplines the Rebellious Generals

When Obregón became president in 1920, he attacked the problem in a roundabout way. While he prepared to suppress the generals in the long run, he moved to co-opt them at once. He brought the irregular generals into the Federal Army. They squirmed and cursed, but Obregón demanded submission. He gave them generals' pay, and soon the army was eating two-thirds of the government's budget! In buying them off he bought time. He encouraged the restless to enrich themselves and faced the bitter truth: no general could resist a cannon blast of 100,000 pesos.

Meanwhile, Obregón trained new officers to replace the wild men of the Revolution. He set up a national military academy and sent the best students to Spain, France, Germany, and the United States for further study. He prepared professional officers loyal to the nation.

Rebellious generals lurked in the regular army and remained a threat to the President's power. As he looked for allies against them, his eye fell upon the Colossus of the North. He decided to win the support of the hated gringos for his struggle against the military chieftains, for he remembered that Mexico's history was a graveyard of parties and factions that had antagonized the United States, and he knew that his government had infuriated American capital. The iron, oil, gold, and copper in the earth, said the Constitution of 1917, no longer belonged to private companies, but to the Mexican government. In the Bucareli Accords of 1923, Obregón promised Washington he would not enforce the Constitution against oil fields and mines already worked by foreigners. The United States then threw its colossal weight behind him.

Obregón made workers and peasants his allies. He favored the peasant league of Antonio Díaz Soto y Gama, the Zapatista ideologue, and protected Luis Morones's labor confederation. During any showdown with the army he could count on mass support.

The showdown came. By 1924 most of the soldiers were up in arms: fires of rebellion had flared up in Jalisco, Oaxaca, and Veracruz. In Veracruz, General Guadalupe Sánchez returned peasants' lands to the hacendados and marched on the capital. While peasants attacked Sánchez's army in the rear, Obregón rallied loyal troops to fight. The United States rushed him rifles, bullets, and airplanes. The common people of the North supported him, Mexico City workers applauded him, and peasants took up arms for him. He snuffed out the military rebellions one by one.

Then began the bloody business of reprisals. Rebel generals faced firing squads, and the president sent politicians into exile. But as he punished with one hand, he rewarded with the other—scores of loyal officers became generals. Disloyal officers fled the country, and graduates of the new military academy took their place. The loyalty of the new men reached beyond local commanders to the nation.

Thus Obregón, the Revolution's leading general, crushed his colleagues with the hammer of the State. Some historians believe this was his greatest deed as president. In four years he cut into military corruption, shaved the army's size, and trimmed its slice of the federal budget to 40 percent.[2] He had seriously weakened the army's power. But though the 1924 bloodletting weakened the military dragon, it continued to breathe fire and smoke. The local generals were often robber barons: corrupt, drunken, violent men who ran haciendas and gambling houses for themselves, and protected landowners against peasants. Someday these violent men could devour the State. Would the next president slay the dragon?

Plutarco Calles Starves the Dragon

In 1924 the new President, took up the challenge. In three years he slashed off a further third of the army's body; the men he let go were of doubtful loyalty. As the army shrank, the government threw it smaller chunks of the federal budget. More federal money was left for schools and public works.

Calles wooed workers and peasants partly from fear of the army; he wanted a counterweight to military power. He distributed land to the free villages and took union leaders into his government. People's militias could help him against rebellious generals.

He modernized the military academy and sent graduates to regiments he did not trust. Between the cowboy generals and their private armies he spread layers of careerist officers loyal to the government. The government gave some generals posts far from their units.

The Mexican foot soldiers, peons saluting *their* generals, lived in ignorance and squalor. If their commander ordered an attack on the government, they followed him blindly. They knew little of the world beyond the barracks. Calles tried to turn the barracks into schools, to occupy the troops with baseball, to put them to work building roads. He improved their living conditions and thus increased their resistance to the promises of disloyal generals.

Yet in 1927 the army still gobbled up one-fourth of the government's pitiful funds while the nation went barefooted.[3] In the giant United States there were 64 generals; in little Mexico, 456. With an election approaching, they grew restless.

In Mexico's political culture elections were fraudulent, for the men who counted the votes always won—they were the governing party. In the 1920s both government and opposition campaigned at election time, then began an armed struggle to decide the outcome. In an election they were cocks strutting their colors before the death fight.

There was opposition to Calles's government: part of the army disliked him; Catholics hated him for enforcing the Constitution against the Church; and landowners resented his program of agrarian reform. In 1927 the election campaign against him began. Fed up with his moves against their power, generals persuaded lower-ranking officers to join them—the death struggle was on. Within a month Calles crushed them. He stood the leaders against the wall, and the dragon bled again.

As Calles stepped down from the presidency, the army had weakened—but not fatally. Many of its generals were murderers, ready to
kill anyone in their way, and they would never be satisfied with provincial commands.

From 1928 to 1934 Calles was the nations's Gray Eminence, moving
puppet presidents across the political stage in Mexico City. He continued his policies of shifting and retiring the revolutionary generals. In
1929, during the election of a presidential puppet, the generals struck
again; they carried away most of the army. Calles took charge of the
fight against them.

He could count on the professional officer corps drawn from the
academy; worker groups supported him; and thousands of peasants
hurried to help the government. The United States again sent large
shipments of arms: chaos in Mexico was bad for American business,
and Washington wanted the rebellion crushed. With aid from the
popular masses, Calles smashed the revolt in two months. Shootings
and exiles followed.

Lázaro Cárdenas Strikes the Death Blow

Was the military monster mortally wounded? President Cárdenas
(1934–1940) was not sure; he continued to undermine the power of the
remaining chieftains. He retired generals, shifted commands, and made
the troops build roads and schools. He passed a law against political
activity by officers and required competitive examinations for promotion. In 1936 he sent some generals into exile. The army's share of the
federal budget slipped to one-sixth. The government saved money for
its modernization program: roads, dams, schools, railways, industry.

In the 1930s the world economic crisis was shaking up societies everywhere, and social unrest spread to Mexico. Cárdenas answered
strike waves and agrarian revolts with labor and land reforms. A few
generals, by now hacendados or businessmen, turned against a president calling for union power and land to peasants. As a check on these
generals, Cárdenas distributed rifles and organized a peasant militia.
The handful of reactionary generals muttered threats. Would the army
follow them? For a generation officers loyal to the president had trick-
led out of the academy into the army. President Cárdenas took no
chances: he also formed a workers' militia, equipped it with rifles and
uniforms. His peasant and worker militiamen soon outnumbered the
soldiers two to one. For the army it was checkmate.

General Saturnino Cedillo, the boss of San Luis Potosí, could not
believe it. Cedillo had entered history as a peasant revolutionary,

gained control of a state, and turned it into his private kingdom. He became rich, Catholic, and conservative. In 1938, with thousands of personal troops, this barely literate strongman rose against Cárdenas and called for army support. But the army was a new creature, staffed by officers loyal to the President, whoever he might be. Cárdenas sent the army against Cedillo, and the peasant militia rushed to support it. The President forced Cedillo's surrender, and shot him. No general ever tried a coup again.

An End to Military Coups?

In the 1940s Mexican presidents suspiciously watched their generals, but the army was a paper dragon. By 1940 Obregón, Calles, and Cárdenas, relying on mass support, had turned the army into a tool of government. The army found enough to do putting up schoolhouses, repairing roads, planting forests, building hospitals, and digging canals. Civilians controlled the ruling party, the big motor that drove the small motor of the military. For decades the army bit out only one-tenth of the budget; it absorbed a smaller percentage of national production than almost any military force in Latin America.[4] (But in the 1990s, with the turn away from the ideology of the Mexican Revolution, spending on the military and its repressive power as an internal police force soared again.)

During the Cold War in the 1950s, the United States built a war economy and expanded its influence and military power over scores of nations; by 1960 Latin American armies had received millions of dollars' worth of U.S. guns, bullets, tanks, and planes. In those days the "Free World" consisted of all those countries that got free arms from the United States. The Latin armies took this aid like alcoholics sipping a bottle of rum. Latin politicians who angered Washington first saw the bottle stoppered, then heard tanks smash the gates of the presidential palace, and finally found themselves in exile. But for decades the Mexican army did not become addicted to U.S. aid. Though the Mexican generals wanted to accept Washington's offer, the politicians pushed the bottle away: they thought it contained a genie beyond their control. Through years of struggle they had tamed the army, and they wanted it weak and obedient. (With the end of the revolutionary tradition in the 1990s, the Mexican army's links with the Pentagon were forged again, and Mexico had many officers studying counterinsurgency in Georgia at the Escuela de las Amércias—called by progressive *políticos* "the School of the Dictators.")

Today the army's task is to enforce the will of the ruling class within Mexico. Every big town has a garrison on the hill, and the troops put down any rebellion. In a nation of suffering millions where violence is common, the army guards banks in the cities, shoots Indian tribes in revolt, hunts guerrillas in the sierra, or scatters demonstrations of striking workers. It has also fired on university students. Though the army cannot legally take part in political struggles, it is hardly neutral—it supports the regime. In the developing world Mexico's army stands out for its servility. In the second half of the 20th century, countries in Asia, Africa, and Latin America have often been run by generals, but Mexico has curbed its officers. The nation broke its century-old tradition of militarism and became the exception among countries south of the Rio Grande.

TAMING THE CLERICAL MONSTER

Alongside its struggle with the army, Mexico waged war against the Church, several terrible battles growing out of the contest between priest and president, a rivalry with roots in the 19th century. Mexico was born in 1821. The new nation suffered from a tumor it carried within—the Catholic clergy. In Europe, before the tumor could become cancerous, it had been slashed by radical surgeons: Diderot, Voltaire, Fouchet, Robespierre. In Mexico it grew ever larger. As the Industrial Revolution hurled Europe forward into the 19th century, the Catholic Church dragged Mexico back into the feudal past. For the Church was an economic power; it owned half of Mexico's land down to Juárez's *Reforma* in the 1860s (then got some of it back under Porfirio Díaz). Mexico had won independence from Spain but was still kowtowing to the Roman Pope. As the nation's banker, the Church sat on the liquid capital or sent it to the Vatican. It controlled education: while the French studied Copernicus, Laplace, and Lamarck, Mexicans learned how the sun goes round an earth created by God in six days. The Church was a political force; priests propped up governments to their liking and sabotaged the rest. No matter what crime a priest committed, he faced a Church court—the State could not touch him. The Mexican Church was a state within the State.

In the 1860s Benito Juárez and the liberals weakened the Church, but in 1910 it was still a major landowner and controlled many schools. It encouraged mass ignorance, supported dictatorial government, and ran medieval convents.

The Revolution of 1910–1920 met an implacable enemy in the Church. The religious hierarchy and the Catholic press backed the dictators Díaz and Victoriano Huerta, sided with the hacendados against the people, and turned a stone face toward Venustiano Carranza's government (1916–1920). So in the Constitution of 1917 the federal government urged the states to limit the number of priests within their borders, declared all religious buildings government property, outlawed the ownership of land by the Church, and banned foreign priests from giving the sacraments. Since many of backward Mexico's priests came from the surplus in Spain and Italy, the Constitution imposed a near-death sentence on the Church. But Carranza refused to enforce it.

President Obregón (1920–1924) took parts of the Constitution seriously. The Church preached disobedience to his government and sneered at the highest law in the land. Priests behaved as if the year were 1820 instead of 1920. Ten years of revolutionary violence had smashed the old political system, robbed the Church of its lands, and raised the hopes of poor peons and hungry miners, of peasants in remote villages and the underclasses in the cities. The voltage of the Revolution shocked Mexico's static society into motion; the people longed for social justice. But justice in this world did not interest the Church. "Blessed are you poor," Jesus had said, "for yours is the kingdom of God." A kingdom in the *next* world, the priests added, for in this life the poor must suffer the wickedness of the rich. For centuries Mexicans had listened to the Church's message: "Obey!"

By 1920 the mood of the people had changed. They welcomed the new programs of land reform and mass education. Obregón began his administration with a literacy campaign based on the simple idea that those who can read should teach those who can't. Soon reading classes were meeting in plazas, in homes, on street corners. Mexico, where eight out of ten people could neither read nor write, had begun to drag itself out of the Middle Ages. The Church frowned on this new progress. Such enlightenment might scatter the shadowy mysteries of faith.

The economic base of the Church had disintegrated during the Revolution, but its ideological superstructure remained as rigid as ever: the priests preached ancient dogma and ritual in a foreign language, fostered superstition and ignorance among the peasants, and fought against education for the people. Like Pope Pius IX in 1864, the priests remained irreconcilably opposed to "progress, liberalism, and modern civilization."[5] The Catholic leadership feared that education would turn millions from the Church, as the schools had done in Europe. But the government needed mass education to build a modern nation. On the horizon loomed a war between Church and State.

In its schools the Church dished out medieval instruction to a few and worked against the government's efforts to enlighten the many. Obregón appointed José Vasconcelos, the Maderista revolutionary who trusted in the bourgeoisie, to be Secretary of Public Education. This passionate democrat represented the liberal tendency in the Revolution. His faith in education as a basis for building democracy was contagious, and he sent volunteer teachers to the villages with no money and a revolutionary mission. For four years the brilliant Madero-worshiping Vasconcelos laid the foundation for an educational program that would astonish the world.

Calles Savors the Blood of Martyrs

The teachers went to live in the villages, and by the end of 1924 the peasants had built themselves a thousand schools. President Calles (1924–1928) deepened and spread this missionary program. The teachers were young idealists who disliked religion—to them it seemed superstition. Soon the villages became arenas for the struggle between teachers and priests. For centuries the priests had argued against Indian beliefs that people had descended from a jaguar; the teachers arrived to say that humans had come from an ape. The enraged priests counterattacked. By pointing to a drought as an act of God against these devilish ideas, the priests sometimes persuaded peasants to stone their teachers. But usually the peasants' thirst for education was too strong, and the priests lost ground all along the line. The Mexican peasants enjoyed their taste of progress.

In the 1920s agrarian agitators organized peasants to demand the land reform promised in the Constitution. The religious hierarchy sided with the landowners against these reformers, and priests undermined the work of peasant leagues in the countryside. The agrarian reformers redoubled their efforts. A few governors helped them regain lands stolen by hacendados.

By 1926 the Church, thoroughly fed up, began to move against the government. The archbishop announced that Mexican priests would never observe the Constitution's regulation of religious activities; the bishops called on Catholics to demand constitutional changes. President Calles urged Catholic leaders to compromise, but the bishops and their conservative supporters wanted a showdown. Calles accepted the challenge: he ordered foreign priests out of the country, closed religious schools, and confiscated churches. He began to enforce the Constitution; he persecuted religion. The Church went on strike and refused to give the sacraments in Mexico—priests walked off the job. Without the sacraments—without confession, absolution, and the last rites—sinful Mexicans would fall into hell. In those days hell had fire in it and the faithful were frightened. Would Catholic Mexico rise in revolt and destroy the government?[6]

There were Catholic rebellions. From 1926 to 1929 violence raged across Mexico in the Cristero War against the government. In this civil war several social tendencies surfaced: in Morelos, peasant radicals fought for land; in Jalisco greedy generals massacred Catholics to seize their goods. But the essence of the Cristero rebellion was conservative. Hacendados rallied to it, as the faithful in Jalisco, Nayarit and Durango rose in arms. The government crushed them, and they took to guerrilla warfare. The guerrillas killed the new teachers or cut off their noses; federal troops hanged peaceful Catholics from telegraph poles; religious rebels murdered agrarian reformers in the countryside. Three years of senseless violence shook Mexico. Jesuit priests with machine guns, teachers without noses, dynamited passenger trains, demolished schoolhouses, burning cornfields, government massacres—scene after scene of the tragedy rushed past. By 1929 the Church concluded that it was no match for the government, for most people did not support the Cristeros. The Church ended its strike and the war stopped. Church and State struck a compromise.

The priests had learned their lesson; they wanted the truce to become a permanent peace. But Calles had tasted blood, and he liked it. As the nation's Gray Eminence he goaded succeeding presidents to revive the antireligious campaign in several states; in 1931 it flared up brightly in the work of the Revolutionary Anticlerical League of Mexico. In Veracruz bombs exploded in churches, and the state government limited the number of priests to one per 100,000 people. In Tabasco the Red Shirts killed Christians and marched with banners that showed fat priests collecting money from the starving poor. In 1932 every state passed laws limiting the number of priests. The Church, worried by the threat of another war it could not win, ordered Christians to avoid violence and condemned sporadic outbreaks of guerrilla warfare against the government.

Cárdenas Supports Socialist Education

Ex-President Calles, becoming rich and politically moderate, wanted to disguise himself as a continuing revolutionary. In 1934 he issued his famous Call from Guadalajara, explaining that Mexico was entering a new period called the "psychological Revolution."[7] He planned to secularize the minds of the next generation through "socialist education"—godless education. President Cárdenas (1934–1940) accepted this plan and tried to implement it.

Tabasco, where Red Shirts terrorized priests, had become the laboratory of the "psychological Revolution." The government's Revolutionary National Party had made six years of "socialist education" for every child in Mexico a constitutional principle.

President Cárdenas set the pace for all those who hated religion. In 1935 waves of government persecution swept over the Church: hundreds of buildings were confiscated; only 300 priests remained in the country. Caught up in the momentum of this de-Christianization campaign, Cárdenas was outdone only by President Calles's terror against the Church.

In 1935 thousands of guerrillas rose again in a second religious insurrection. For three years Cristeros murdered agrarian reformers, wrecked schools, killed teachers, and cut off 200 pairs of ears. But the priests condemned these religious warriors and ordered the faithful to turn them in: the Church had learned that it could not beat the government. With radios and airplanes the federal armies hunted down the guerrillas to give them a martyr's death.

At last the Church had become a loyal supporter of the government. Cárdenas called off the campaign against religion and ended rationalist propaganda in the schools. Socialist symbols vanished. The strains of the *Internationale* no longer floated from classroom windows.

By the end of Cárdenas's term Church and State were at peace. The Church accepted the Mexican Revolution as irreversible; the government stopped enforcing the Constitution against religion. Since 1940 part of the Church has drawn closer to the poor of Mexico, and today some of the clergy are the vanguard in the people's struggles. The clerical engine has jumped its 500-year-old track to break new paths.

FINISHING THE FATTENED ARISTOCRACY

Revolutions are fought over the distribution of the economic surplus. The economic surplus is what is left over after the workers in fields and factories produce enough for their food, clothes, and shelter; it is what is left after used-up machines, tools, and materials are replaced with a fund set aside for reinvestment. In every society what is left over is taken by upper social strata who dedicate themselves to law and government, to science and art, to business and entertainment. They make up a ruling class. In Mexico the transfer of the bulk of the economic surplus from the landowning oligarchy to a rising class of capitalist farmers and industrialists took place in the 1930s and 1940s.

Between 1910 and 1940 the Mexican Revolution resulted in a dramatic change in social relations. The old native and foreign landowners had possessed 60–70 percent of the nation's wealth; this class almost completely disappeared. By the 1950s thousands of new millionaires had replaced them.[8] This transfer of the economic surplus from one class to another, from landowners to capitalists, was a structural change in the ship of state: a capitalist engine replaced the feudal sails, and the new pilots (who had thrown overboard the old navigators Díaz and Huerta) continued to guide Mexico toward industrial development. These pilots were not entrepreneurs, bankers, rentiers, investors, brokers, merchants, agrocapitalists—in a word, the business community. They were the New Class of bureaucrats and professionals who had seized the helm of state in 1920.

This historical transformation was a social revolution by default: with a land reform the new pilots flushed the old oligarchy into the sewer of history and left the young business class in charge of the economy. Unintentionally, they carried through a social revolution. History is a cumulative sequence of causes and effects that are not always deliberate. In the 1950s Mexicans woke up in a new social order, a society going through rapid industrialization. History awarded the developmental State a report card with high marks—a 6 percent annual rate of economic growth.

In the 1930s the pilots brought about a social revolution not out of love for the people but in order to keep the social volcano's erupting agrarian revolt from blowing them out of the National Palace. The governing class rode the inevitable explosion upward and directed it against the hacendados; the bureaucrats led the land-hungry peasants to destroy the inflexible aristocratic elite. In doing so, they leveled the volcano once and for all, and created a political system of remarkable stability.

Obregón and Calles Grapple with the Landowners

The change in social relations on the land began under Obregón. In 1920 he confronted the land barons, a bloc that had come through the military phase of the Revolution unbroken. Individual landowners had not always survived the fighting; some had been killed or had fled abroad. But their haciendas rarely went to peons who worked them. Sometimes a rising mestizo warlord seized the hacendado's land for himself. Sometimes peons abandoned a great estate to join Villa's armies. Sometimes the exiled landowner returned to his fallow fields, rebuilt the ruined hacienda, and put the jobless to work. The age-old methods of production, clumsy and primitive, continued as before. Abuses like debt peonage were against the new Constitution, but the law was rarely enforced. How much had really changed in Mexico?

The faces of some landowners had changed. During the decade of revolutionary battles, foreigners had fled the country in tens of thousands; some were landowners, leaving forever. The Church, the greatest landowner of all, became a target for those who helped themselves to its goods. In Puebla alone the government confiscated 59 mortgages and 9 haciendas belonging to the Church; the men of God lost their lands to the men of war. And finally there were revolutionary generals turning into landlords.

Though some of its members had changed, in 1920 the landowning oligarchy was still intact. In the populous areas most of the land still belonged to the huge estates called haciendas, covering thousands of acres. At the center of the hacienda stood the great house, surrounded by a high stone wall, with a church, a workshop, and a store. There were filthy huts for the workers. The landowner carried a gun and lorded it over the peons, as he had for centuries. The owners held sway in the central and northern states: Michoacán, Jalisco, Nayarit, Sinaloa, Guanajuato, Querétaro, San Luis Potosí, Zacatecas, Durango, Coahuila, and Nuevo León. Against these powerful people Obregón could do nothing. His shaky government dared not begin land reform in their states, for it would mean class war that might split the country and topple the President.

In Mexico one-fifth of privately owned land still belonged to foreigners (usually Americans). In some northwestern states, for example, they owned 40 percent of the land, some of it fertile, some of it rich in minerals. The new Constitution threatened the lands of foreigners, who held a big chunk of the nation's wealth in metals and ores, in crops and oil. The U.S. State Department ordered Obregón to announce formally that he would not enforce the Constitution against property already owned by foreigners. He delayed; and the United States refused to recognize his government. With the sword of intervention hanging over him, Obregón could not think of land reform in the areas run by Americans. Near the end of his term, facing internal revolts, he formalized the hated promise to Washington: Mexico would never touch Americans' land if the U.S. government would shore up *el Presidente*. The Bucareli Accords were a bitter bargain.

In the field of agrarian change, history tied the hands of Mexico's President. People threw him proposals for land reform, which he kicked away as smoldering dynamite. He was consolidating his young government. And he did not really believe in dividing the great estates into small plots producing for a family's need, for then who would feed the cities?

Yet he needed land reform as a safety valve for mass anger, for the restless men throughout the South where the Zapatistas had led the agrarian revolution for "Tierra y Libertad." In the South the peasants were not helpless peons. There free villagers occupied the plains and valleys; they wanted back their ancestral fields and woods. The great owners were weaker in the southern states: Guerrero, Morelos, Puebla, Veracruz, Oaxaca. There Obregón could distribute token bits of land without fear of reprisal from the hacendados.

His government walked a tightrope, balancing the demands of workers and peasants against those of foreigners and landowners. The landowners were clever and powerful. Could the peasants drive the government to move against the hacendados? The land barons hired armed bands to terrorize the peasants. In a nation charged with violence, the armed bands (called White Guards) kept the poor cringing in fear. To this threat of bullets priests added the fear of hell: they warned the peasants that poverty was blessed, that land seizures were robbery, and that the government was run by rebels and atheists. Would the peasants act?

Throughout Mexico during the 1920s, people moved about the countryside, demanding the land promised in the Constitution. These were people who sympathized with the underclasses: urban intellectuals, schoolteachers, agrarian reformers, labor agitators, peasant leaders—the *agraristas*. To rouse the masses into action, the agrarians risked their lives for a generation, and thousands died under the bullets of Cristero guerrillas and the landowners' gunmen. No agrarian was safe; sometimes White Guards hanged government officials. But the agitators kept the peasantry in ferment.

Rural Mexico divided into two regions. North of Mexico City the hacienda peons were born on the plantation and died on it; the master ruled over their work, fiestas, and prayers; theirs was the psychology of dependence. In the South, where Zapata rode his white horse over the mountains in popular legends, men lived in free villages—they had the courage to revolt. There Díaz Soto y Gama, the Zapatista intellectual, founded the National Agrarian Party in 1920. The agrarians supported President Obregón, who promised a land distribution program: free villagers were to get their stolen lands back. But Obregón was in no hurry to keep his promise to the South.

His government handed the land reform to judges who entangled it in red tape. Every village had to become a legal person and put its claim through the courts. The villages, spurred on by agrarians, fed their claims into the bureaucratic machine; the rusty gears clanked in endless court cases. The Mexican peasantry was tormented by the fires of land hunger, and Obregón sprinkled drops of water on the flames.

In the southern states the peasants went so far as to occupy land in Morelos, Veracruz, Yucatán. In Yucatán the state government had curbed the power of the hacendados and begun to regulate the hemp industry. Hemp brought high prices on the world market, and the profits gave Yucatán room to maneuver: its government toyed with radical policies; the rural masses prepared for action. The Socialist Party of the Southeast and Felipe Carrillo Puerto's Resistance Leagues were struggling to shorten work hours and raise wages for the Mayan serfs who cultivated hemp. In 1922 Carrillo Puerto became governor. The organized workers and peasants helped push through reforms, including distribution of land to villages. Carrillo Puerto translated the Constitution of 1917 into Mayan languages and taught peasants their rights. For two years the peasants struggled forward. In 1924 the landowners carried out a counterrevolution and shot Carrillo Puerto and his associates.

In Veracruz, Governor Adalberto Tejeda supported peasant movements, while the state's army commander sided with the landowners. When the hacendados tried to drive villagers from newly won lands, the peasants counterattacked. They seized great estates; they welcomed socialists pouring out of the cities to organize the countryside. In 1923 a congress of peasant leagues sent agrarians throughout the state, and soldiers killed many organizers. The landowners' hired thugs burned peasant villages while army cavalry destroyed their crops. Obregón ignored the defenseless peasants, yet they supported him when General Guadalupe Sánchez and the landowners rose in revolt against Mexico City. Obregón distributed rifles to the peasants, who harassed rebel columns from the rear as they marched toward the capital.

Not only in the southern states was there an agrarian struggle. Here and there across Mexico agrarians organized peasant leagues. In Michoacán the peasant Primo Tapia tried to organize Tarascan Indians to demand the return of ancestral lands to their villagers. Governor Francisco Múgica supported his efforts, but the state army commander sided with the landowners. So did the priests. When the governor wanted to return lands to the villages of Pátzcuaro, the priests persuaded the Indians that God would curse them as robbers— and they turned from state aid. Agrarians traveled around teaching the rural masses about land reform, and White Guards and soldiers hunted them down. But the landowners could not catch Primo Tapia. He slipped in and out of peasant villages, explaining their constitutional right to former lands. To the villages Governor Múgica distributed 50,000 acres—a drop in the sea. Yet he had made a beginning. In 1922 generals and landowners carried out a counterrevolution and drove Múgica from the government. They searched for Tapia in vain; by 1923 he was leading a secret peasant association. The rich murdered its leaders, castrated peons, and cut off ears—but the league grew. In 1924 Tapia's native village got its land back. And rebellious generals faced a firing squad.

Peasant leagues across Mexico sent delegates to the National Agrarian Congress; Obregón's government paid their fares to Mexico City. At the Congress the Zapatista intellectual Díaz Soto called for arming the peasants, and warned that many generals and priests were holding back agrarian reform. The peasants were moving toward a nationwide organization.

When Calles became president in 1924, he believed that land for the peasants might prevent revolutions. Calles developed programs that echoed his old slogan: "Land and books for all!"[9] He expanded the literacy campaign and distributed land to the villages three times as fast as Obregón. But he, too, was attacking the flames with a sprinkler.

In the countryside the class struggle raged on. In 1925 in Aguascalientes, General Rodrigo Talamantes, working with big landowners, killed peasants or drove them from their lands. The labor organizer Miguel Ricardo arrived to investigate, and Colonel Enrique Estrada shot him. The next year the colonel tried the same approach in Nayarit and died in a peasant ambush. Violence crackled across rural Mexico. The social volcano smoked and smoldered, streaked with bloody lava.

The peasant leagues spread. From 16 of the 27 states, leaders poured into Mexico City to found the National Peasant League. This organization decided for cooperatives and socialism. It endorsed Article 27 of the Constitution, and declared for any government working to free peasants from priests and landowners. The League called for solidarity with proletarians around the world in their fight against capitalism. The leaders of the League, Manuel P. Montes and José Guadalupe Rodríguez, were later assassinated.

In 1926 the Cristero War broke out, and landowners supported the rebellion of the priests. But in Morelos, the country of Zapata, landless peasants raised the flag of agrarian revolt and joined the uprising against a government they hated. Their leaders carried the guerrilla war into Guerrero and raided near Mexico City. Old Zapatista generals rode again: Benjamín Mendoza, Maximiliano Vigueras, Victorino Bárcenas. The roads of Morelos were unsafe; guerrillas attacked buses and trains in broad daylight.[10] Dwight Morrow, the American ambassador, narrowly escaped capture on the road to Cuernavaca. His limousine flying the American flag roared into the state capital, wearing a tail of whooping riders on horseback with the guns smoking.

Calles neared the end of his term. While Zapatista peasants fought on in Morelos, clouds of reaction gathered over the nation: foreign interests screamed that Calles was a Bolshevik; American businessmen demanded intervention against him; the Church encouraged Cristeros to overthrow his government; and landowners plotted to do him in. So in 1928 he cut back on land reform. He was also worried by the rising agrarian debt, for the government was compensating the expropriated landowners with 20-year bonds. Where would backward Mexico find the money to pay?

The governor of Tamaulipas, an agrarian named Emilio Portes Gil, became interim President in December. He stepped up land distribution in the South, and the powerful Calles tried to restrain him (for Calles himself was becoming an hacendado). The new President answered that the government depended on peasant loyalty. In Morelos the Zapatista commander, Vigueras, seemed to be everywhere at once: his secret network of peasant supporters used telegraphs in the cities to track regular army movements, and weapons streamed to him through the underground from the capital. On December 27 fate caught up with Vigueras—capture, torture, death. But his Zapatista guerrillas continued the war for land and freedom.

The power behind the throne was Calles. During 1929 this Gray Eminence protested the land distributions of Portes Gil, the interim President. Portes Gil warned him that another election was approaching with its inevitable army coup, that the government had to arm peasants to help fight off the military, and that only land grants could gain supporters from the tillers of the soil. The coup came. Peasants fought the army, and the government survived, stronger than ever.

In the early 1930s weak presidents danced from the strings of Calles, who pulled them as best he could from his mansion in Cuernavaca. He and his cronies, acquiring estates for themselves, had grown rich and conservative; they tried to slow the machinery of land reform to a crawl. The result was growing unrest among peasants. Popular pressure increased on the remaining reformers in the ruling party; workers and peasants pressed for a turn to the left. Calles saw the handwriting on the wall, and in 1934 allowed a young reformer to run for president.

Cárdenas Tramples the Hacendados

Lázaro Cárdenas took the election seriously (though the ruling party could not lose) and campaigned thousands of miles across Mexico. He visited villages in the valleys, hamlets in the mountains, and peons on the haciendas. He heard the peons and peasants of Mexico threatening, he listened to their demands. Was a revolutionary storm like that of 1910–1917 brewing, a hurricane that would sweep away landowners and president in a new civil war?

In 1935 Cárdenas surveyed the enemies of the ordinary people of Mexico. He saw foreign interests crippled: the national income of the United States down from $87 billion to $39 billion; one of every three American workers out of a job; breadlines spreading. The Colossus of the North showed feet of clay. The Mexican Church, that old friend of landowners, lay defeated in the Cristero War and begged the government to call off the de-Christianization campaign. Obregón and Calles had so reduced the army that generals-turned-landowners had not tried a coup in several years—a sign of weakness.

Cárdenas sensed the impatience of the underclasses. Strike waves rolled over the nation. In 1933 there were 13 strikes; in 1934, at least 200; in 1935, some 650. (Unofficial sources reported more than 1,000 strikes during Cárdenas' first year in office.)[11] Violent strikes of agricultural workers exploded around the country: on the commercial haciendas in Michoacán, on the hemp plantations of Yucatán, and in the cotton-growing regions of north-central Mexico the people working from dawn to dark had reached the end of their tether—they demanded better wages and shorter hours. Groups of landless seized soil for their use; the peasants were on the move. From the thunderheads of peasant anger, lightning flickered over the countryside as agrarians and big owners clashed throughout the land.

For 15 years the time bomb of peasant frustration had ticked under the nation. Cárdenas and his government wanted to detonate it, but under controlled conditions. The regime prepared to unleash the rural masses against the landowning class.

The landowners affected by reforms had received compensation in 20-year bonds, but the rising agrarian debt made it ever harder for the government to carry on land distribution in good conscience. Cárdenas' government sent the agrarian debt to the devil; land would go to the peasants whether the owners got paid or not. Before this, land had gone only to free villages. But almost half the rural families did not live in villages—they were hacienda peons. The government turned to these peons in central and northern Mexico with the slogan "Land to the tiller!" The hour of the hacendados had struck.

The President was embarking on an unknown and risky course, a revolution in the countryside. What if it ran away from him? In July 1935 he ordered the creation of peasant leagues in every state, then the merging of all existing leagues in a confederation run by the government. The peasants, working through local committees, could petition the government for land; the state would grant land and organize these committees into peasant leagues. Cárdenas wanted top-down control of land distribution.

Landlords destroyed peasant villages to keep them from asking for land. White Guards burned peasant crops and killed men, women, and children. Peasants organized for self-defense. "I will give to the peasants the Mausers with which they made the Revolution," said Cárdenas, "so they can defend it and the village and the school."[12] On January 1, 1936, he ordered governors and army commanders to distribute weapons and to organize a peasant militia. The landlords tried to win over army officers commanding the militia; in Chihuahua, Guanajuato, and San Luis Potosí such tactics worked. Sometimes rifles meant for the militia went to the White Guards. There were battles between the landowners' mercenaries and armed peasants throughout Mexico—thousands died in the struggle. The peasant militia grew, and by 1940 it numbered 60,000 men, all with arms, half with horses.

Without waiting for the government to grant the lands promised, some groups of peasants began to occupy them. Cárdenas struggled to retain control of the movement: in March 1936 he ordered army commanders to repress all spontaneous land seizures. He rushed to grant land to the peasants.

The distributed land took three forms: small plots, *ejidos*, and collective farms. *Ejidos* were village communities that owned land in common; each family, assigned its plot, could neither rent nor sell it—an Indian tradition. The *ejidos* struck a blow at private property, but even more radical were the President's collective farms. He remembered the recent general strike in north-central Mexico, with its million acres of cotton and wheat. In October 1936 he broke up the scores of plantations there, most of them belonging to foreigners. He gave the land to the workers and organized them into collective farms. Then came the turn of other areas boiling with discontent: Yucatán's hemp plantations, the haciendas of Sonora's Yaqui Valley, and the big sugar-growing area of Los Mochis in Sinaloa. Foreign owners gnashed their teeth.

With these radical agrarian measures—*ejidos* and collective farms—Cárdenas' ruling party was leading Mexico into agrarian socialism. "Madero proposed a very mild program in regard to land, speaking only of the restitution of lands to the small owners who had been deprived of the properties through the abuses of the laws. . . . There was no general idea of reconstructing the landholding system in its entirety," writes one of the great historians of the social revolution. "No one, not even the drafters of Article 27, had this objective clearly in view, and certainly the governments of the Revolution up to the time of Cárdenas (1934–40) resisted the growing pressure to make the law mean what it has since come to mean, the destruction of private property landholding in Mexico and the substitution of communal village ownership."[13] By leaning so far to the left, Cárdenas was straining the social pact of the Revolution—the constitutional program of Obregón and Calles.

As plotting against the government increased, Cárdenas armed a workers' militia in the capital. In 1938 General Saturnino Cedillo, allied to landowners and foreigners, rose against the government. He was defeated and shot. In the United States a reformist president, Franklin Delano Roosevelt, was busy fighting economic paralysis at home; and voices for intervention against Cárdenas cried in vain. The Mexican leader moved to take over American oil in Tampico. His country united behind him.

From 1935 to 1938 half the landowning class lost its holdings to the peasants. On tiny plots most peasants raised food for their families; not much was left over to feed the towns. To feed the rising cities in the 1940s, the government irrigated vast tracts in the North and turned them over to agrocapitalists. Big capitalist farms, using new seeds, fertilizers, and tractors, spread through the northern states. Today these have evolved into modern agrobusinesses flourishing in Baja California, Sonora, Sinaloa, Chihuahua, and Tamaulipas. The giant factories and farms of Mexico are run by modern professional managers and collectively owned by numerous stockholders. The wealth of the nation is in such hands; the old aristocracy of landowners has either disappeared or gone modern. The "little people" barely get by: mass unemployment, subsistence farming, migrant labor, pitiful wages, poor food, illiteracy—misery is their lot. This misery is surprising in the tenth largest country in the world. One-third of its 100 million people are functionally illiterate; almost half live in dwellings with no running water and six people to a room. Half the nation is without proper medicine. At least one-third of the labor force is unemployed, and that means frightening poverty; three-fourths of the people must divide among themselves the one-third of Mexico's personal income left to them after the elites have take their huge slice.

In the 1920s Mexico was an agricultural country. In the countryside, power and riches depended on possession of large tracts of land, on personal ownership of haciendas. From father to son the haciendas passed down through inheritance. But after the agrarian reform of the 1930s, riches no longer came from private ownership of these estates. During the reform, half of these big owners vanished. The rest soon found that owning haciendas was no longer enough, that traditional large-scale farming was doomed. The ancient methods of production were slowly disappearing in the face of modern agrobusiness. The new business farmers of the North drew wealth from capital and technology: control of credit, knowledge of the market, management ability, soil engineering, tractors, fertilizers. To learn to compete, the remaining hacendados sent their sons to Texas A&M University. Today the old barons of the soil are gone; in both agriculture and industry Mexico's wealth belongs to the multinational corporations and to native millionaires—capital and technology rule. A professional-managerial class is administering the fields and the packing sheds.

In 1920 life on the hacienda went on in the centuries-old way. The peon was born into debt: the hacendado loaned token coins (redeemable in the hacienda store) for his baptism, his first white clothes, his marriage feast. The peon built his hut on the hacienda and drew corn, candles, and pulque from the company store. From there came the white *manta* to make his clothes; he rarely saw money. If the hacienda was sold, his debt was transferred to the new owner—the peon could never escape. Should it surprise us that some historians have called him a serf?

Article 123 of the new Constitution had ordered an end to debt peonage and the closing of company stores. But enforcement depended on the state governments, and throughout most of the country peonage remained the reality, if not the law. The Revolution of 1910–1917 had weakened the debt system; there were fewer hacienda peons than under the old dictatorship. But the system still survived.

The agrarian struggles of the 1920s brought a gradual enforcement of the law. By 1933 the system of token coin, payment in kind, and the *tienda de raya* (company store) was still to be found, but it was confined to isolated places. The land reform of 1935–1937 dealt the debt system a mortal blow, and the rise of agrocapitalism finished it off: a rural proletariat had grown up in the Mexican countryside, with migrant labor and mass unemployment. The old semifeudal system of dependent labor was gone. The rest of the rural population lived in semicommunal *ejidos*.

The Social Revolution

In the 1930s and 1940s Mexico underwent rapid industrialization. Mexican business had no competition from foreign producers, as depression and war in the developed countries halted their exports. Since 1940 Mexico's businessmen have made fortunes in steel, chemicals, cement, banking, bottling, brewing, textiles, hotels, supermarkets, consumer goods, real estate, department stores, and sports arenas. Most of the big entrepreneurs began to accumulate their fortunes in the 1920s and 1930s.[14] During those years the bulk of the nation's wealth passed from landowners to rising businessmen. The traditional haciendas were replaced by either subsistence farmers or modern agriculture, and the nation entered a new epoch, an age of entrepreneurs and large corporations.

Between 1920 and 1940 Mexico shook itself free from army, Church, and oligarchy, built schools and factories, and stepped into the modern world. Though one foot dragged behind and the other sank into the mire of dependence on the power to the North, who can deny that the nation lurched forward?

This advance came through leadership and mass struggles. Obregón, Calles, and Cárdenas worked to rid the army of disloyal officers while peasant and worker militias fought down military uprisings. Most Mexicans withheld support from the Church during its showdown with the government; Calles could therefore isolate the Cristero rebels and crush them. By the 1930s Church and army had bled into weakness, and the government dared to unleash peasant leagues against that great enemy of the people, the landowning oligarchy. Without allies, the landowners went down to defeat.

Soldier, priest, and landlord: thundering down a historical track of misery, that huge troika had pounded Mexico for centuries, until the Revolution smashed it. Out of the wreckage the Mexicans built a modern vehicle that would carry them through the twentieth century—a corporate state.

FIRST STEPS TOWARD THE CORPORATE STATE

Almost 900 years ago John of Salisbury offered a theory of stable society by comparing the state to a body. The king was its head, the senate its heart, soldiers its hands, tax agents its stomach, and workers its feet. All must cooperate, urged John, for the good of the total interrelated society; each organ, in doing its job, would help toward the happiness of the whole body.[15] This metaphor of the state formed into a sinewy, healthy corpus took root in political theory. *Corporatus*, in Latin, means "formed into a body." Political scientists often refer to a society run on this model as a "corporate state."

Obregón, Calles, and Cárdenas were not theorists; they had read history but little political science. Yet in Mexico between 1920 and 1940 they slowly built a corporate state. They started with a turbulent society full of class struggles, religious rebellions, internal colonies, army coups, racial strife, peasant uprisings, workers' strikes, and widespread violence. How could they fuse the hostile groups into a single nation? They worked from the Mexican tradition that sees the President as dictator and struggled for top-down control of society. Each president followed the age-old tactic of divide and rule with increasing success. Obregón and Calles herded the people into organizations run by the government, and Cárdenas scooped them up with the net of the catchall ruling party.

Obregón Co-opts Workers and Peasants

In the last years of the Porfiriato strike waves lashed Mexico. In 1906 workers in the railway yards rebelled against starvation wages. The strikes leaped from city to city: Chihuahua, Torreón, San Luis Potosí, Monterrey, Aguascalientes. At the railroad station in Cárdenas, San Luis Potosí, a violent clash left 18 dead in 1907; a huge strike exploded in protest. In 1908 strikes sizzled over the nation's railway grid, and the workers won sympathy from people in many walks of life.

From 1903 to 1910 federal troops spattered bullets on strikers in the mine pits of Mexico. The largest of these strikes flared up in Sonora. At Cananea, in the copper mines owned by foreigners, the workers laid down their picks in 1906 and American foremen fired on unarmed demonstrators. The workers searched for weapons and fought back as the Americans shot them down with dum-dum bullets. Both American volunteers and the Mexican *rurales* rushed to Cananea to slaughter workers.

In 1906 and 1907 workers struck in the textile factories of Veracruz, Tlaxcala, and Puebla, where working conditions made every mill an inferno. This general strike caused a nationwide lockout of textile workers. The strike movement led to the government massacre of men, women, and children in Rio Blanco.

In mines, railways, and factories Mexico's workers showed fighting spirit against the dictatorship. Their economic strikes took on a political tone, an anti-State bias encouraged by anarchists. These agitators preached direct action to bring down the government.

In 1911 Madero chased the dictator Díaz into exile, then fell as a martyr. In 1914 Carranza's Constitutionalists stormed down the railway lines to Mexico City. Obregón urged the workers to join Carranza's movement against Villa and turned over the telephone company to the striking laborers led by the electrician Luis Morones. Finally, many labor leaders accepted Obregón and formed the Red

Battalions. To get food, workers joined up and left the starving capital. In 1915 they fought battles, and in the wake of Obregón's advancing armies they organized unions. Unionism swept the nation; soon there was hardly a branch of industrial activity without a labor union.

In 1918, as the military phase of the revolution drew to a close, Mexico's workers had proven themselves a social force. Red Battalions, militant unions, anarchist ideology, general strikes, sabotage—the workers waved the red flag of socialism and the black flag of anarchism. Mexico had stepped into the 20th century with a fighting proletariat.

That same year, after the fighting died down, Obregón set in motion the machinery for co-opting the workers into the social pact of the Revolution. He persuaded President Carranza to sponsor the Congress of Workers' Organizations, and out of it came the Regional Confederation of Mexican Labor (CROM). When leaders of the Zapatista movement organized a rival peasant party in 1920, Obregón gave it his blessing. Behind the scenes Obregón reached an agreement with both the CROM and the new National Agrarian Party. He got the government to subsidize the CROM; he rewarded its leaders with government posts in return for keeping the lid on labor discontent. And he promised a radical program of land reform if the peasant party would support the government. With great skill Obregón divided workers from peasants and prepared to deal with their leaders separately.

The CROM

Díaz, Huerta, and Carranza had failed to tame the workers with bayonets and police clubs. Then Obregón suggested to President Carranza a new tactic: an offer of friendship. Grudgingly Carranza agreed to pay the workers' fares to the Congress of Workers' Organizations in Saltillo. In 1918 more than 100 organizations sent their people to the government-sponsored Congress. A key figure in its executive committee was Luis Morones, once an anarchist revolutionary, then a man in contact with the American Federation of Labor in the United States, and finally an organizer working to help labor through government action. Obregón was soon plotting with Morones; both labor boss and revolutionary general rode the workers' movement to power. Obregón had switched the proletarian locomotive onto tracks leading toward a government station. In the birth of Mexico's large labor central (the CROM), the government acted as midwife.

Obregón's star was rising. The nation expected him to become President when Carranza's term expired in 1920. Luis Morones and his

Action Group inside the CROM secretly proposed a pact to Obregón. In the struggle over the presidency, the CROM would support Obregón in return for guarantees: the creation of a Ministry of Labor headed by Morones, material and moral support for the CROM from the government, presidential consideration of the CROM's views on all proposed reforms affecting the nation, and government money to build links between the Mexican proletariat and the international working class. Obregón signed this pact with the Action Group. Neither rank-and-file labor nor the Mexican public knew what had happened in a smoke-filled room.

In 1920 the workers, feeling their power, pounded the nation with strikes—90,000 walked off the job: the oil workers of Tampico, the railwaymen of the Veracruz-Mexico City line, the miners of Zacatecas and Coahuila, the farm laborers of the haciendas in north-central Mexico. These workers toiled for foreign companies, and an interim Mexican government adopted a hands-off policy toward labor disputes. Washington machine-gunned the Mexican regime with threatening diplomatic notes (14 in 6 months). The cannon of foreign intervention pointed into Mexico.

Into this turmoil walked the new president, Álvaro Obregón. Caught between a militant proletariat on his left and the formidable United States on his right, he stepped onto the tightrope of his presidency and began a clever balancing act. Impressed by the power on his right, Obregón moved to divert the seething energy of the proletariat into government channels. He began to carry through his secret promises to the Action Group inside the CROM.

Huge sums of government money flowed to the CROM for organizing workers. Communists and anarchists organized a rival labor central, but they were cut off from the nourishing rays of Obregón's sun: massive financial aid, protection in disputes with employers, and, for CROM leaders, posts in government.

What kind of posts? Obregón made Morones chief of the Manufacturing Establishments. The CROM's Ricardo Treviño (an anarchist) was elected to the Chamber of Deputies, along with the brilliant lawyer Vicente Lombardo Toledano (who would later become a leading Marxist). The CROM put the socialist Juan Sarabia in the Senate and gained 50 percent of the municipal offices in Mexico City. Two years later Morones and a host of CROM leaders were in the Chamber of Deputies—they dominated the Congress on vital questions and passed laws favorable to labor. Obregón made CROM men governors of states: thus Lombardo Toledano came to power in Puebla. Observers began to speak of a Workers' Government in Mexico. It seemed that the social pact of the Revolution was tilting to the left, away from the liberal business groups.

Was it a Workers' State? In 1921 the number of strikes reached 310. That was too many for Obregón, and both he and Morones worked to strengthen their control over the unions and to organize more workers. In 1922 the strikes were fewer, and usually not for higher wages or shorter hours—the workers struck to gain recognition of unions by management.

Obregón developed a carrot-and-stick policy toward the working class. In one hand he held a whip: jail for Communists and anarchists, troops against strikes by "red" unions. In the other he held rewards: money and posts for friendly labor leaders, pay hikes for "yellow" unions. The president—a master politician—oscillated between repression and co-optation. He was holding the workers firmly in the social pact of the Revolution.

The Agrarians

Obregón labored to keep the urban workers divided from the peasants. The division had roots deep in the Mexican Revolution. When bands of dark-skinned Zapatistas thundered into Mexico City late in 1914, the white working-class leaders in the capital looked upon them with suspicion. The workers' leaders had recently arrived from Spain, and their heads were filled with anarchism and atheism. They watched the peasant guerrillas gallop past with religious flags, the Virgin stamped on their huge sombreros, capes flying in the wind. The Zapatistas celebrated victory amid the pealing of church bells, the churches anarchists had just sacked. The workers sneered at these country yahoos. The workers poured into Obregón's Red Battalions and marched off to fight Villa's agrarian armies. Obregón had deepened the split between workers and peasants.

In 1920 Díaz Soto y Gama, the Zapatista intellectual, founded his National Agrarian Party. President Obregón quickly threw his weight behind Díaz Soto. The President made a deal with the National Agrarian Party.

When running for president, Obregón had favored land for the people, but warned against breaking up the productive estates into tiny plots for a family's needs. For land to the tiller meant parcelization, smashing haciendas into subsistence fragments. Obregón did not really believe in "dividing up," though he consented to the formation of a country of farmers who were small but efficient.

Once in the presidency, he saw that some land would have to be returned to the people in order to prevent revolution. So he promised

Díaz Soto's agrarians that free villages in the South would get their stolen lands back—a radical program. Then he produced a tangled legislation about the way this would happen, and turned the process over to the courts. The bureaucrats fulfilled his hopes; the reform soon struggled in a swamp of treacherous and annoying legalities. The peasant villagers marched into this wilderness to attain the promise on the other side.

While the agrarian knights worked off their energies jousting with the bureaucratic dragon, Obregón thought up another way to keep them busy. He handed the land distribution agency to the National Agrarian Party. The party used the regional agencies to organize peasants, and soon Leagues of Agrarian Communities were flourishing in many states. In these leagues Obregón spotted a means of controlling the turbulent countryside, so he invited leagues and agrarians to a national congress in 1923, with the government paying the bill. Over 1,000 people, representing hundreds of thousands of peasants, gathered in Mexico City. The high point of the Congress was the ending, Obregón's rousing speech. The agrarians applauded wildly. Obregón was pleased, too: peasants were staying within the social pact of the Revolution. But for how long?

Calles and the Workers' Regime

Obregón's measured pace had finally exhausted the peasants' patience. Under Calles there was increasing violence in the countryside: more clashes between agrarians and White Guards, and in 1926 the resurgence of a Zapatista revolt in Morelos. Calles raised the pace of land distribution from a walk to a trot, enough to keep the peasant nag from breaking the bit.[16] But he dared not allow the agrarian left to gallop ahead, for the power on his right was rising steadily. The Church idealized feudal land tenure and encouraged armed rebellion against Calles's government. Generals-turned-landowners threatened him with their guns. And the agrarian debt was soaring, for the government paid landowners for confiscated acreage with bonds. The bonds drifted into the hands of bankers in the United States. Where would the Mexican treasury find the money to pay? Yet, some day, pay it must: in the dozens of armed interventions by the United States in Latin America, Mexico had often suffered the whip. In Washington, ruling Republican Party's conservative politicians looked at Revolutionary Mexico with hostile eyes.

"Since the government did not persecute any form of enterprise except large landholding, the rich began to get out of land and to reinvest their capital in banks and industries," writes a historian of the Revolution. Calles fostered the growth of incipient native capitalism. He encouraged the monied people "to invest in the new Mexican consumer-goods industries, oiling the wheels of industrialization with a capital that once went abroad or into inefficient landholding."[17]

Under Calles's administration there continued the contest between the National Agrarian Party and Morones's CROM, a struggle for the allegiance of people in the fields. For example, in Morelos the CROM had formed a peasant union in Tepoztlán; in 1925 two government agents from the Agrarian Party came to Tepoztlán to distribute hacienda land but died suddenly, probably by the hand of the CROM. In 1926 the CROM claimed 1,500 peasant workers' unions as its own.

Though Calles did not encourage the CROM's work among peasants, he had raised labor leaders to the pinnacle of power in the cities. In 1924, during his campaign for the presidency, he made a deal with Morones for CROM support. The labor boss was licking his wounds after a shoot-out in the Chamber of Deputies. Calles and Morones reached a secret understanding, then later signed a pact: the CROM promised to warn the State of all strike plans and to support government decisions and decrees; the presidential candidate agreed to finance the labor central, to back its actions, and to make Morones the Minister of Labor. In power, Calles quickly took Morones into his cabinet. In the Congress the CROM got one-fifth of the deputies and of the Senate, two governships, and control of Mexico City's administration.

There were more secret agreements between the President and labor chief. To stabilize Mexico, the CROM agreed to suspend strike actions, and the government locked the CROM workers into the social pact with wage hikes, better conditions at the workplace, and other favors from the state.[18] The number of legal strikes slowly fell to zero.

What is a legal strike? The Constitution of 1917 allows for strikes that "aim to harmonize the relations between capital and labor." The government spots such a strike and declares it legal. "Harmony" is for the government to define.

The government nourished the CROM with huge sums of money and improved the conditions of its rank and file. During the first two years of Calles's reign, people spoke again of a Workers' State. B. Traven's proletarian novels called the government a Workers' Regime; international monopolies screamed against Calles's "bolshevism." There was widespread belief that Mexico aimed at socialism. Honest socialists provided moral cement to hold the CROM together. They gave Mexico City one of the best municipal administrations it had seen. Lombardo Toledano worked as governor of Puebla to serve the people.

Ezequiel Salcedo was a model senator. Calles, who had always called himself a socialist, was not only holding the workers in the social pact of the Revolution, he was tilting the coalition's balance toward the left. The liberal businessmen complained that he was a Communist.

What kind of socialist was Calles? He and his reformers believed they had discovered in revolutionary nationalism a third road to industrial development, a socialism compatible with the social pact and class struggle within the framework of the 1917 Constitution, a socialism coexisting with a modified and reformed capitalism. Calles conceived this mixed economy as a capitalism without capitalist exploitation and a socialism without a proletarian revolution. (Capitalism without capitalist exploitation is a contradiction in terms, but socialism without a proletarian revolution—from the top down under the leadership of professionals—is the normal state of affairs.)

In 1926 one of the CROM's top leaders, Vicente Lombardo Toledano, explained how revolutionary nationalism inevitably leads to socialism. "To the extent that the Mexican governments really are revolutionary," he wrote, "they bind themselves more firmly to the nationalist thesis." They dictate measures converting the country's natural resources into national property, "the land, the rivers, and mineral products, which in the hands of private owners seriously threaten the nation's freedom and the socialists' freedom of action." To the extent that the government implements this program of national recovery, therefore, "the labor movement deliberately and instinctively becomes united with the government," for "they have the same internal and external enemies . . . [and] they seek the same ends."[19]

But the CROM soon dropped its class-struggle philosophy to call for class peace. The nation was approaching a new time of troubles. Foreigners threatened Calles with intervention; the Church preached rebellion; generals waited for their chance. Calles told labor leaders that he needed the support of the working class. Since the workers were too weak to seize power, reasoned the leaders, they should back a government that favored the proletariat within capitalism. The President persuaded them to accept "class peace" during the industrialization of Mexico. Employers applauded the new policy. The balance of the social pact shifted once more toward the center.

Corruption had been growing in the CROM leadership since its collaboration with Obregón. How could labor bureaucrats resist diverting some government aid, big and secret, into their pockets? Morones set the pace. He drove about in a large automobile, flashing diamonds on his fingers. The diamonds, he explained, were the worker's funds kept safely away from shaky banks. His sparkling fingers were their revenge upon greedy capitalists who wanted to see workers in rags. Or his riches were an inheritance from his father![20]

Corruption ate into the hull of the CROM and cracks appeared throughout—it began to sink. The rank and file tired of Morones. In 1928 Obregón campaigned for the presidency, firing volleys of criticism at the CROM, and unions jumped from the sinking ship to join the next captain of state. Then, as Obregón dined at a garden banquet, a fanatical Catholic sidled up and blew his head off. Interim President Emilio Portes Gil, an enemy of Morones, pounded the disintegrating CROM with government power. Police and troops went after its unions; in the CROM's disputes with employers, the State ruled against it. Without Calles's protection the CROM slowly went under.

CÁRDENAS BUILDS A CORPORATE STATE

Political Crisis

In 1929 the CROM lost its hold over the labor movement, and by 1930 the peasant leagues were losing control over people on the land. The movements of the underclasses split up. Rival factions competed for the allegiance of the workers, and peasant groups squabbled among themselves. The early 1930s saw a babble of tongues among the Mexican masses. The nuclei of new labor centrals failed to grow; peasant organizations sputtered along, out of gear. A firm hand at the helm of state was missing: a series of weak presidents sat out two-year terms while strongman Calles pulled the strings from Cuernavaca. When Lázaro Cárdenas, Mexico's greatest President, took charge in 1935, the situation quickly changed; he organized workers and peasants into huge, new confederations of leagues and unions. He set out to sew the social pact back together.

Obregón had emerged from the chaos of the first revolutionary decade to become a strong President. Under him people's organizations flourished: CROM for the workers and the National Agrarian Party for the peasants. Calles was stronger, and he raised the CROM to new heights, while peasant currents built up their power. Next came Obregón's assassination in 1928, triggering a political crisis that stretched into six years of division and weakness at the top. At the base the big organs of popular will fell apart—confusion was king. A deepening economic crisis drove the masses toward an explosion like that of 1910. Then President Cárdenas, a populist leader of great ability, repaired the state engine, hitched people's organizations behind it, and steered them against landlords and foreigners.

After the lid blew off in 1910, the desperate and illiterate Mexican masses became a steaming sea of social energy, churning up revolutionary storms that threatened to sweep away all elites. Slowly the new state learned to channel that energy in different directions, collect it into organizations, and turn these against military, religious, and propertied interests. Thus the bureaucrats sought to divide and rule. In government, strong leadership brought the nation through the agony of budding industrialization, maintaining the social pact—but weak presidents drifted into crisis.

The death of Obregón, the presidential candidate in 1928, opened a period of weakness. For a year an interim president, Emilio Portes Gil, attempted to rule with Calles looking over his shoulder. Pascual Ortiz Rubio, an engineer, then tried to govern with Calles's approval. People were not sure where the decisions came from—until Ortiz suddenly resigned. Calles appointed a general to take his place. General Abelardo Rodríguez lasted until 1934, but checked his actions with the shadowy power in Cuernavaca. The government remained divided.

In 1929 Calles had tried to seal the cracks opening in the state structure by founding a national party to hold together the progressive groups thrown up by the revolution: small parties and their splinters, political leaders and their local followers, state governors with administrative hierarchies, restless generals commanding divisions, labor chiefs with union bureaucracies, congressional leaders and their clients, the president himself surrounded by top officials. In March they were called to meet in Querétaro: "The Revolution has created an organic peace, resulting from the equilibrium achieved between the living forces of the country. . . . It needs an organism of expression and support. This will be the function of the Revolutionary National Party."[21] The summons went on to say that Madero, Obregón, and Calles had completed their historical mission, and that the new party should be responsible for the coming historical duties of the Revolution and the interests of the Mexican people. As the Action Program put it, the Revolutionary National Party would protect big industry, but that protection would not hurt the working class; the party would work for a "just equilibrium between the factors of production, capital and labor." The party "ratifies all the doctrine advanced in Article 123 of our Constitution."[22] The key concept is equilibrium: the balance among the social forces and tendencies in the social pact.

Since 1924 the nation's leading intellectual, the liberal José Vasconcelos, had bitterly criticized Calles's administration. The Maderista Vasconcelos ideologically represented the liberal business tendency in the Mexican Revolution. A passionate democrat, in 1929 he opposed the new Revolutionary National Party in the name of democracy.

At first the Revolutionary National Party (PNR) was a weak alliance of many groups, but it gained in strength every year, and by 1934 it had developed a bureaucratic machine for directing the new men of power. Yet the machine lacked a skillful conductor.

In 1929 General Lázaro Cárdenas, the governor of Michoacán, was one of the main personalities among the men of power; he would quickly become the leader of the ruling party's left wing. The right wing of the party rallied behind Calles, who grew more conservative with every passing year. He inclined the balance in the social pact back toward business. He openly said that Mexico must be capitalist; he slowed agrarian reform to a crawl and announced to the peasants that land distribution would stop. Mexico was still a nation of huge estates: of the privately owned land, a few thousand landlords held 80 percent; 700,000 in the semicommunal *ejidos* held only a tenth as much; and 2.3 million peasants had no land at all. So after 1930 peasant support for the government melted away, as the rising cry for land got a deaf ear from Calles and the party's right wing. There was growing trouble in the countryside, and by 1933 land seizures and strikes of farmworkers were spreading. Peasant uprisings exploded in Zacatecas, Guanajuato, and Michoacán; in the state of Veracruz 15,000 people revolted. In rural Mexico gusts of discontent were blowing up a tornado of mass anger while the government drifted before the wind.

Economic Crisis

In 1929 the crisis of world capitalism gripped the Mexican economy. On the world market the price of silver tumbled, and a vital sector of Mexico's mining industry sickened. The disease got worse, as gold, copper, lead, and zinc lost value. Oil production, already dropping in the 1920s, fell ever faster; plantations in the cotton-growing regions of north-central Mexico slid into bankruptcy. Around the nation, layoffs and wage cuts dragged the proletariat toward starvation. Food prices were rising; floods, droughts, and frosts ruined a third of the corn crop and cut the bean harvest in half. Mexico's economy, based on export, had always swung with the ups and downs of the world market. In the 1930s it collapsed.

In the disorganized working class there were spontaneous struggles and strikes; the government answered with swift repression. Layoffs led to workers' claims against companies, jacking up the number of labor conflicts year by year. Starting in 1929 with 13,000, the number of conflicts rose annually from 21,000 to 29,000 to 37,000. Workers' demonstrations for a return to policies favoring labor met rebuffs from Calles. In Cuernavaca he toasted his political cronies with tequila and amused them with poker and parties, with women and song. Whenever the puritanical General Cárdenas visited Calles, he refused to join in the fun and sulked in his room. A military man who would not drink? Calles, who admired Cárdenas for his suicide charges during the civil war, found the likable young general amusing.[23]

By 1933 a practiced eye could spot the elements of a revolutionary situation: repressive government, political crisis, economic disaster, increasing misery for masses of people with a fighting tradition, and a sharp rise in their actions against existing conditions. In the cities there were labor disputes, suppressed strikes, marches, speeches, demonstrations; in the countryside, roaming migrants, squatters' movements, land seizures, clashes between peasants and big landowners, and armed uprisings setting thousands of people in motion.

While Calles and the right wing of the ruling PNR remained blind to the abyss opening beneath their feet, the left wing gazed into the depths with fear. The social pact was splitting open, but a turn to the left might close the gap. By 1933 the left had converted the bulk of the party to its vision. A Six-Year Plan vaguely calling for socialism was drawn up, and the left's leader became the next candidate for President. Lázaro Cárdenas was to become the greatest agitator in Mexican history.

Cárdenas had rocketed out of a poor family to become a general of division at age thirty-two. Riding the wings of the Revolution to glory, he showed all the strengths of the populist commander along with the usual weaknesses. A man of the people, he lived simply and worked long hours to serve the peasants he loved. He knew how to listen to their problems and hopes; he was patient with their slowness. He often spent whole nights talking with peasants in a remote village, only to continue, sleepless, on his journey the next day. As governor of Michoacán he mobilized people to fight for their rights; together they distributed land and built schools.

He was a self-educated man, not an intellectual, and he took his political views from the grab bag of leftist ideas available in Mexico. Like all radical populist ideologies, Cardenismo was a bag full of contradictions: the state would mix capitalism and communism into a brew called Mexican socialism; the President would protect some private enterprise while educating people to hate it; producers' cooperatives would slowly multiply through decades to form the new order emerging from the shell of the old. Cárdenas was a passionate democrat. He trusted the elemental power of the masses to right wrongs and to rebuild the country. At the same time he believed in a strong state supported by the popular classes, but also obeyed by them, as the only way to avoid chaos. (The memory of the civil war and its horrors ate at his mind.) He wanted to organize the masses in defense of their class interests and to make the state work for them. He was an active socialist.

In 1934 Cárdenas launched his campaign for the presidency. In this campaign his ruling party could hardly lose the election, but something more than votes was at stake. The nation was a primed mine, and an explosion might come at any minute; the presidential candidate was struggling to defuse the bomb of the people's wrath threatening the government. Cárdenas moved over the length and breadth of his vast country, traveling thousands of miles to talk with peons and Indians, with miners and ranchers in remote areas. He made speeches off the top of his head, using simple ideas, and he listened to peasant committees stammering out their griefs and hopes. He saw that many no longer believed in the promises he was making for the government, and he knew that when he became President, he must do something quickly. Everywhere he preached that a new deal was coming to Mexico, promised land for the people who tilled it, and shouted against the foreigners exploiting the nation's ores, factories, oil, and agriculture. In the fields and factories he never tired of telling laborers to organize themselves, to press their demands on their enemies, and to throw their weight behind their government. He urged atomized workers and peasants to unify their fragmented organizations into leagues and centrals; he took a hand in healing their quarrels. He met peons, migrants, unemployed, workers, women, and youth with the same slogan: Get organized! A man of the people, he felt their suffering and dreamed with them of a new order; he convinced many that he was leading the nation toward a just society.

The hour had produced the man.

The Confederation of Mexican Workers

At the end of 1934 Cárdenas became President and looked around for allies. His eye fell upon the fragmented working class, and he encouraged the unification of the labor movement. For two years union leaders had called for unifying the pieces of the old labor centrals, and here and there they had formed larger blocs. In 1933 there had been more than a dozen confederations, scores of federations, and hundreds of loners. Then the eloquent Lombardo Toledano formed a new central from dissidents of the ghost of the CROM. His central called for the overthrow of capitalism and returned to the idea of direct action: meetings, demonstrations, boycotts, sit-down strikes. To fight low wages, the central organized walkouts, and in 1934 a general strike. The Marxist-Leninist Toledano and his workers became a center of attraction for the drifting unions.

In 1935, with President Cárdenas in office, waves of strikes encouraged by the government shook up the industrial system. In the summer Calles publicly warned the President away from socialist policies and threatened him with a military coup; this won huge applause from the business community. But Cárdenas dismissed conservatives in his cabinet and retired generals of doubtful loyalty. As the crisis deepened, he ousted congressmen suspected of plotting, fired a number of state governors, and purged the ruling Revolutionary National Party of its right wing. Among the workers there sprang up a Committee for Proletarian Defense, aiming at a single labor central to back the President. The Committee directed more and more strikes, demonstrations, and unity meetings. It threatened to drive Calles out of the country with a general strike. Around it rallied workers of all tendencies: socialists, Communists, syndicalists, reformists, and former anarchists. In December it filled the streets of the capital with 100,000 workers, peasants, and students in a giant demonstration that was led by Lombardo Toledano to the central plaza, where Cárdenas swayed the masses with words. To support him they might unleash a general strike. The agitation swept out of the capital across the country; there were marches and meetings for Cárdenas in cities throughout Mexico. Labor was getting together under radical leadership.

At the beginning of 1936 several thousand delegates met to form the Confederation of Mexican Workers (CTM) with the brilliant Lombardo Toledano at its head. He dissolved his own central in this big one, and many others merged with it. Although some unions stayed out, such as the corrupt CROM and the anarchist General Confederation of Workers (CGT), a single central was uniting the Mexican proletariat. The CTM built itself out of industrial unions and ordered craft organizations to regroup in the new way.

At the Confederation's founding congress Lombardo Toledano declared independence from the government. The CTM was supposed to grow on its own. The new central began with 200,000 members and carried on organizing around the country. Fidel Velázquez, the secretary of the organization, sent propaganda and agitators into every corner of Mexico. The CTM umbrella opened over the working class: by 1937 it counted half a million members, and its growth went on year by year. By 1940 it contained more than a million. The CTM sucked in the unattached unions in the country.

The labor central's leaders publicly denied government aid during this spectacular growth, but somebody was paying huge sums for organizers and buildings, and it was hardly the Mexican workers earning subsistence wages. Government and party officials spoke of aiding the CTM. Historians have guessed that Cárdenas was financing the astonishing growth of the labor central. Those familiar with Mexican politics would agree.

At least the CTM leaders were honest. Fidel Velázquez was a tireless organizer who made the young central grow into a giant. From the organizing secretariat he built a bureaucratic machine inside the central and gathered power into his hands. Above his bureaucratic advisers was suspended the central's charismatic General Secretary, Lombardo Toledano. He matched Cárdenas as the other mass leader of the period, but with a difference: behind Lombardo's word-magic lay a mastery of Marxist theory.

Unlike Lombardo Toledano, President Cárdenas did not expect that the proletariat would someday seize power to push the nation rapidly toward a classless society. Mexico would evolve toward state-regulated socialism over several decades, as producers' cooperatives and capitalist factories existed happily side by side. For the time being, thought the socialist President, the State must undertake to free the nation from economic dependence on the United States; it must also stimulate Mexican entrepreneurs to expand industry and modernize the country. This last point was the essence of Cárdenas' tactical program: the creation of a consumers' market by jacking up wages through pressure from organized labor.

Lombardo Toledano and Cárdenas agreed that an immediate proletarian revolution was not the task at hand—socialism lay somewhere beyond history's next turn. They also agreed that the pressing problem was to raise the workers' starvation wages and to force the business bosses to make concessions. So Cárdenas made a pact with Lombardo: the CTM would back the President in his struggle against landlords and foreigners, and the State would support labor's strikes. The president would share power with the organized proletariat, or at least with its leaders.

The misery of the industrial workers worried Cárdenas. Their wages were so low that they lacked food; their desperation was turning into rage. In the explosive atmosphere of the 1930s the urban proletariat was inflammable material, and the reformist President wanted to soak that dry tinder in food and drink. He gave a green light to the engines of social integration, the militant unions. They pushed ahead with strikes.

Remember that under the Mexican Constitution, in labor disputes the State holds the whip: the government can declare a strike illegal and smash it with troops, or recognize it as legal and arbitrate in favor of labor. From 1935 on, workers paralyzed railway yards, mine pits, and factory floors in the anarchist tradition of seizing the means of production during strikes. Often they merely raised their fists to threaten a strike. Unions threatening a strike informed the government; state arbitrators then rushed in to settle the dispute before a walkout. Between employer and workers slipped the government official, ready to oil the machinery of collective bargaining. Cárdenas was determined to have the workers eating enough to keep them at their jobs.

Cárdenas pushed through social reforms. He struggled to enforce the minimum wage law and passed legislation requiring pay for workers on Sundays. Sunday pay boosted the power of mass consumption by 16 percent. The President said he was trying to restore social equilibrium. In fact, the economy picked up rapidly, as the new buyers demanded goods from industry. As output soared, even bankers stopped calling Cárdenas a Communist.

The National Peasant Confederation

Notwithstanding his support of the new labor central, Cárdenas threw the weight of his government against a CTM project to swallow up peasants in one big union. The Mexican State reserved for itself the right to organize peasants, and he urged agrarians to boycott the CTM's efforts. He played on the old suspicion of peasant leaders who feared the labor movement. The biggest peasant league ordered its members to stay out of the CTM, and the government raced ahead with the construction of its own nationwide organization on the land.

How did Cárdenas build his National Peasant Confederation (CNC)? He and organizers from the ruling party traveled up and down the country, calling for peasant unity. The President spent half his time on the road, visiting villages in the mountains and jungles where no top leader had ever gone. For an hour daily he opened the telegraphs to Mexico City so that peasants could talk to *el Presidente*. His populist style invaded Mexican politics, and state governors went out to meet the people.

For several years Cárdenas's agrarian revolution and the construction of his Peasant Confederation marched hand in hand. To get land, peasants had to organize a committee to petition the government; then the state granted land. Once the agrarian committees appeared, the ruling PNR brought them together into regional committees. Next the regional committees in each state were united into a peasant league.

And finally the ruling party merged the leagues into a national confederation, the CNC.

To keep the revolution from sweeping beyond the government, Cárdenas revved up the machinery of land distribution to meet peasant demands. Before some peasants could ask for land for their *ejido* village, big owners sent White Guards to kill, burn, and destroy. Villages vanished. The State distributed rifles to villages, for a militia to defend the land reform. Over the Cárdenas years the militia grew into a people's army with 70 battalions and 75 regiments of cavalry—firearms protected the new acquisitions. While the men worked in the fields, their women stood guard with Mauser rifles and fought off the hacendados' gunmen. Once again, gunfire lit up the map of Mexico as battles between agrarians and White Guards exploded around the nation.

By the end of 1937 the Revolutionary National Party had organized 28 peasant leagues. Across Mexico rural teachers from peasant families brought the tillers of the soil into agrarian committees. The teachers' work helped the ruling party catch over a million people in its organizing net. These agrarian cadres often died in the struggle. During the first years of the reform, White Guards murdered 2000 agrarians in Veracruz state alone. The teachers never tired of explaining to peasants what the government was doing, and their ideas undermined the work of hostile priests and political bosses. When the Catholic General Saturnino Cedillo rose in arms to stop Cárdenas's reforms, he called for support from the confused peasants of San Luis Potosí. As peasants rallied to his cause, rural teachers marched with them to explain what was happening. They went over to Cárdenas.

By the summer of 1938 there were 37 peasant leagues and unions; and the government called them to the capital to found the National Peasant Confederation. The CNC was to remain a creature of the state. To the end of the century its members, grateful for the land, backed the ruling party.

The base unit of the CNC was the *ejido*, the semicommunal village rooted in the mythical past. The village owned the land and assigned a plot to each family; the peasant could till the land but not rent or sell it; forest and pasture land were held in common. An *ejido* assembly was supposed to run the common affairs of the village and to send delegates to the peasant league. In theory the CNC was democratic.

In December 1935 the State founded the Ejido Bank to give the villages credit for fertilizer, seeds, and tools. From the beginning Cárdenas planned to use the bank to organize production and distribution in the countryside. His revolution would go beyond a change in land tenure to rebuild the economic and social life of rural Mexico.

The State would slowly lead the peasants into the new world of agrarian socialism.

The Ejido Bank became more than a lender. It stored and sold harvests, bought machinery and taught peasants to use it, fought crop plagues and developed new seeds, built power plants and repaired irrigation canals. The Bank set up consumers' cooperatives. It grew into a giant brain for administration and planning, with bureaucratic nerves linking it to a thousand villages. Through this monster the government got more of the seething countryside under control.

The Laguna cotton-growing area in Jalisco and Aguascalientes, a million acres cultivated by over a hundred haciendas, saw bloody strikes throughout 1935. The foreign owners refused to meet their peons' demands. In 1936 a general strike brought the crisis to a head, and the government decided to turn the haciendas into collective farms run by workers. So the foreign owners wrecked irrigation canals and carried off machinery. Workers' detachments guarded the canals while the State reorganized two-thirds of the area into 300 collective farms. These collectives used land, water, machinery, and credit in common. Everyone in the collective had a card noting the number of days each labored, and profits were distributed according to each person's work. The collectives got massive aid from the Ejido Bank.

A strike movement shook up the rice plantations of Lombardia and Nueva Italia in Michoacán; the President handed over the farms to workers' collectives. In Yucatán the big hemp growers had created chaos to sabotage Cárdenas's struggle for agrarian change, and by 1937 reformist efforts there were paralyzed. The frustrated peons threatened to break loose against the husks of the old order. The president rushed to Yucatán to give the land to the workers, along with the hemp growers' machinery; to the emerging collectives he promised big credits from the Ejido Bank. The wheat fields of the Yaqui Valley in Sonora, the sugar-growing region of Los Mochis in Sinaloa, the coffee plantations in Chiapas—all these areas sprouted collective farms. The foreign landowners were going down under the blows of Mexico's greatest nationalist. And the bourgeoisie was terrified by the impending socialist revolution. Cárdenas had tilted the social pact to the extreme left, beyond its original limits. Would it hold?

The Federation of Bureaucrat Unions

Cárdenas believed in the magic of organization and early offered its blessing to the state civil service. He attacked the spoils system and gave some public employees tenure, then urged them to form unions.

These white-collar workers wanted to join Lombardo's CTM, and in 1936 the labor central declared it would organize the civil service. This would give the CTM great power, for a strike by the bureaucrat unions could paralyze the government.

As the organizing moved forward in 1937, the government worked to bring the office workers into unions outside the CTM. The labor central repeatedly attacked the official policy, and between the State and the CTM there developed a struggle for public employees. Cárdenas maintained that since public employees formed part of the state organization, their duty was to identify with its interests. He threw the weight of his office against Lombardo, and in 1938 the CTM's bureaucrat unions transferred to a new labor central, the Federation of Unions of Workers at the Service of the State (FSTSE).

The organization of teachers also took place outside the CTM, but the labor central complained that it was a violation of their right to associate freely. Cárdenas was determined to check the CTM's power, for he feared that his pact with its Marxist leader would someday break down. But once the chief of state had lined up the peasant CNC and the FSTSE behind the government, the CTM was likely to go along; Lombardo would go where the power lay. Thus Cárdenas continued the policy of divide and rule.

THE CORPORATE STATE IN ACTION

The CTM continued to back Cárdenas. The most dramatic example of its power to rally Mexicans behind the President occurred in 1938. In Tampico the foreign oil companies refused to obey a government ruling, and Cárdenas plotted to seize the petroleum industry. He worried that the U.S. might send its fleet to Tampico to stop him. He had already taken the lands of U. S. owners to build collective farms, and President Franklin Delano Roosevelt had done nothing. The engines of the U.S. economy barely idled, and the American President was busy with repairs. Peace was needed on the border. But the oil might bring U.S. warships snarling down the Gulf, and Cárdenas wanted Mexico to back him up. He asked the CTM to mobilize the nation.

The CTM prepared its unions for demonstrations around the country and urged other organizations into action: the CROM, the CGT, the socialist youth, the Communists, the ruling party. They shifted into gear, and drove more and more Mexicans into the demonstrations of March 1938. Cárdenas fired off his decree nationalizing oil. Like a rocket burst it signaled a national fiesta: Mexico City schools vomited students into the streets; shopkeepers closed up to join the crowds; 200,000 workers surged down thoroughfares to paralyze the capital. Demonstrations broke out in cities around Mexico. The press applauded while peasants, women, youth, professionals, bureaucrats, and labor unions declared for the President. On March 18 the oil became Mexican.

Retooling the Ruling Party

Riding this wave of popular enthusiasm, Cárdenas stepped up his efforts to turn the ruling party into a working democracy. For two years he had struggled to strip the party of its old image. To Mexicans it had always seemd a bureaucratic machine, the instrument of an elite, a tool for settling disputes among the groups in power. But President Cárdenas preferred a political organization controlled by the masses. So in 1937 the ruling party arranged for assemblies of workers and peasants to ratify the people's candidates for office. At the party's national assembly after the oil expropriation in 1938, Cárdenas herded millions of celebrating workers into the fold of a new political party, the Party of the Mexican Revolution (PRM). The President marched them into what he called a "labor" sector, a "peasant" sector, and a "popular" sector. (There was also a "military" sector, but the party soon dropped it.) At the center of each sector he placed a large organization orbited by smaller groups. In the labor sector around the giant CTM hovered the smaller centrals and independent unions: the CROM, the CGT, the Miners' Union, the Electricians' Union. The peasant sector was roughly the CNC and its leagues. In the popular sector was the bureaucrats' FSTSE, surrounded by associations of professionals, intellectuals, women, youth, artisans, shopkeepers, and small manufacturers.

Every worker in a union, each peasant in an *ejido*, every *oficinista* with a desk, every artisan with a workshop, every doctor with a consulting room, every shopkeeper with a store, every tiny manufacturer with a business became a member of the ruling party (PRM). Cárdenas thought he was turning the elitist PNR into a mass party, but in fact it became a party of social groups called "corporations"—the political and economic bodies that make up a corporate state. Working people belonged to the PRM because they were members of the CTM, or the CNC, or the FSTSE. A migrant laborer on the land, a street vendor in the city, a prostitute in the street, an Indian in the high sierra, a peon on a big estate, a maid slaving in the kitchen, an errand boy in the market, all the drifters, the unemployed, the illiterate, the wretched of the earth—they were not members of the party. But anyone in the labor, peasant, or bureaucrat unions could not escape it. To get a civil service job an eighteen-year-old woman had to join a union and thus become a card-carrying, dues-paying member of the PRM.

The three sectors were supposed to control the workers' party from the bottom up. On the national level they would elect a candidate for President; on the state level, candidates for governors; and on the local level, candidates for municipal offices. The labor, peasant, and popular sectors would serve as pressure groups on the President, pushing him to make state policies in favor of working people.

The reformed and reconstructed PNR, said the PRM's declaration of principles, "considers as one of its fundamental objectives the preparation of the people for building a workers' democracy, for arriving at a socialist regime."[24] It identified the "class enemy" as big business. The great industrialists, merchants, and bankers could not join the workers' party, but the law required them to organize in associations: the Chamber of Industry, the Chamber of Commerce, and the Bankers' Association. Through such associations they could express their interests in an orderly way before the People's State. The workers' party was supposed to lead the nation toward socialism by struggling to transform the country's economic institutions.

Democracy Backfires

Cárdenas's attempt to transform the ruling party into a working democracy backfired. In the big unions at its base the party suffered all those tendencies that organization produces: the emergence of bureaucracies and chains of command, the shifting of control into the hands of internal oligarchs. ("Oligarchy," in case you have forgotten your Greek, means the "rule of a few.") Modern sociology has concluded that the base of every organization tends to dump control into the laps of bosses, for the rank and file are too exhausted by the demands of work, family, and leisure to inform themselves about the aims and problems of their movement. Nor are they competent to manage complicated matters requiring expertise, such as strike funds, pension plans, labor law, collective bargaining, union organizing, and political strategies. Most sociologists believe that direct democracy is technically impossible.[25]

The barely literate Mexicans were unable to make the party unions work for them, and the politicians did not encourage participation at the base. Cárdenas was a man of action, not a political scientist; he did not realize that control from below must be institutionalized by requiring that union leaders receive no more than the wages of a skilled worker and that leaders in key positions regularly rotate back to jobs in production. Without such checks, the bureaucracy in a popular organization elevates itself above the base and becomes a lower stratum of the new bureaucrat-professional class that lines its pockets through privileged salaries—at other people's expense.

The 1930s drew to a close, and the economic crisis ebbed away. As the excitement of the popular clases cooled, party men manipulated their organizations from the top down. In an economy with little to offer the average man, the workers' leaders discovered the road to well-paid jobs in the ruling party. In the election of 1937 large numbers of worker and peasant leaders had been taken into the government to become members of Congress. Their privileged salaries made them eager to do what the party wanted, in hopes of being chosen for other posts. With bursting billfolds they enjoyed the fleshpots of the capital and discovered that they, too, were privileged members of society. These newly prosperous bureaucrats had switched class position as easily as changing shirts.

In the elections at local, state, and federal levels, democracy never developed beyond assemblies of workers and peasants ratifying candidates proposed by the ruling party. The President picked the candidates for governorships, and the party sectors approved his choices. This process also worked at lower levels. Cárdenas thought it a transitional phase that must pass into full democracy, but his expectation was not fulfilled. For the rest of the century, nomination of candidates for office occurred from the top.

In 1938 Cárdenas approached the end of his term. He wanted as his successor the socialist Francisco Múgica—even more radical than himself—but most of the generals, the governors, the senators, the deputies, and the party elite preferred the more conservative Manuel Ávila Camacho. The social revolution against feudalism was over; the new rulers longed for a stable social democratic regime and wanted to tilt the balance of the social pact back toward the center and toward the nascent business community. The masses had calmed down, and to encourage them to advance was dangerous—what if they suddenly raced toward a classless society? Such egalitarian madness would eliminate the high salaries of the governing professionals and bureaucrats.

In 1939 the struggle over the presidential succession continued. To Cárdenas's astonishment, the bureaucratized leaders of the proletarian CTM and the peasant CNC turned their backs on the radical Múgica and threw the weight of the people's organizations behind the conservative Ávila Camacho. What could Cárdenas do except bow to the will of his party? Too late, the great socialist discovered that he had built a prison and cast his people into it. The cells were the bureaucratized corporations of the Corporate State.

After 1940 the revolutionary, idealistic, puritanical, egalitarian, charismatic Cárdenas stepped into the background of history, where his light continued to shine dimly in the top levels of the ruling elites. Later the fiercely independent Lombardo Toledano was forced from the General Secretariat of the CTM, and the organization man Fidel Velázquez took over. The new General Secretary was more interested in a post in Congress than in pressuring presidents to meet labor's needs, although he did enough to keep the workers' loyalty. For the rest of the century the party raised labor leaders into fat jobs in government, and the CTM became a cushion between the proletariat and the State.

The peasant CNC had been a creature of the State from its birth. Authority flowed down to its *ejido* base, where the Agrarian Department manipulated village assemblies. The poor and ignorant peasants slipped under bureaucratic control. But as the land reform crawled forward under later presidents, the CNC continued to take new *ejido* peasants under its umbrella. In order to keep the loyalty of the peasants, the CNC bureaucrats struggled to represent at least some of their interests.

The better-educated members of the FSTSE and professional associations showed more energy than the other sectors, so the ruling party carefully took their interests to heart. It showered the civil service, the teachers, and the state doctors with adequate medical care, retirement pensions, and low-priced goods in special commissaries. But the bureaucrat unions did not democratize the party.

The worker, peasant, and popular sectors failed to become pressure groups moving later presidents on a radical course. They turned into interest groups: the ruling party took into account their needs, made concessions to the rank and file, and co-opted the organizational leaders. These leaders always had a toehold in the underclasses they represented before the State, but their juicy salaries also made them representatives of the State to their own supporters.

The Mexican working people were locked in the cages of the Corporate State, and the ruling party had the only key. What would the bureaucrat-professional class do with it?

3

Administering the Social Pact

Cárdenas's Mexico was a revolutionary society. A people in arms defended the *ejido* and the school, the nationalized oil and railways, the collective farms. Cárdenas' government protested against Mussolini's invasion of Ethiopia, supported the Republican cause against Franco more than any other country, accepted refugees when the Spanish Republic fell, stood up for the suffering Jews at Geneva, condemned the Japanese invasion of China, was almost alone in rejecting Hitler's snatch of Austria, and took in the revolutionary Trotsky fleeing from Stalin's terror.

In 1940 Cárdenas left the Chair of *el Presidente*; he and his disciples took lesser posts in the ruling party. Although they remained an important current in the reorganized Party of the Mexican Revolution (PRM), the radical tide of the Revolution was ebbing: the workers with doubled wages became politically lazy; the peasants with corn patches began to yawn. The masses had gotten something at last; on the city block and in the rural village they relaxed. For the Revolution to gallop toward socialism they needed leadership, but most of the bureaucrat-professionals had had enough of radicalism—they wanted social peace. The bureaucrat-professionals decided to tilt the social pact of the Revolution away from workers and peasants, and toward business interests. As administrators of the social pact they hoped to restore the social balance. They aimed to hold the business class in a political coalition with workers, peasants, and *oficinistas*. They also thought to

maintain an equilibrium between capital and labor. In turning socialist under Cárdenas, the Revolution had swung to the left, but adjustment toward the center was next on the agenda. As a result of this
adjustment, the Cardenista move toward socialism would be reversed
at the top while pressure from below would slowly build up. The shifting of revolutionary gears took place under President Manuel Ávila
Camacho.

THE GENTLEMAN PRESIDENT

Ávila Camacho, an amiable man who had a heart attack during his
campaign for the presidency (and two more soon after), was a leader
seeking national unity. For the first time in the 20th century a Mexican President declared publicly, "I am a believer . . . I am a Catholic by
origin, in moral feeling."[1] Religious processions appeared in the streets,
and Catholic schools opened.

Promoting Capitalism

At the helm of state Ávila Camacho turned the policy wheel and began to steer in a capitalist direction. The government's Ejido Bank no
longer worked with socialist norms of agriculture to help the *ejidos*; instead it struggled to turn a profit. It gave credit to the few *ejidos* and
collectives that promised returns. Those who got money for machinery and fertilizer found themselves working for the Bank, which sold
their harvests on the market, sent bureaucrats to regulate production,
and forced peasants into a new kind of bondage. The number of *ejidos*
receiving credit dropped, for the government was spending more
money on dams and roads to service agribusiness.

In the cities businessmen applauded the new direction of the Bank.
Through it they invested in the collective farms, and profits flowed into
their pockets. The Bank forgot its old mission. In its huge body the can-
cer of corruption spread; it floundered in a swamp of fraud and red
tape. Its officials got rich off peasant sweat.

The State suspended the Cardenista project of slowly expanding the
public sector of industry across the economy. The public sector would
slowly grow, yes, but the private sector would fatten even faster. The
government was content to invest in energy, transportation, and communication, leaving the profitable areas to private enterprise—production in mines, factories, and farms. The State provided oil and dams,
railways and roads, while businessmen went after the profits in industry: textiles, cement, food, chemicals, beer, steel. The Mexican government set the table, and private enterprise came to the feast. But the

program worked: the industrialization of Mexico took off like a rocket and curved across the economic sky at an average 6 percent rate of growth until 1970. The rest of Latin America's developing nations gaped in envy.

In the social democratic tradition, Ávila Camacho believed in a strong, interventionist state. He set up the Nacional Financiera, a government bank that would give cheap credit to industrialists and watch over the development process. In 1944 he sent a law to the rubber-stamp Congress that invited foreign business to come to the feast but not to be greedy at table: the stock in any mixed corporation would be under Mexican control. American interests could eat their fill but not take over the restaurant. The Revolution's nationalism was alive and kicking.

Shoring up the Social Pact

The Revolution's literacy and vaccination campaigns had raised life expectancy in Mexico; more children survived infancy. But the practice of having many children in hopes that some would live, continued in Catholic Mexico, and a population surge began. In 1940 there were 20 million people; by 1950 the population had exploded to 28 million. This fateful demographic upsurge would continue to hold back growth in the standard of living until the government applied population control policies in the late 1970s.

Although Ávila Camacho was more interested in irrigating lands for agribusiness in north-central Mexico than in providing water, seed, tools, and fertilizer to the peasant *ejidos*, he continued to give out corn patches to the expanding population. He distributed only a third as much land as Cárdenas had done, but the distribution continued. Article 27 of the Constitution proclaimed that peasants had a right to land. Two-thirds of the Mexicans lived in the countryside, and the government wanted to keep this political force in the social pact of the Revolution.

In the irrigated North the desert bloomed like a rose, and Rockefeller-sponsored Norman Borlaug arrived to begin the Green Revolution with miracle seeds. Mexico's economy shifted gears and spurted forward in agriculture and industry. Mexico exported tomatos, avocados, sugar, and coffee to the United States; money flowed back to build factories. The nation prepared to urbanize as the Revolution climbed off its horse and got into an automobile.

On May 23, 1942, Mexico entered the war against the Axis Powers on the side of the United States. A squadron of Mexican "eagle warriors" shot down Japanese planes in the Pacific, but economic support for the war effort was more important: zinc, copper, and lead flowed into U.S. war plants; sugar went north to make chocolate bars for American soldiers at the front; fuel followed to drive Sherman tanks. Mexicans formed long lines to buy scarce energy for their little stoves, and children cried because there were no toys. Scarce goods in Mexico sent prices through the roof while CTM bureaucrats loyal to the government held wages level. Ávila Camacho had replaced the Marxist leader of the CTM with the cigar-smoking bureaucrat Fidel Velázquez. The President needed labor's loyalty.

As the Revolution climbed off its horse, inflation leaped on it and galloped away. Inflation sent the workers' buying power through the floor, wiping out the gains made under Lázaro Cárdenas. The business community celebrated with horn-tooting mariachis. (When an economic pie is divided up, inflation favors the monied people.)

To hold labor within the social pact of the Revolution, in 1943 Ávila Camacho created the Social Security Agency (IMSS). At first the *seguro*, as Mexicans call the institution, had only limited funds. But it was a promising beginning, and over the next generations the beefed-up *seguro* bettered the lot of Mexico's ill-paid workers.

In 1946 the President changed Cárdenas's Party of the Mexican Revolution (PRM) into the Institutional Revolutionary Party (PRI). What did "institutionalizing" the Revolution mean? It meant that the aim of the government was to maintain the balance in the social pact between capital and labor. The new party abandoned the slogan "For a democracy of the workers." Capital gained influence.

Until 1940 armed attacks on the Revolutionary state had come from the political right: military coups, religious guerrillas, and White Guards. As the government turned ever rightward, attacks started coming from the left. In 1943 the old Zapatista commander Rubén Jaramillo rose in a guerrilla war in Morelos. His socialist program demanded the nationalization of all sources of Mexican wealth and its equitable redistribution. The Mexican army chased him around the mountains of Morelos until he accepted an amnesty a year later. Jaramillo, who for a time was a secret member of the Mexican Communist Party, was also a Methodist minister. With the Bible in his palm and a rifle on his shoulder he preached the gospel of equality to the peasants.[2]

As Ávila Camacho, named by historians "the Gentleman President,"[3] finished his term in 1946, Mexico was chugging down the track of "Stabilized" Development. On December 1 he wrapped the green, white, and red presidential band around the chest of Miguel Alemán, a smooth lawyer from Veracruz who had not fought in the Revolution.

Alemán proclaimed that "what was good for business was good for Mexico."[4]

THE ENTREPRENEURIAL PRESIDENT

Immediately Alemán made clear to all that he was abandoning Cárdenas's socialist legacy. He reformed Article 3 of the Constitution and dropped "socialist education." He opened an attack on labor by arresting the leaders of the oil workers' union. The PRI eliminated all talk of socialist goals and of the bourgeoisie as the class enemy. Alemán considered the rising industrialists his class friends.

In the Great Depression of the 1930s, as goods stopped flowing in from the paralyzed economies of the northern developed countries, home industries had appeared in Mexico; and the government had put up a few tariffs to protect such products as women's clothes—although Mexico's woolen goods could compete with anything produced by the United States. Ávila Camacho added more tariffs, and President Alemán raised the wall higher. Mexican entrepreneurs produced consumer durables such as radios, stoves, refrigerators, and washing machines for the home market. Alemán gave tax breaks and subsidies to capitalists, a policy later presidents would continue. Hiding behind tariffs, businessmen often produced shoddy goods for a captive market. Women's dresses were made with inferior patterns that lacked the zip and style of New York or Paris; Mexican washing machines whirled with limited cycles. Mexican consumers made do with what was available to them, but the stuff could hardly be shipped abroad.

As the government continued to set the table for the entrepreneurs' feast, the smell of profits drew foreign companies into Mexico. U.S. multinational corporations arrived to invest in the production of TV sets and automobiles, to invest in raising tomatoes for export to the United States. Mexican women learned the delights of shampoo and hair spray. For international business the feast was rich indeed.

In the Mexican countryside typhoid is as common as the common cold; drinking water systems in rural Mexico are polluted. When advisers suggested to President Alemán that he improve the water in tropical Mexico, he decided instead to subsidize the sale of sugar to the soft drink manufacturers—Coca-Cola is safe. Today in the most remote mountain villages poor peasants meet in the plaza to drink Coca-Cola, to them a sign of modernity. Nowadays the 35 brands of soft drinks are made by foreign companies, and Mexicans drink more soda pop than any nation on earth: the increased sugar content makes the drinks addictive. We're glad they do drink them—the water is dangerous. This example of the decades-long developmental attention to profit-making started by Alemán, rather than providing necessary services, is an example that can be multiplied: Kimberly Clark makes the best toilet paper on earth, but millions lack toilets; the Kleenex is of the highest quality, but millions lack textbooks; the automobiles run with a tiger in the tank, but millions lack transport; half the nation survives in huts and shanties, but those shacks contain TV sets; industrialized Mexico City is the worst ecological catastrophe on our planet, but in manufacture for export the nation ranks twelfth in the world. Mexico may not be a developed country, but it is certainly an industrial society. In the year 2001 the 190 countries below Mexico in economic status find its economic "miracle" more astonishing than the appearance of the Virgin at Tepeyac.

Under Alemán low taxes encouraged entrepreneurs to reinvest their earnings in Mexico's development, and they were anxious to do so in such a promising new market. His don't-tax-the-rich policy set a fatal precedent that has continued to this day, turning Mexico into a tax haven that cynics now compare with the Cayman Islands. But during the industrialization drive from 1940 to 1970, Mexico successfully applied the formula SAVINGS + INVESTMENT = GROWTH. During this period of economic stability, reinvestment of business profits became profitable. (In the 1980s, however, when the economy began to toss about in a globalizing world money market, lashed by the storms of devaluations, inflations, recessions, speculations, and stagflations, capital fled the country like monarch butterflies migrating north. Just as the butterflies preferred the green hills of Canada for feeding, so investors preferred the greener pastures of Wall Street for profiting. The towers of Wall Street were solid compared to the Mexican stock exchange, bouncing around in economic earthquakes.)

Keeping the Social Pact Alive

It was Alemán who decisively pointed the nation down the track of savage capitalist development, passing each switching point with ever increasing speed. Yet even as he shifted the social pact heavily toward businessmen, he tried to hold the popular classes in it. As the industrialization drive accelerated, the workers' wages began to creep upward. The President gave out almost as much land to the remaining landless as Ávila Camacho had distributed. New schools dotted the countryside. Hundreds of small factories appeared in Mexico City, Monterrey, and Guadalajara as the middle social layers slowly grew. For them Alemán placed the National University in the lava flow south of Mexico City on a campus so beautiful that it seemed to have been dropped from another world. (But he forgot to put books in the library!) And if the underclasses did not get drinkable water, at least they got Coca-Cola. Inspection brigades rushed through the Coca-Cola plants; if they found a single fly, management was fired.

Alemán continued to mix a dose of state socialism into the cocktail of a market economy. The state sector of the economy continued to expand, though not as fast as private business. The state oil corporation doubled production; electricity output tripled; highways crisscrossed the nation. The state built harbors, airports, railroads; it irrigated huge tracts of land in the northwest, and more of the desert blossomed like a rose. Under Ávila Camacho and Alemán, Mexico's gross national product expanded 100 percent.

Alemán tilted the social pact of the Revolution so far toward business interests that he needed to mask reality with rhetoric. The son of a revolutionary who died in the mountains, he never stopped hailing the Revolution. On his lips the revolutionary slogans may have been empty, but he never forgot to mouth them.

He mysteriously became a millionaire. Millionaires popped up all over the place, including top officials who were looting the government till: estimates of dollars hidden in foreign banks by the *políticos* ran as high as $800 million.[5] Under Alemán a politician who remained poor was a poor politician. The cabinet played follow-the-leader. The business President made the Mexican economy boom, but it benefited the rising capitalist class and not the little man, while political theft clouded the nation with fumes of corruption. The stink was too much for workers and peasants, who found that Coca-Cola was not satisfying their basic needs. They wanted the next president to turn the policy wheel to the left. To the left? Yes, toward boosted wages and credit for *ejidos*. Back to symmetry in the social pact of the Revolution!

The Cardenista current in the ruling party had also had enough, and demanded that Alemán choose an honest man as his successor. So in the election of 1952 the outgoing President launched the incorruptible Adolfo Ruiz Cortines as the official candidate. (Ruiz Cortines could be an honest politician because he had no living relatives.)

THE HONEST PRESIDENT

General Miguel Henríquez Guzmán, a rich businessman who was a friend of Lázaro Cárdenas, campaigned against Ruiz Cortines with a Cardenista program: attention to peasant needs, labor reforms, a purge of corrupt officials, and a swing toward socialist ideals. There was an explosion of labor and campesino support for Henríquez's Federation of Parties of the People (FPP). As a mass movement erupted, the ruling party repressed it with violence. For example, a peaceful caravan of 15 busloads of peasants approaching Puebla for a Henriquista rally was shot up by armed men in an ambush; in Mexico City federal troops scattered a peaceful Henriquista demonstration with gunfire. In Morelos the Mexican Workers' Agrarian Party (PAOM) of the Zapatista Rubén Jaramillo joined Henríquez's Federation, and the state governor unleashed official terror, torturing and assassinating some of the 15,000 Jaramillistas. Ruiz Cortines won the presidential election amid widespread accusations of fraud at the polls.

In protest against repression and electoral fraud in Morelos, in 1953 Rubén Jaramillo again rose in guerrilla warfare against the regime. With 30 guerrillas he entered the village of Ticumán on March 7, 1954, captured the police chief and two merchants accused of torturing peasants, tried them in the plaza, and shot them. Jaramillo's guerrilla band slipped in and out of villages throughout the state, protected by the Mexican Workers' Agrarian Party. The state of Morelos is a gigantic valley ringed by mountains, and for five years the Jaramillistas galloped through the sierra and the ravines, pursued by federal cavalry and airplanes. Only in 1958, during the presidential campaign of Adolfo López Mateos, did Jaramillo accept a second amnesty: the new candidate promised to solve the problems of the peasants growing cane in the sugar bowl.

In 1953 President Ruiz Cortines had begun his rule facing these armed attacks from the left. Was the social pact falling apart? Something had to be done to preserve it. So Cortines demanded strict honesty from his bureaucrats. When the President is honest, he can frighten his cabinet into incorruptibility. Ruiz Cortines ordered all officials to make public their financial holdings, and year after year he fired the better-known grafters. Irritated businessmen complained that no one would take their bribes.

Under Alemán the pendulum of Mexican policy had swung far to the right of the political spectrum, but Ruiz Cortines barely moved it back toward the center: wages continued their upward creep, the *ejidos* languished with little credit. Nevertheless, he cleaned up the filthy image of the government and threw sops to small businessmen, workers, peasants, and women.

Underpinning the Social Pact

Women? Yes. Women are the oppressed sex in macho Mexico. The culture is a synthesis of four strands: Mayan, Aztec, Spanish, and Arab. The Moors ruled Spain for seven centuries and implanted Arab machismo there; the Spanish stamped it on Mexico. Although women had fought and died as *soldaderas* in Pancho Villa's army, not a single woman was allowed in the revolutionary government formed in 1920. For decades feminist movements had demanded the vote, and in 1953 Ruiz Cortines gave it to them. This raised the status of women in Mexico and opened the door for future struggles.

The president progressively expanded the state medical program (IMSS) that guaranteed care to industrial workers: the number of clinics rose from 42 to 226, hospitals from 19 to 105. Workers' wages kept pace with inflation. Until near the end of his administration there were few strikes, and Adolfo López Mateos, the young Secretary of Labor, managed to settle them quickly.

The demographic explosion continued, alarming sociologists and intellectuals. In 1950 the population was 28 million; by 1958 it had jumped to 33 million. The new peasants appearing in the countryside demanded land. Ruiz Cortines distributed slightly more land than Alemán had done. And for the first time the medical service of the IMSS reached into the countryside.

More than half of Mexico's exports were still avocados, tomatoes, lettuce, strawberries, asparagus, pineapples, sugar, coffee, chocolate, cotton, beans, and corn. Much of the rest consisted of minerals from the mines. Although profit was reinvested in the country for industrialization, it hardly seemed enough. The economy needed to export manufactured goods to help finance the industrialization drive. But most of the economy was still small and medium business; protected by tariffs, these entrepreneurs were not making goods that would be competitive on the world market. Americans would not buy Mexican footwear. To sell more to the United States, the tariff wall would have to come down, but small business begged for protection. To maintain its support, Ruiz Cortines swathed the economy in even more tariffs.

Why not? Foreign investment was pouring into Mexico's economy like fuel into an engine. In Monterrey, Guadalajara, and Mexico City there were signs advertising General Motors, Chrysler, Kellogg, Dow Chemical, Campbell Soup, Pepsi Cola, Colgate, Goodyear, John Deere, H.J. Heinz, Ford, Procter & Gamble, Sears, and—well, you know the names. These giant corporations flexed their industrial muscles and the economy raced ahead. They also sucked huge profits out of Mexico, but the factories, bottling plants, and department stores stayed put.

Big Mexican capital also marched forward. Fortunes were made, and the number of entrepreneurial millionaires crept upward; but the state sector of the economy also expanded, and an infrastructure of new roads helped farmers reach urban markets. Meanwhile, the main beneficiary of the industrialization drive remained the business community.

The Shaken Social Pact

In the legends of the peasants of Morelos, Zapata still rode over the mountains on his white horse, and many believed him alive. Others saw Jaramillo as his reincarnation, and Rubén was very much alive—shooting at the government and demanding socialism. So Ruiz Cortines continued verbally to honor the Constitution, implying that someday the workers and peasants would be invited to the feast. Distributive justice might be a dream, but can't dreams come true?

In the last year of Ruiz Cortines's administration, the stabilized development of Mexico began to destabilize. In April 1958, Othón Salazar Ramírez led a demonstration of underpaid teachers into the central plaza of Mexico City—they demanded a 40 percent raise. Club-swinging police invaded the plaza and scattered the teachers like pigeons. They dispersed to mobilize support from their pupils' parents, and soon 90 percent of the government primary schools in Mexico City were on strike.

The labor leaders running the National Educational Workers Union (SNTE) inside the FSTSE—the organization of government bureaucrat unions in the base of the ruling party—were enraged because the teachers had broken out of their cage in a wildcat strike. The press and the labor leaders allied to the government immediately applied "the police theory of history" to the movement, proclaiming that Communist agitators had stirred up the foolish teachers in an attack on society. Mónico Rodríguez, who was advising Salazar,[6] was in fact a Communist, but did this one man, who had accidentally joined the spontaneous movement, trick thousands of poorly paid teachers into demanding a raise? (Salazar became a Communist only in 1965.)

As the strike dragged on and the hungry teachers demanded wages to keep up with inflation, the Secretary of Public Education stonewalled and refused to meet with Salazar. At the end of April thousands of teachers marched to the Secretariat of Public Education, a block-wide, three-story building with murals by Diego Rivera around a huge courtyard. Salazar, "the little giant," made an explosive speech, and the teachers voted for a sit-in at the Secretariat.[7] For weeks they camped in the courtyard under the Revolutionary murals, supplied with food by sympathizers and their pupils' parents. To discredit the movement, the press and the government roared that Communists were at work. (Mexican authorities agreed that if the Communists did not exist, it would be necessary to invent them.) As students and workers proclaimed solidarity with the teachers, Ruiz Cortines decided to end the strike.

On May 15, a traditional holiday for all Mexican educators, President Ruiz Cortines suddenly announced that he was granting a 17 percent raise to all the teachers in the nation. Towering above the hardhearted education bureaucracy, the President appeared as the kindly father of his people, taking their needs to heart. (Everyone, remarked Machiavelli, sees what you seem, but few know what you are.)[8]

Many of the striking teachers wanted more than a raise, they wanted to democratize their union. The strike continued. But the government would not concede control of the union to the base, and as vacation time approached, the strike ebbed away. The Revolutionary Teachers Movement (MRM) would remain an important popular current in the official union and would launch more strikes in coming decades.

From June 26 to August 7 the workers paralyzed the national railway system with a turbulent strike that was finally settled by a pay hike: the railroad grid was the framework of the economy, and the freight had to roll. Workers were thrashing about in their cages and tearing them apart. Strikes flashed here and there in the last months of Ruiz Cortines's presidency.

As President and later, Ruiz Cortines always lived simply, and did not die a millionaire. When he retired, every Mexican Diogenes waved his lantern and applauded: at last they had found an honest politician. But who would succeed him?

The pendulum of Mexican policy had been stuck on the right during three presidencies. It was high time for a swing toward the center of the political spectrum. What would the ruling PRI do? Cárdenas and Alemán were fighting each other for control of the party. Most of the party officials understood that the desired balance in favor of social justice and capitalist development had inclined too far in favor of the business community. A shift toward the left was needed. The nomination went to Adolfo López Mateos, Ruiz Cortines's Secretary of Labor, who stood for healing the sickened social pact and had the backing of Lázaro Cárdenas.

THE POPULAR PRESIDENT

As the ruling party's electoral machine turned out a landslide vote for López Mateos in the summer of 1958, the Revolutionary Teachers Movement in the capital was electing Othón Salazar head of the Executive Committee of Section IX of the National Educational Workers'

Union. The officials of the government-controlled union refused to recognize Salazar's victory. In September a teachers' march demanding recognition was joined by other workers; Ruiz Cortines's government smashed the demonstration and arrested Salazar and the leaders. As Ruiz Cortines's administration ended, the President elect watched a rising wave of strikes. López Mateos was sworn in as the strikes continued and infected parts of the countryside—landless peasants tried to take over big private estates. He took office and released Salazar from prison. Soon afterward he proclaimed, "I am left within the Constitution."[9] He meant that he would try to return the ruling party to the path forged by Obregón and Calles, holding the business class by one hand and the working class by the other.

Mexican Society in 1959

What was Mexican society like during the new president's first year in office in 1959? In Mexico City a typical working class tenement had 25 rooms (without toilets) surrounding a courtyard. In each room lived a family with six or more children. The bathrooms, where lines formed, were in the corners of the courtyard, and there were basins for washing clothes by hand. On tiny grills the inhabitants cooked beans and tortillas; chiles were a source of vitamins. Meat, eggs, and milk were rare luxuries.

Mexico is a street culture; people play in the street, often eat there, sometimes even work on the sidewalks. For some the tenement was only for sleeping and for refuge during the summer rains. Most of the older tenement children attended school, but finishing the sixth grade was a difficult achievement.

In peasant huts in mountain villages in the sugar bowl of Morelos, a family lived in one room with a dirt floor. There was no bathroom. Hanging on the wall of the hut were pots, grills, and *petates*, the straw mats that peasants have slept on since Aztec times. Here, too, was a monotonous diet of corn and chiles, but chickens yielded eggs and there were a few turkeys. On feast days pigs were slaughtered to prepare *carnitas*, tasty bits of fried pork.

The villages lacked electricity. During the summer rains a family made eight trips a day to the well, and during the longer dry season, 20. In the village school the only teacher taught the first grade from 9 A.M. to noon, the second grade from 1 P.M. to 4 P.M., and the third grade from 5 P.M. to 8 P.M.

Peasants and rural laborers who had fled the lifelong poverty of the countryside to look for work in the metropolis might be found living in tin and cardboard shanties in eastern Mexico City. Upon arrival they often stayed under a canopy on the roof of a relative already living in the shantytown. Their next problem was to build a shack of their own and to tap a line into a power source. There were no bathrooms, and gaining access to a water faucet was not easy. If illiterate, they were not only unemployed but sometimes unemployable, and survived by selling lottery tickets in the street or collecting paper and cans for recycling. But others might land a factory job with the help of a friend. Many believed they had made a step up from the misery of rural life. On Sundays they sat in giant movie theaters watching American films with Spanish subtitles; those who could read translated out loud for their illiterate friends. (The official national illiteracy rate was 40 percent, but the actual rate was probably closer to 50 percent.)

Often a worker's family would save and scrimp all year in order to invite their many relatives and friends for tamales and tequila to celebrate a baptism or a wedding; the peasants also had feasts on saints' days and during rites of passage. The joy of poor Mexicans lay in inviting or being invited to these endless fiestas. On Sundays in the capital the poor might picnic in gigantic Chapultepec Park and take their children to the zoo for free.

In 1959 two-thirds of Mexicans lived in pinching poverty. They had never known anything else, and although they were class-conscious enough to understand that the upper social layers were exploiting them, many thought the gap between the poor and the rich was as inevitable as the gap between earth and sky.

The middle strata were widening. In 1959 there were forests of TV antennas on the apartment buildings of petty bureaucrats. (In those days black-and-white television sets were expensive, beyond the reach of three-fourths of the population.) Office workers, tradespeople, small businessmen, successful professionals, and ambitious intellectuals were still firmly in the social pact of the Revolution, a cushion between the poor and the rich.

In the mansion of one of the nouveaux riches who had made a fortune running guns during the Revolution, there were parquet floors, a showy library, a huge kitchen, eight bedrooms. In the grounds were three garages, well-kept lawns, heated pools, flowery terraces, frontón tennis. The staff included chauffeurs, servants, gardeners, nannies, cooks, and guards. The rich don't live in Mexico, they live above it!

The Carrot and the Stick

Twenty years after 1940 the train of the Revolution had changed its makeup: the engine of the ruling party was now connected to a Pullman car and a luxury diner containing happy politicians and bourgeois gourmets, followed by a few coaches of middling professional and technical workers, clerks, and petty bourgeois. It pulled a long string of boxcars full of ragged workers and peasants, tailed by a caboose with marginalized Mexicans riding on the roof and hanging off the sides. In the boxcars were agitators urging the ragged poor to demand better accommodations. On December 1, 1958, Adolfo López Mateos sat down in the engineer's seat and put his hand on the throttle. He wanted to improve the lot of workers and peasants, and to kick the agitators off the train.

As his administration began, the real trains ground to a halt. In March 100,000 railwaymen stopped work, demanding that the Constitution's Article 123 guaranteeing housing to workers be observed. Again the workers were breaking out of their cage with a whirlwind strike, but this one convulsed Mexico: without transport, the economy idled. Once more the government did not have to invent the Communists—they were leading the strike. López Mateos crushed it with troops and jailed the Communist leaders Valentín Campa and Demetrio Vallejo for violating the law against "social dissolution." What kind of law? Social dissolution was whatever the president said it was—in this case, leading a strike paralyzing the nation.

While traveling in Venezuela, David Siqueiros, the internationally famous Communist muralist, violated a Mexican taboo by criticizing, in another country, *el Presidente's* repression at home. When he returned to Mexico City, the police came for him. Siqueiros fired at them and fled, but they chased him down and salted him away in Lecumberri Federal Prison for four years. He first painted the walls of his cell and then did 250 portraits of himself. Meanwhile, López Mateos kicked other agitators off the train.

Mending the Social Pact

The President then moved to improve the lot of the workers and peasants by putting teeth into Article 123 of the Constitution. He injected funds into the Social Security Medical System and it stretched to cover more workers, he built more clinics throughout the neglected countryside. Vaccination teams scratched the arms of peasants in remote areas, and cholera was wiped out. A war on mosquitoes brought victory over malaria. Polio retreated before the attacks of public health campaigns; TB microbes died, and coughing stopped. Between 1958 and 1965 the Mexican Institute of Social Security increased the number of people covered in its programs by 250 percent.[10] More aging workers, instead of being thrown into the street or onto the mercy of their offspring, were cared for by pensions.

To turn the policy wheel left and do more for the underclasses, the state needed money. But López Mateos ran into a brazen wall: the bourgeoisie laughed at the tax collectors. Decades of low taxes on booming business had concentrated personal income at the top of the scale. By 1963 Mexico had one of the steepest income distributions of any nation on earth. In the slicing up of the personal income sandwich, peasants and marginalized groups, making up 60 percent of the population, nibbled on a tiny bite amounting to 21.7 percent. Factory workers and the middle strata, making up 30 percent of the population, gnawed on an ample portion amounting to 36.7 percent of the sandwich. The upper elites of business tycoons and bureaucrat-professionals, making up 10 percent of the population, devoured a fleshy slice amounting to 41.6 percent.[11]

Around the world during the 1950s and 1960s, in the Keynesian theory of the welfare state the rich were to be taxed in order to redistribute national wealth to the underclasses through free education, public health, retirement pensions, unemployment compensation, mass transit, subsidized housing, and basic services. The Mexican leaders knew their Keynes, but Ávila Camacho, Alemán, and Ruiz Cortines had taxed business so lightly that there was little to redistribute. From 1940 to 1970 most of the 25 Latin American countries had tax burdens bigger than Mexico's: on the scale of countries trying to make the rich pay up, Mexico lay at the bottom of the heap with Guatemala and Paraguay. By the time of López Mateos, the Mexican rich resisted tax reform like tigers defending a lair. A tax reform would be equivalent to another social upheaval.

It is not easy for a government to build a tax base and an efficient and honest Internal Revenue Service. A national civic spirit, a norm internalized in the culture—"We ought to pay our taxes!"—is even more difficult to create. López Mateos knew that the PRI was in no mood to start a fight with the business community over its booty: such folly would surely result in an investment strike, a flight of capital, and a collapse of the booming economy.

The government was short on money, and for social spending López Mateos had to do with what little money he had. As the nation's top leader read and reread the Constitution containing the social pact, he decided to enforce Article 123's declaration that every business must share profits with its workers. The Constitution is potentially socialist; it does not define the percentage of the sharing but leaves that question to be decided by political struggles. If the share were 51 percent, the bulk of the profits would go to the workers, and Mexico might no longer be a capitalist society. In 1962 López Mateos entered this portentous road by setting up the National Commission for Profit

Distribution to work out a plan. By 1964 many workers had increased their pay 5 to 10 percent a year by biting into the bosses' profits. The business community was not amused.[12]

Urbanizing Mexico had turned into a nation of reeking slums and shanty towns. The President stepped into the ring with this monster problem and delivered it a well-aimed blow by starting housing projects in the big factory towns. Some of the housing developments contained schools, clinics, and nurseries. In Mexico City one slum gave way to single-bedroom apartments renting for $6 a month. In spite of the hammer blows of the President, the slum monster kept growing, fed by the population explosion. Sociologists wrung their hands as the government failed to institute population control in Catholic Mexico. The President resembled a dermatologist removing skin cancers but encouraging sunbaths.

In a shanty town a woman from Oaxaca had given birth to 30 boys. These 30 would grow up to father more than 100 children: in a macho culture, the more kids, the bigger the man. Mexico's population was growing faster than that of its cultural mother—the Arab world. After the state built a low-cost housing project, two more shantytowns appeared on its rim. If a new factory hired 100 laborers, 100 more appeared at the gate with upraised arms, begging for work. As the arms grew in number, they became skinnier.

In the countryside a typical peasant produced a flock of children as his workforce. He had as many as possible, in hopes that some of them would care for him when he was too old to work. The birthrate was outrunning the land available for cultivation by new generations. In order to keep pace with population growth, Ávila Camacho, Alemán, and Ruiz Cortines each had distributed about a third as much land as Cárdenas had done. Now López Mateos whipped the pace of distribution from a trot to a gallop and gave out two-thirds as much as Cárdenas. It was not always the best land: without water, the peasants had to wait for the rainy months of June, July, and August in order to get in a corn crop. But the summer crop could be stored and eaten in the dry season—it was the difference beween life and death. If the peasants lived near a city, they looked for menial work there during the dry season; one of their daughters might be taken on as a domestic laborer. In the Mexican countryside, life was a grim struggle to stay alive.

Ávila Camacho, Alemán, and Ruiz Cortines had irrigated desert land in the North in order to encourage agribusiness to feed the sprawling cities and to export food to the gringos for profit. López Mateos turned his attention to the deep South of Mexico, where forgotten indigenous peoples, breeding in the tropics like fruit flies, needed corn patches. There he cleared and opened up new lands for cultivation.

God commanded, "Be fruitful and multiply, and replenish the earth" (Genesis 1:28). Catholic priests assured Mexicans that God was talking to *them*. Medieval theology, Mexican machismo, cultural lag, and the fear of final abandonment in a society without enough old age pensions combined to fuel the baby boom. And the boom gave birth to another monster problem.

When the Revolution began, eight out of ten Mexicans could not sign their names; but four decades of missionary teachers and rural normal schools had cut illiteracy in half. Yet because of the continuing baby boom, in 1960 there were more Mexicans without the ABC's than in 1910. López Mateos squared off against the monster of growing illiteracy, and struck two aggressive blows.

First, he multiplied the number of country schools by giving villages building materials and know-how; peasants then built the classrooms themselves, and in every schoolhouse put rooms for a teacher to live in. Second, the energetic executive printed millions of textbooks for the first six grades and required every school in Mexico to use them—they were free.

The religious schools had to teach the textbooks, too; inspectors dropped by with exams to find out if pupils knew what was in them. They told of the Spanish Inquisition during the colonial period; they described the Church's war against liberal Benito Juárez and its betrayal of the *patria* to the French imperialists in the time of Maximilian; they reported the efforts of religious guerrillas to overthrow the new government. Outside of the totalitarian Stalinist societies to the east, Mexico was the only nation to impose a universal obligatory textbook on its people.

A roar of rage went up from the priests and the faithful, but López Mateos hung tough and the free textbooks became standard fare in Mexican education. As the decades rolled by, the textbooks glorified revolutionary presidents and leaders like Mao and Gandhi, Nasser and Tito. In order to combat the racism that Spain had inculcated in Mexican culture, the books contained pictures of white, black, yellow, and brown children playing together.

Sustaining Economic Growth

López Mateos peppered the society with labor and land reforms. If these barely touched the misery of the masses, at least they signaled to millions that workers and peasants were still in the social pact of the Revolution. He operated in the Revolution's social democratic tradition of enlarging the state's role in the economy. His government bought controlling stock in several foreign industries. U.S. companies held the switches of the power grid, but he soon gained control over this productive energy. The nationalization of the electrical industry brought howls from the right about creeping socialism. New petrochemical industries stabbed the clouds with their stalagmite towers: Petróleos Mexicanos was reaching for the skies. Mexico was producing its own steel and oil—in those days the basis of an industrial society. Like his forerunners, the PRI leader blew strength into the infrastructure servicing production, and the business class sailed before the wind.

Foreign companies had built two separate telephone systems in Mexico City. If you were on the same line as a friend, you could call him; if not, you had to ask a neighbor on the other line if you could use his phone. You can imagine what this meant for business. Mexican private enterprise gained the upper hand in the telephone system; its rationalization was the order of the day. Local enterprise also built first-class hotels in Acapulco, when the pelicans still dived into waters clear as glass. Tourists spent millions at new resorts, and the money flowed into the arteries of the economy.

The labor President struggled to bind workers to the social pact. A clever populist, he projected an image of caring for them. In the traditional initiation of the soccer football season by *el Presidente* (corresponding to the American president's throwing out a baseball), he appeared in the stadium to watch the game, a sports aficionado like his people (although in fact he was sitting there with his cabinet, engaged in official duties). The president, handsome as a movie star, spread many stories about himself as a Don Juan (and did just enough to convince macho Mexico that there was fire behind the smoke). He had a winning personality, and when the time came to spout revolutionary rhetoric, he could make a speech that sounded like Fidel Castro. Workers could easily identify with this "man of the people," who had come from an impoverished family. López Mateos bought the movie industry from American interests and kept the price of tickets so low that workers could afford them. As he wound up his term, he had achieved a short-term stabilization of the social pact.

Rubén Jaramillo had risen in guerrilla warfare in 1943 and again in 1953. Nine years later, disgruntled by López Mateos's failure to keep his promises to the peasants of the sugar bowl, Jaramillo was preparing for a trip to revolutionary Cuba. He had just rejoined the Communist party and was sharpening his guerrilla knife for another thrust at the government. So on May 23, 1962, dozens of soldiers and police surrounded his house in Tlaquiltenango, then carried him and his family to Xochicalco and shot them. This official murder made news around the world. The crime would have been impossible without the knowledge and consent of López Mateos. He was still throwing Communist agitators off the train.

Carrying on Revolutionary Nationalism

In foreign policy the President remained true to the nationalism of the Mexican Revolution. Venustiano Carranza was the father of this nationalist tradition. Never a social revolutionary, he was Mexico's greatest revolutionary nationalist. During his presidency he faced down Woodrow Wilson's armed intervention against Villa in Chihuahua, sneered at Washington's ultimatums, and thundered, "Out Now!" In 1917 General John J. Pershing went home with his tail between his legs. Carranza imposed ever increasing taxes on the foreign oil companies in Tampico, thumbing his nose at their threats of armed intervention. When in 1917 Washington pressured him to declare war on Germany, he proclaimed neutrality instead, proposed an immediate end to the world war, and urged all neutrals to stop selling anything to the warring powers. In 1918 Carranza denounced the Monroe Doctrine and demanded that diplomats stop intervening in the internal affairs of other nations. This "Carranza Doctrine" of nonintervention guided Mexico's foreign policy for seven decades. In 1919, when the League of Nations accepted the Monroe Doctrine in Article 27 of its charter, Carranza roared that Mexico would not join it.

National sovereignty, the self-determination of peoples, and nonintervention became the cornerstones of Mexico's foreign policy in the 20th century. Obregón, Calles, and Cárdenas continued this posture.

In 1959 Fidel Castro entered the history of the Western Hemisphere like a thief in the night, and before Washington could lock the door, he had stolen one of its economic colonies. By 1962 an enraged Uncle Sam was demanding that every Latin American president break diplomatic relations with Communist Cuba and join the U.S. economic blockade of the island. All fell on their knees before Uncle Sam except López Mateos, who remained on his feet, urging "No intervención!" He saved Cuba from complete isolation: instead of having to fly from Caracas all the way to Paris and then back again to Havana, Venezuelans could catch a plane to Cuba from Mexico City. Cubans could likewise visit Latin American capitals without making a detour through Europe.

The President's revolutionary nationalism did not mean that he sympathized with communism, a contagious disease that might infect more of the Mexican left. On April 17, 1961, came the CIA-sponsored invasion of Cuba at the Bay of Pigs, and in Mexico City there was a protest march of 20,000 on April 18. The head of the demonstration was marching down narrow Madero Street when a phalanx of tanks throwing tear gas canisters appeared in front of it, pushing the leaders back against the thousands streaming forward down the canyon of buildings. In the closing vise one slip meant being trampled to death. With canister shrapnel stuck in their heads and blood-streaked faces, the radicals in the lead struggled to stay on their feet. López Mateos was still throwing agitators off the train.

In trying to govern as a leftist within the Constitution, the most popular President since Lázaro Cárdenas maneuvered to maintain the social pact of the Mexican Revolution. His successor, Gustavo Díaz Ordaz, suffered from an authoritarian personality that had hardened during his service as Secretary of the Interior, a cabinet post demanding an iron hand on radical dissent. The Secretary is in fact the nation's top cop and the PRI government's man in charge of social control. Throughout López Mateos' administration, Díaz Ordaz had been the tough guy throwing the agitators off the train: the railway workers' Communist leaders, the Communist painter David Siqueiros, and other radicals who became guests of the government in Lecumberri Federal Prison. The Zapatista Rubén Jaramillo was not so lucky; he was thrown under the wheels.

THE DESPOTIC PRESIDENT

In 1964 the business community applauded Díaz Ordaz's campaign for the presidency and expected him not only to share a bit of the economic surplus with the popular classes but also to use a cutting whip. He would not disappoint them. He was the ugliest President Mexico had seen since Benito Juárez, and during his administration some of the middle strata would find his policies to be the ugliest since the earlier Díaz and his dictatorship.

The Weakening Social Pact

The rising tension between worker-peasant needs and bureaucrat-business interests had threatened the social pact of the Mexican Revolution, but López Mateos had once more tried to tighten the pact. Díaz Ordaz understood what the labor President had been doing. With limited funds the buck-toothed leader struggled manfully to persist in some of the same programs. He pushed the policy of profit-sharing with the workers—insisting they should have 8 percent. He kept on distributing land to peasants. He continued urban renewal. He spent even more money on education. He nursed the health of the economy for the business community, and profits and reinvestment held growth at a vigorous 6 percent—jobs were created. But time was running out for the PRI government: Mexico still resembled a luxurious mansion in which the feasting few toasted one another, while outside the wretched many begged for crumbs and scratched their sores. Already, more than one Lazarus was beating on the door. How long before they decided to break in?

Although he needed money, Díaz Ordaz did not stoop to printing new bills to pay the state's old bills. (A temptation later presidents did not resist; and because too much money was chasing scarce goods, their economies sickened with inflation.) Like Ruiz Cortines, Díaz Ordaz also refused to fill his own pockets with state money (another temptation later presidents yielded to). But these virtues were canceled by his vice: incurable authoritarianism.

Under an umbrella of protective tariffs Mexican business, especially small enterprise, was producing shoddy goods for a captive market. The stuff could not be exported, and smuggling of U.S. goods into Mexico was rising. The Tepito market sparkled with contraband electrical gadgets. Díaz Ordaz proposed to lower tariffs on many goods to make business more competitive. But small and medium business began to bawl, and the President backed down. He wanted to hold the middle sectors in the social pact.

The Bankrupt State

In the period from 1880 to 1935, Mexico had exported oil and minerals and imported consumer goods for the upper class. From 1935 onward, Mexicans tried to found infant industries making the things sold in the stores, keeping out competitive imports with a tariff wall. But "import-substitution industrialization," as the economists called it, was not enough to build a strong economy: the time had come for Mexico to start making capital goods, to make the things that make consumer goods—machinery, instruments, factories, and spare parts. The new domestic industries producing consumer goods were importing most of their machinery from the United States. "We are worried," said Díaz Ordaz in a speech to the U.S. Congress, " by the disparity in prices between the natural products that we export to you and the capital goods which are our principal imports from you."[13] To make expensive capital goods were needed bigger plants, more technology, and costly machines. But only a strong State could finance a program of building capital goods; only a government with money could finish the industrialization drive. And the rich refused to pay the needed taxes. Díaz Ordaz found that by strengthening the bourgeoisie, the state had pushed itself into a corner.

The problem was always the same: not enough money for Social Security, not enough for public health, not enough for the Ejido Bank, not enough for housing projects, not enough for education, not enough for the State sector of the economy, not enough to finance ongoing development. In his desperate search for money Díaz Ordaz doubled the number of income taxpayers by hitting more of the growing middle layers.

When a tax collector walks into a private clinic he can count patients, ask questions, observe equipment, talk to nurses, check salaries, estimate the profits—if tax cheating is going on, he can smell it. When he enters a small ceramics factory, he can look at the sheds the workers are under, see what type of ovens they are using, peer into storerooms. He can guess at the boss's evasion and turn the screws. It is even easier to collect taxes from managers, professors, bureaucrats, engineers, professionals—you simply take 30 percent of their salary. But what do you do with the Coca-Cola Corporation, operating in a hundred countries with half a million employees? How do you check its sales and profits when it is doing business in almost every grocery store in Mexico and tens of thousands of villages reached only by mule trains? How do you know that the giant Cementos Mexicanos is showing you the real set of books when Lorenzo Zambrano claims that a bad year has left it operating in the red? Just as the tax collector takes on faith the priest's promise of eternal reward, so he takes on faith the big company's account books. But with this difference: he can check out the priest by dying to see what happens, whereas the company remains forever mysterious with its sibylline books.

In Mexico the account books of small businesses and the employers' lists of professional salaries were an easier prey for tax collectors. The middle layer tried to hoax the tax collectors but found its bag of tricks almost empty. The government also fleeced it by piling heavy sales taxes on consumer goods. The superrich hardly noticed the tax on cosmetics and shampoos, but bank tellers on meager salaries felt the pinch. Unlike the superrich, the middle layer could not threaten the government with an investment strike and capital flight. Therefore the State gobbled up a third of its income.

During the fruitless hunt at home for money to run the State, Mexican Presidents had been borrowing money abroad. So in the period from 1960 to 1969 they had to shell out $4 billion in debt payments and interest. In those days that was a lot of money for Mexico—where did it come from? When Díaz Ordaz began his regime in 1964 the public debt was $2 billion; when he finished in 1970, it had doubled to $4 billion. You have heard of borrowing from Peter to pay Paul? To service its growing debt, Mexico was borrowing from Peter to pay Peter. Instead of money flowing into the country, the net result had become a hemorrhage of value to financial creditors in the United States and Europe.[14]

Trapped in the Conventional Culture

Díaz Ordaz found himself locked in the cultural establishment. Culture is a system of beliefs, attitudes, and practices, a system that makes individuals think, feel, and act in certain ways. For generations entrepreneurs had paid little taxes, and the resulting business culture of Mexico now made them hide profits, find loopholes, demand exemptions, bribe collectors, keep two sets of books, and threaten capital flight if they were equitably taxed. The State backed down before their power, and by 1970 Mexico had one of the most regressive tax nets in the world.

Another face of the system was the political culture. For generations a single party had run the nation, keeping others out by force or fraud. It was impossible to remove people in power except by shooting them, so corruption and irresponsibility were growing throughout the bureaucracy. The local and state political bosses had too much power and wealth concentrated in their hands. Criticism of the president, who appointed governors, senators, and successors, was taboo. Mexico was a one-party dictatorship with a new face in the presidency every six years.

Liberals, intellectuals, professionals, teachers, and students were yelling for freedom and democracy. At first Díaz Ordaz seemed to understand the need to democratize the ruling party, for he appointed the charismatic Carlos Alberto Madrazo as President of the PRI. Madrazo tried to bring the base of the party into decision-making, to sweep out the cobwebs of corruption, to recruit more women, and to undermine the power of political bosses. His reforms were ground to pieces in the state political machines, and the bosses rose up as one man against him. Díaz Ordaz got cold feet and failed to back him up. Forced out, the populist Madrazo started a campaign for reform, and his oratory swayed the masses until he died in a fatal "accident."

Still another face of the system determining social behavior was Mexico's macho Catholic culture. The population explosion accelerated, eroding government efforts to maintain the social pact with the masses: the birthrate gained upon food supply, stole a march on land distribution, strained health programs, shot ahead of job creation, outstripped the building of schools, overburdened basic services. As the underclasses suffered want and the economic elite wallowed in luxury, the pact tilted back in favor of Big Money.

Attacks on the Political Regime

During the reign of Díaz Ordaz, the patience of many Mexicans ran out and they began to rebel against the government. Díaz Ordaz was a man of the system, so he shook out his whip and prepared to defend it. He would use the lash to frighten the masses into the pact.

In the Social Security Medical System the 8000 young resident doctors working in five hospitals in Mexico City and throughout the states were paid low wages and treated as if they were under military discipline. In 1965 the outraged professionals paralyzed the Medical System with a wildcat strike against their insulting working conditions, and Díaz Ordaz answered with the lash. As their government-controlled union tried to intervene, the doctors extended their demands to include an independent and democratic union of their own.

In 1966, during an outbreak of student unrest in the University of San Nicolás in Morelia, Díaz Ordaz sent soldiers to the campus to arrest dissidents and cart them off to prison—including the rector of the university, Eli de Gortari. The next year the despotic President laid the same whip on the student rebels at the University of Sonora. Students in Durango, Morelia, Guerrero, Ciudad Juárez, and Mexico City were fed up with the blows of the ruling party. A national movement for change was forming.

There was standing room only when in May 1966 the Aztec Stadium, holding 100,000 people, was inaugurated. Mexico was playing a soccer game against Italy. The President arrived late, and as he walked into the stands, he was greeted by prolonged booing and catcalls. The lash was not popular.[15]

But it was needed against counterelites in the underclasses that were mobilizing resistance to the ruling groups. In 1964 and 1965, in the Chihuahuan mountains near Madera City, the rural teachers Arturo Gámiz and Pablo Gómez rose in a guerrilla war. They recruited peasants, blew up bridges, ambushed police, attacked a radio station. They were applying Che Guevara's theory that by such actions a guerrilla band can trigger a peasant war against the State. On September 23, 1965, they imitated Fidel Castro's legendary assault on the Moncada Barracks that had begun the Cuban Revolution. With 17 guerrillas they attacked 120 soldiers at the Madera Barracks, then fled, leaving 8 dead. Soldiers and paratroops hunted them down and Arturo Gámiz fell in combat. A few survivors continued the armed struggle in the sierra between Chihuahua and Sonora for several years. Martyrs are symbols, and Arturo Gámiz's sacrifice generated a social myth of the heroic guerrilla. It would influence generations of youthful revolutionaries. For the next 35 years the tradition of guerrilla warfare—both rural and urban—would flow throughout Mexico, surfacing now here and now there, but with some amazing continuities.

For example, the People's Union, a secret group committed to armed struggle, was formed in 1965. It aimed at the radical transformation of society and the establishment of socialism. Organizing in the underground, it escaped the chief executive's whip. In 1974 it became the People's Union: Clandestine Worker Revolutionary Party (PROCUP), and carried out armed actions in the 1970s and 1980s, sabotaging military installations and placing bombs in government buildings. It kidnapped a billionaire for a payoff to buy arms. In 1996 it launched a guerrilla war in the impoverished state of Guerrero as the Revolutionary Popular Army (EPR), and continues to ambush state police and federal army patrols. Its original socialist program is now updated to demand an end to "neoliberalism" by whatever means, including electoral struggles.[16]

In 1967 the southwestern state of Guerrero, where half the poor peasants speak the Aztec language, was an image of the nation: the squalid poverty of the western sierras surrounded the rich resort of Acapulco. The peasants tilling survival corn patches needed schools, clinics, electricity, water, fertilizer, credit, and roads. In 1967 at Atoyac the rural schoolteacher Lucio Cabañas was organizing peasants to demand attention to their needs when on May 18 the state police opened fire on a peaceful meeting, killing 7 and wounding 20. This time the deadly whip had descended from the hand of the PRI governor, and it provoked a stinging backlash. Cabañas fled to the mountains and took up arms. His guerrilla band—later known as the Party of the Poor—began ambushing the state police and local bosses known to be killing peasants. Kidnappings of the rich for ransom and bank robberies to finance his movement followed, and his populist program became openly socialist.

Díaz Ordaz threw more and more federal troops into Guerrero. The army tripled the number of roads there in order to chase Cabañas, but these also helped peasants to reach markets. Guerrilla ambushes of the army resembled a flea biting a jaguar. Several times the military proclaimed that Cabañas was dead—until he reappeared. Once Cabañas stopped tourists driving to Acapulco to stick his head into the car window with a smiling, "Buenas tardes," just to show that he was still alive. He became a living legend, and throughout Mexico the left studied his example. Would others imitate him? In 1974 he fell in combat, and his Party of the Poor merged with the underground PROCUP in order to continue subversive activity to this day.

The whip cracked regularly on the bleeding state of Guerrero. In the early 1960s the rural teacher Genaro Vázquez had founded his Civic Association to help reform the miserable condition of the peasants, but after a massacre of his followers, he went underground. He continued political work and interviewed Rubén Jaramillo in order to coordinate their efforts to organize poor peasants. His secret organizing ended with his capture in 1966 and his imprisonment in Iguala. Vázquez was feeling the whip. In 1968 Lucio Cabañas' band attacked the prison and freed Vázquez, who then fled to the sierra and started his own guerrilla war. He proclaimed that he would answer the brutal whip with bullets. He expanded his organization into the Revolutionary National Civic Association. It, too, had a socialist program.

Peasants joined Vázquez's guerrilla band. It operated for several years on the Costa Grande between Acapulco and the Balsas River, pursued by army battalions, helicopters, paratroops, and counterinsurgency technology developed by the United States in Vietnam. The army could not catch him, which meant that he had support from the region's peasants. His guerrillas were fish swimming through the sea of the people. The eyes of the nation focused on Vázquez's kidnappings of millionaires in order to exchange them for ransom and for the release of political prisoners. He became a romantic revolutionary figure for Mexican university students, who often hung his portrait in their rooms. The youth of Mexico turned away from the PRI in disgust and cursed the ugly president, who they nicknamed "El Chango"—the monkey.

In 1972 Vázquez suffered a dreadful automobile accident. Badly injured, he fled from the wreck, was captured by the army, and died of his wounds.

In 1969 in Monterrey, César Yáñez and Alfredo Zarate founded the National Liberation Forces (FLN), inspired by the guerrillaism of the Cuban Revolution. Organizing in secret, the FLN escaped the whip of "The Monkey" and launched guerrillas in the southern jungles. Although in 1974 President Luis Echeverría's secret police wiped out the FLN's headquarters near the capital, the FLN continued its clandes-

tine work in Veracruz, Puebla, Monterrey, and Mexico City. In 1983 it
set up another guerrilla band in Chiapas with the name Zapatista
Army of National Liberation (EZLN), joined in 1984 by Rafael
Sebastián Guillén Vicente, who as "Marcos" would lead the Indian uprising of 1994 that electrified the world.[17]

Rebellion of the Middle Strata

In the late 1960s the PRI government continued to rule with its old
tactic of carrot-and-stick. With one hand Díaz Ordaz was feeding carrots into the social pact: profit-sharing, land distribution, urban renewal, expanded education. With the other hand he was beating
people with his stick. The carrots were skinny but the pact was still
holding—if badly. Between the worker-peasant interests grinding
against the bureaucrat-bourgeois interests there were buffers: the CNC
and the CTM. The really bitter opposition to the bureaucrat-bourgeois
marriage was coming from those fighting in the mountains and in the
underground. It was also increasingly coming from middle strata—
students, teachers, youth, intellectuals, journalists, professors, writers,
liberals—angered over the absence of democracy in Mexican political
and social life.

To criticize either the President or the army was forbidden, and elections were managed by the corporate state. Workers and peasants were
snared in the corporative net, squirming and kicking but unable to
escape. The prisons were stuffed: the Argentine revolutionary Adolfo
Gilly, who had done nothing to Mexico, and the leaders of the 1959
railway strike, Valentín Campa and Demetrio Vallejo, slowly withered
away behind the gloomy walls of Lecumberri. What crime had such
men committed? There was informal censorship of Mexican movie-
makers and television journalists. The press was kept tame by government subsidies that could be withdrawn at a whim. When Mexico's
prestigious Fondo de Cultura Económica decided to publish Oscar
Lewis's *Children of Sánchez*, an anthropological study of slum life in
Tepito, Díaz Ordaz fired its editor, Dr. Arnaldo Orfila. Mexico's upper
half should not find out how miserably the other half lived. A scream
of pain arose from the whole intellectual community: to flog the have-
nots was one thing, but to whip intellectuals who were trying to inform the haves about how the have-nots lived—that was a horse of
another color. The expanding universities agreed that it was a horse
not to be whipped.

In the late 1960s a knowledge explosion was taking place in dozens of countries, and everywhere growing student bodies were protesting against bureaucratization. They hated bureaucracy as a plague

infecting the State, the giant corporation, and the "knowledge factory." Demonstrations, marches, sit-ins, and rallies for freedom were in vogue. Around the world students waved portraits of Rosa Luxemburg and Che Guevara, of Ho Chi Minh and Mao.

University "Red Guards" were dragging down bureaucrats in China; with barricades students rose up against their administrators in Paris; they hauled them from their offices at Columbia University and San Francisco State; they rioted in Amsterdam and Belgrade, throughout Latin America and Western Europe. Globalized world news reported these movements to Mexicans: images of street fighting on the barricades of Nanterre reached National University students the next day. It was deliciously contagious. And there in the National Palace sulked the Big Bureaucrat, threatening the youth of Mexico with his gigantic whip.

In July 1968 police beat students marching to commemorate Fidel Castro's storming of the Moncada Barracks in Cuba; students answered the truncheons with street fighting. Heads cracked under the billy clubs. To protest these beatings, strikes broke out in the high schools, the Polytechnical Institute, and the National University. The authorities shouted that Communists were at work, and unleashed a cycle of police violence followed by further student radicalization. Paratroops attacked several high schools, and hundreds of people were arrested. Several were killed. To protest government violence, on August 1, 100,000 citizens and students marched silently through the capital to University City. Cooler heads in the government managed to get the police off the streets, and during August peace returned to the capital.

Students launched the National Strike Council; provincial universities and Mexico City campuses elected their delegates subject to total recall. The education strike was spontaneous and libertarian—no political party could control it. The Strike Council demanded an end to the law of "social dissolution," the firing of Mexico City's police chief, the indemnification of the families of killed students, the abolition of the military riot police, and the freeing of all political prisoners. For a month brigades circulated in Mexico City asking for, and winning, support from the middle social layers. On August 13 there was a support march of 200,000; on August 27 half a million people filled the main plaza—the largest protest demonstration in Mexican history. Most of the workers and peasants watched quietly from their cages, for this was a libertarian movement of the middle sectors.

The Strike Council demanded negotiations with the government on national television. Díaz Ordaz would not accept such an open debate before the nation (television, like so much else, was heavily censored). Most of the students expected his refusal; many wanted to keep the strike going. Some hoped to awaken the worker and peasant masses, and trigger a revolutionary explosion.

The President saw that the student-popular movement was isolated. During September he took out his whip and beat the movement down: there was street fighting across Mexico City between police and students with sticks and bullets; the army seized the National University and captured the Polytechnical Institute; hundreds of people were arrested and jailed; the capital was littered with burned buses and barricades. In Europe frightened sports fans began to cancel their trips to the Olympic Games scheduled for Mexico City in early October. On the evening of October 2, 1968, 5,000 students, supportive families, and curious bystanders massed in a peaceful demonstration at the Plaza of the Three Cultures in Tlatelolco to hear speeches by the Strike Council. The army was sent to surround the plaza and to arrest the speakers—peacefully.

But the President had another whip under his coat. General Luis Gutiérrez Oropeza, chief of the Presidential General Staff, was running a secret death squad that hit people Díaz Ordaz was angry with. The President ordered ten of these terrorists placed on top of and within the buildings surrounding the plaza. As the peaceful meeting started and the army peacefully encircled the plaza with tanks, the hidden death squad opened fire with automatic rifles on both the crowd and the soldiers. Believing that armed students were shooting at them, soldiers panicked and blasted the defenseless crowd with machine guns. On and on they sprayed with their automatic weapons: hundreds were mowed down and there were uncounted wounded.[18]

The massacre of Tlatelolco shocked the world. Next day a terrified Mexico City was as peaceful as a cemetery, and the Olympic Games were held on schedule. But "the 1968 movement," writes a leading historian, was "the most serious challenge to the authority of the Mexican state in thirty years."[19] And the massacre opened a breach between the government and the middle layers that would endure for a generation. From 1968 to 1985 radicalized intellectuals, students, academics, and professionals turned their backs on the ruling PRI. As late as 1989 Marxism had more influence in Mexico's institutions of higher learning than in any other universities of the West. To this day there is a march of 100,000 students every October 2 to commemorate the massacre.

Mass arrests, prison sentences, censored publications, and general repression of the political left followed the tragedy of Tlatelolco.

Díaz Ordaz ended his term in 1970 as the most feared and despised President since the Revolution.

From Tlatelolco thousands of Mexican youth drew a bloody conclusion—to arms!

THE POPULIST PRESIDENT

In 1970 the transition toward a new presidency began. The Marxist insurgencies that had begun as a response to Díaz Ordaz continued to resist the government: the People's Union, the FLN, the Party of the Poor, the Civic Association. And besides these, beginning in 1970 new urban guerrilla formations opened a campagn of terror: snatching millionaires for ransom, robbing trains, killing police, robbing banks. These "expropriations" continued for several years. The young guerrillas were overly impressed by the success of Fidel Castro's armed movement under different conditions in the 1950s and by Mao's guerrilla victories in China. In these years the Mexican intellectual community was enamored of French Marxism, and university students had drunk deeply of the revolutionary wine. Many were inebriated with utopian visions, others were acting out their rage over the hammer blows of the Mexican state.

Into this storm Díaz Ordaz launched the official candidate of the PRI for the presidency, a cold politician who had silently risen through party ranks like an invisible man—Luis Echeverría Álvarez. Knowledgeable Mexicans gazed at him with fear and trembling, for he was the Secretary of the Interior.

Popping out of the storm clouds, candidate Echeverría curved over the nation like a rainbow: smiling, talking, gesticulating, backslapping, glad-handing, baby-kissing, speechifying, campaigning, dialoguing, and politicking. He romped up and down the vast length of Mexico, covering tens of thousands of miles, visiting cities, towns, and villages in every state. Mexico had not seen such a campaign since the days of Lázaro Cárdenas. Everywhere he went, Echeverría promised Mexicans the moon, promised that change was coming.

On an official vehicle carrying Echeverría and his aides toward a whistle-stop, a reporter covering the campaign asked one of the *políticos* what was going on. Enrique González Pedrero, director of the Faculty of Political Sciences at the National University in 1968, explained:

The PRI is a coalition of forces guided by the spirit of equilibrium. The middle class (Madero, Carranza, and Obregón too) that began the Mexican Revolution made a compromise with the masses, the people who carried through the Revolution on the field of battle. That compromise was lodged in the Constitution of 1917 with individual guarantees as protection for the middle class and with the social articles 3, 27, and 123 as protection for the masses. . . . The country has always had to struggle for equilibrium. Under Obregón, Calles, and Cárdenas it inclined to the left, and since then it has swung to the other extreme because of the processes of industrialization and market expansion. . . . The PRI is a coalition and our presidential candidate observes the different forces within it. His mission as governing leader will be to reestablish equilibrium.[20]

Shortly afterward, Echeverría "arranged" for González Pedrero to become the PRI's new senator from Tabasco.

Even scholars who hate Echeverría, such as the conservative historian Enrique Krauze, admit that Mexico's stability had eroded: "the abandonment of the peasants and the unequal distribution of income were another and deplorable face of the 'Mexican miracle.' They had to be corrected."[21] Echeverría thought of himself as the corrector.

His metamorphosis from a loyal apparatchik into a flaming populist horrified Díaz Ordaz, who tried to withdraw his candidacy. The tyrannical president feared that if Echeverría shelved the whip, Mexico would sink into chaos. But withdrawal was against the rules of the political culture, and the PRI stuck with candidate Echeverría. As a student he had drunk deeply from Marxist fountains: he had studied at the Workers' University under the great Leninist, Vincente Lombardo Toledano. This forgotten fact was something Díaz Ordaz had missed when he picked the gray organization man as his successor. Echeverría dropped his gray bureaucratic mask to reveal a pink Marxoid agitator.

During the populist campaign, Echeverría's endlessly repeated slogan was *Arriba y Adelante!* (Up and at 'Em!) On December 1, 1970, he sat in the Presidential Chair, swiveled it to the left, leaped to his feet, and started moving. He walked out of the National Palace to meet the people, talking to workers on the shop floor and to peasants in forgotten villages—wearing a tropical shirt. He emptied the cells of political prisoners. Some of the Marxist students and professors got work in the government; others returned to their universities. He lifted much of the censorship, and the nation found its voice. University classrooms resonated with debate. A bitter muckraking movie showed the miserable life of the underclasses, and it played to packed cinemas. An explosive play attacking the PRI as a gangsterlike elite began its 15-year run. *Excélsior* turned into a critical informative newspaper, digging deep with the shovels of social criticism. The bookstores bulged with Marxist treatises. Progressive priests preached liberation theology to the poor.

Reformist Policies

To help the poor, Echeverría put rigid price controls on tortillas and milk. Searching for money to finance social programs, he slapped a 10 percent tax on yachts, limousines, diamonds, caviar, porcelain, mahogany, private planes, mink coats, and Aztec art. Customers of ritzy night clubs and luxury restaurants suddenly discovered a 15 percent surtax added to their bills.

In the countryside Echeverría built roads and brought power lines to remote villages without light. For the pathetic *ixtleros*, crawling over the northern deserts to gather the fiber of the istle plant to sell in the cities, he organized a medical program. He gave more attention to *ejidos* and set up peasant cooperatives (for example, in salt production).

In the cities he nationalized the tobacco and telephone industries. He built state steel mills. Anaconda had the biggest copper mine in the country at Cananea—Echeverría nationalized it. The public-owned sector of industry, increasing decade after decade, got another big boost.

He beefed up tourism and opened new resorts to make jobs (for waiters, cooks, bartenders, cleaners, bellhops, beach boys, cabbies, accountants, managers). The labor unions gained hefty pay raises. And Echeverría tried to strengthen the law about profit-sharing with workers, a law that employers had become experts at evading. (As profit-sharing time arrived, the managers usually presented account books in the red.) He widened the Social Security system to cover 10 million more Mexicans. He enlarged the National Company of People's Subsistence that doled out subsidized beans and rice to the starving poor.

Echeverría fattened the state bureaucracy and thus invented jobs for the professional class. He constructed low-cost housing projects for the petty bureaucrats and schoolteachers. An apartment that could be paid for over the long term was now within reach of poorly salaried government employees. He tried to curb real estate interests by regulating the urban land market. He operated state stores with goods at low prices for workers and bureaucrats. They could buy sofas and beds at cut rates, afford stoves and refrigerators. To protect small business, he wrapped the economy in a cocoon of tariffs; it became difficult for other countries to send goods into Mexico.

The education budget jumped fourteenfold, and new schools appeared to keep up with the unbridled population growth. For poor Mexicans, Echeverría established a system of 857 vocational technical schools and technological institutes throughout the nation; in the countryside these schools trained *técnicos* to erect small rural industries (for instance, to turn tomatoes into canned sauce before they spoiled). He gave generous subsidies to the National University, enlarged it to accommodate tens of thousands of new students, and founded huge high school systems that he turned over to the Marxist "generation of 1968" to work in as teachers. Echeverría built the Metropolitan Autonomous University for another 60,000 upwardly mobile youth in the capital. There Marxist ideology took root. His rapid expansion of free public higher education occupied radicalized students and intellectuals in academic study. With their noses in books, they had less time for revolutionary plotting.

In the 1970s a feminist movement got under way among Mexico's elites. In public Echeverría always referred to his wife as "my *compañera* María Ester," thus placing her on an equal level with himself. He took seriously Mexico's revolutionary Constitution and its social program that presidents were supposed to enact into law. Article 123 declared equal pay for equal work. Echeverría wrote a law promising women equal salaries and job openings. Enforcing the law was tough going, but it slowly had effect. In the 1980s, city governments accepted women into the police forces (and found that they took fewer bribes than men).

The Mexican Revolution had always had a strong nationalist tendency, and Echeverría created an image of himself as a Third World leader. He recognized Communist China. He supported Salvador Allende's Marxist government in Chile, and after Allende's overthrow, he accepted hundreds of Chilean exiles who found jobs in Mexican universities or in government. He broke diplomatic relations with the new Chilean dictator. He continued refusal of recognition to the Fascist government in Spain. He went to Cuba in order to show his friendship for the Revolution. He speechified in the UN and pushed his Charter of the Economic Rights and Duties of States that aimed to equalize the difference between rich and poor nations. He denounced economic imperialism and deplored his country's dependency on the United States (70 percent of Mexican trade was with that one country). To reduce this commercial dependency, Echeverría developed new export-import connections abroad and lowered Mexico's trade with the United States to 50 percent. He founded a think tank, the Center for Third World Studies. These "Third Worldist" efforts brought frowns from the business community, which looked upon Uncle Sam as a friend. Uncle Sam began to snarl and scowl.

Nationalism penetrated economic policy. The economy was dependent on patents and innovations in the technological field, assuring juicy profits to the multinational corporations operating in Mexico. So

Echeverría founded the National Council of Science and Technology to help overcome the painful dependency on northern research. He also wrote a law regulating the transfer of technology and patents. In 1973 came another law aimed at promoting Mexican investment in industry and at regulating foreign investment. These stopgaps were supposed to slow the deepening industrial dependency of Mexico on foreign capital.

Echeverría styled himself a new Cárdenas, often citing the socialist president in his speeches. There is no doubt about it: during his administration the balance in the social pact swung leftward and reached the center of the political spectrum. Meanwhile, the guerrillas lurked in the background of the historical action like ominous scenery. Echeverría's policies aimed to isolate them. He stole bits and pieces of their program until they faded from the picture.

Crushing the Terrorists

There was a darker side to the treatment of the revolutionaries, for the regime carried on a "dirty war" against the terrorists. Its secret White Brigade used terror, torture, assassination, and intimidation to hunt down radicals and wipe them out. In 1972 Genaro Vázquez fell in combat; in 1974, Lucio Cabañas.

The 23 September Communist League had taken its name from Arturo Gámiz's legendary attack on the Madera Barracks in Chihuahua. It was the umbrella organization for the new urban guerrillas: Mexico City's Comando Lacandones, the Chihuahua-based Guajiros, the Student Revolutionry Federation of Guadalajara, the Movement of Revolutionary Action in Morelia, Los Procesos in the Netzahualcóyotl slum, and the Zapatista Urban Front. Sabotage, kidnappings, robberies, assassinations, destruction of machinery, and gunfights with police were their revolutionary tactics. In their youthful vision they were inspiring Mexico with examples of resistance to a despotic government, lessons that would inspire the rest of society to launch general strikes and elect people's committees to govern Mexico—in the style of the student movement of 1968.

By 1973 the League had created secret local action committees in Sinaloa, Chihuahua, Oaxaca, Tamaulipas, Sonora, Monterrey, and Veracruz. Most of the armed actions were in cities. They did not win the support of the conservative, family-oriented Mexicans struggling to pay their bills and rent. To most people the League seemed a band of robbers and killers—nothing more. In Monterrey the guerrillas killed Eugenio Garza Sada, the head of the most powerful group of millionaires in the country, and the enraged business class demanded a full government campaign against the terrorists.

The army and the police hammered the Communist League to pieces on the anvil of the people's indifference. During the "dirty war" against the terrorists, some 1500 of them were killed or captured, "committed suicide" in their cells, or "disappeared." By 1975 it was over.[22]

The repression was carried on in secret, while the populist President continued his reformist campaigns, hardly noticing the latent civil war in the cellars of society. *El presidente* was, so to speak, "above it" (except when his father-in-law was captured and held for ransom).

The population explosion flamed ever brighter and more terrifying. It burned away many of the gains made by the populist reforms. Echeverría's Population Commission recommended a national program of birth control, but *el Presidente* dallied and delayed. (He had nine children.) In a traditional society of convinced Catholics, he was afraid to institute population control: he feared the reaction of a macho culture under the sway of conservative priests. When, near the end of his term, he finally attacked the problem, it was too little and too late.

Financing Social Welfare

The reformist President faced another problem that had plagued previous administrations: how to finance social programs. In the social stratification, the upper 10 percent of Mexicans, who had the wealth of the nation under their control, mutinously refused to pay taxes. By the 1970s the business class, pampered for decades, had grown into a giant that wielded most of the economic power in the country. The giant brandished its weapons: a potential investment strike, flight of capital, closure of factories, paralysis of the economy, a media campaign against the government. Understandably, the President shrank from fighting the monster. He dawdled at tax reform but dared not dig into the capitalist profits.

For two decades economic growth had roared ahead at 6 percent annually with little inflation. Economic stability was something everyone had come to expect. No one understood that in the early 1970s the world market was changing, that the first signs of globalization would bring increasing instability to Western economies: inflation, devaluation, recession, stagflation. During Echeverría's term a surprised Mexico would be caught in this international whirlpool.

Echeverría had studied Marx and a class analysis of society, but he never mastered economics. In the cabinet his minister of the economy,

José López Portillo, also was not an economist. The two populists saw a quick solution to their finance problem without grasping the economic results that might follow in the long run.

In the 1970s the Arab states had made tens of billions of dollars with their oil cartel and had stashed the money in the big banks of the northern industrial countries. The banks, bursting with money, offered cheap loans to nations that wanted finance. Echeverría and López Portillo gaily borrowed billions of dollars to pay for their welfare programs. Mexico's debt soared from $4 billion dollars in 1970 to $20 billion in 1976.[23] That was still not enough money. So Echeverría told his mint to print extra pesos, and with this depreciated coin he paid the state's bills.

In the early 1970s world inflation was contagious, and Mexico had already caught the virus. But Echeverría unwittingly worsened the ailment with his massive injections of borrowed and created money into the arteries of the economy. When too much money is chasing scarce goods, prices go up. The business community, hostile to the President's *socializante* policies, made goods even scarcer by cutting back on production. By 1974 inflation had topped 20 percent.

As prices continued rising, Mexico's products became more expensive on the world market while imports from the United States cheapened. A trade deficit opened: the money flowing out of the country to pay for increased imports was greater than the money coming into Mexico from fewer exports. As money rushed out of the country, devaluation loomed on the horizon. (Devaluation makes imports expensive and stops the hemorrage of value.)

The business community was infuriated by Echeverría's economic policies. In 1975 the industrial, commercial, and financial elites created the Business Coordinating Council, which would become the strongest representative of the private sector of the economy. Echeverría and the Council threw mud at each other faster than either one could wipe it off. The talkative president accused business interests of looting Mexico, and the Council complained that he was an enemy of entrepreneurship.

So in 1975 private investment in the economy dipped dangerously and economic growth ground to a halt. That, and especially the detonating population bomb, meant that too many people were looking for too few jobs. Economists found that 45 percent of the economically active population had fallen into underemployment.[24] Economically active people are those who get up in the morning, have coffee, open the door of their dwelling, and go out to earn bread for their families. Underemployment means that they have no fixed work with a paycheck and fringe benefits: they are in the street running errands, shining shoes, pushing drugs, washing cars, hawking soft drinks, begging, selling hot dogs, peddling lottery tickets, picking pockets, following the harvests, migrating to the United States, cultivating poppies, and doing a thousand and one things to stay alive. In Mexico almost every other working person was in that condition.

In 1976 the trade deficit and threatening inflation signaled the need for devaluation of the peso. The rich began putting their money into Wall Street securities, San Antonio real estate, and U.S. banks: that way the money would not lose value. Instead of devaluing at once, Echeverría delayed and let capital escape from the country like a frightened deer. Without capital, without investment, the economy went to its knees. Mexicans were struggling to get it up again when two massive devaluations knocked it flat.

In the Northwest, landless peasants seized several hundred thousand acres from big owners and Echeverría declared their action legal. To protest their loss, agrobusiness interests sent more capital abroad and lined up 250 tractors in Culiacán in a strike; the business community, screaming curses at Echeverría, joined the farmers.

On December 1, Echeverría slunk out of the National Palace, leaving a nation gripped by political and economic crisis.

THE INTELLECTUAL PRESIDENT

José López Portillo, a former professor of law at the National University, took over the reins. Echeverría and López Portillo had been close since childhood, and the populist president believed that his friend would implement his popular policies. The Business Coordinating Council stared at the new leader with icy eyes. The business community was determined to punish populism with capital flight and a ruined economy. What could López Portillo do?

He announced that Mexico was sitting on a sea of oil. This was at a time when the industrial countries were hungry for petroleum, and the Arab oil cartel had jacked up the price. Mexico was set for an oil bonanza. The new President flew to Monterrey and made a conciliatory speech to the millionaires, begging them to bring back capital. The vision of government oil profits revving up the economy seduced Big Money back into Mexico: businessmen wanted to get in on the oil boom.

The professorial President continued the policy of Echeverría: if the rich would not pay taxes, then the government would simply borrow money abroad. The World Bank forked over to Mexico the largest loan it had ever made. The giant commercial banks in the northern countries, bulging with Arab petrodollars, were only too glad to finance the

President's programs and purchase of technology to suck oil from the bowels of the earth. Billions of idle dollars could be loaned out for interest. Since the interest rates were low, López Portillo used the loans to throw money at Mexico's social ills.

The government entered the economy like a successful bank robber on a spending spree in Las Vegas. To deal with the terrifying transport problem in the urban sprawl of the capital, the executive expanded the subway system and crisscrossed the city with rapid lanes for cars. Superhighways snaked across the nation. New buildings rose, and the construction projects created jobs. Mexico's first atomic power plant appeared. The poor ate better, for the government subsidized basic foods. The price of tortillas was half their real market value, and even the colorful "Marías"—Indian women begging in the streets of the capital—grew fat.

López Portillo doused the nation with social welfare projects. The Plan for Deprived Zones and Marginalized Groups coordinated government efforts to help the poor: the Federal Electricity Commission brought power lines to shantytowns, the Secretariat of Public Health providing charity hospitals, the Secretariat of Public Education built schools. The 1980 census showed that at last illiteracy had nose-dived. The efforts of López Mateos, Díaz Ordaz, Echeverría, and López Portillo had finally paid off.

The National Company of People's Subsistence, the government agency that provided low-quality beans, rice, sugar, and cooking oil to the poor at cut rates, stretched its network of stores over the nation. The state made its bureaucrat and labor unions open commissaries with lower prices for teachers, oficinistas, and workers. (And later on, in state stores the sales tax vanished.) The commercial elites grouched that these stores were unfair competition.

Four thousand years before Christ, the people of Middle America discovered how to raise corn. It resists droughts and plagues, it contains more calories than wheat or rice, it is Mexico's gift to the world—and in 1965 the nation was still exporting the rich grain. But as the capitalist economy piled up wealth for the affluent classes, they demanded tasty beef. Agricultural lands were converted for grazing, and corn farmers cultivated fields of sorghum to feed cattle for the tables of the rich. Soon Mexico was importing corn from the United States. What if the gringos decided to cut it off? Without tortillas the nation must either submit to Uncle Sam or die.

Nationalists denounced the new food dependency, and the President set up the Mexican Food System. Big investment in agriculture plus heavy rains brought in a bumper corn crop. Mexico was freed from the dependency trap. (Temporarily, for in later years, when the money dried up and the clouds did too, huge food imports returned.)

In his 1978 State of the Union message, the President admitted that "in 1968 an epoch opened that is still with us."[25] The "generation of Tlatelolco" had given up armed struggle, but the intellectual community—artists, writers, actors, philosophers, scholars, scientists, professors, students—remained firmly Marxist and actively leftist. The President's populism aimed to co-opt as many as possible to work for the government in reformist programs.

He also integrated radical parties into the political system. The Mexican Communist Party, founded in 1919, was the dean of Marxist parties. It gained registration and began to participate in electoral politics (in a system in which the government laid down the rules of the game so that only the PRI could win). The Socialist Workers Party was also legalized. Later, the Trotskyists were registered. Right-wing parties also got legal status, such as the Mexican Democratic Party of the Cristero peasants with its emblem of a yellow rooster.

López Portillo, who had written Hegelian interpretations of Mexico's history, was determined to maintain a synthesis of the left and the right in the dialectical process of the Mexican Revolution. If the business class remained economically powerful inside Mexico, the President would balance that with revolutionary nationalism in foreign policy. In 1979 he broke diplomatic relations with Anastasio Somoza Debayle's dictatorship in Nicaragua. When the Sandinista revolution triumphed, he sent his presidential airplane—named *Quetzalcoatl* for the Aztec wind god—to bring the Sandinista leaders to Mexico City, and promised material aid and diplomatic support to the Marxist government. Mexico also promised oil to Nicaragua. During a meeting in Cancún, Portillo embraced Fidel Castro. In El Salvador a Marxist-Leninist insurgency was spreading through the countryside, and in 1981 López Portillo joined France in recognizing the guerrillas as a "political force." In Washington the Republican Party and President Ronald Reagan gnashed their teeth—helplessly. Washington was irritated by López Portillo's continued resistance to U.S. pressure to rip down Mexico's tariff wall. Uncle Sam wanted Mexico to enter the General Agreement on Tariffs and Trade, but Portillo repeatedly refused. His protectionist policy was also hated by giant Mexican corporations. Inside Mexico, as Portillo waved the red flag at the bourgeois bull, it stomped angrily and pointed its horns. When would it charge? López Portillo, who in private life was a good boxer, was flexing his regime's new oil muscle, and in the ring of political relations was threatening its enemies.

The President fed Petróleos Mexicanos (PEMEX) with borrowed dollars until it grew into a giant. Clusters of drilling platforms dotted the Gulf of Mexico. The sea of oil gushed to the surface. Mexico marched down a developmental road paved with black gold. As the wheels of the economy spun ever faster, the entrepreneurial class invested in the production of clothes and toys, washing machines and refrigerators to meet rising consumer demand. Economic growth reached a whopping annual 9 percent.[26] The chatter at business breakfasts was all of oil and profits. Everyone expected PEMEX to be the motor of economic development right up to the end of the twentieth century. López Portillo would develop Catholic Mexico into a modernistic cathedral honoring the goddess Progress. In the dome would be an oil derrick instead of a keystone.

Economic Difficulties

When López Portillo had taken office in 1976, the roaring demographic explosion was scorching Mexico with unemployment. The President used the fire extinguisher of contraception to spray the raging flames with an effective population-control policy. (He had only five children.) Although for political reasons he consciously maintained a macho image, throwing javelins on television and openly carrying on an affair with the dark brown beauty Rosa Luz Alegría, he cleverly developed a program of birth control that undercut machismo by appealing to women. The Social Security Medical System offered contraceptives and often urged women to use them without telling their husbands. The government put big sums into this effort, and the soaring growth rate of 3.4 percent in 1977 slowed in eight years to 2.4 percent.[27]

That was progress. But half of all Mexicans were children, and almost a million were arriving on the job market every year. "By the late 1970s López Portillo was faced with an unemployment rate of almost 25 percent and an underemployment rate of almost half of the country's work force."[28]

In 1982 more chickens came home to roost. To finance his populism the President had increased the debt from Echeverría's frightening $20 billion to $60 billion.[29] Much of this money, as subsidies for basic consumer goods, was creating demand but not supply. Portillo's mint was also making extra coin to pay government bills, and as this money entered circulation, Mexicans with jingling pockets rushed to the stores. Voracious consumer demand gulped goods like a shark chasing sardines. Prices in the stores hopped onto the escalator of inflation for a ride out of reach of the poor. As prices climbed, they pushed the value of Mexico's goods above the world market while imports from the United States cheapened. Money rushed out of the country to pay for the bargain imports, and devaluation again raised its ugly head.[30]

In 1982 the business community saw the devaluation coming, and began sending billions abroad so that they would not lose value. López Portillo played Echeverría to the business elite's defensive action—he delayed devaluation. A President who devalues the currency devalues himself. Kicking, squirming and darting his eyes about for a way of escape, López Portillo refused to devalue. Only after much of Mexico's capital had given him the slip did he face the inevitable. A series of devaluations dropped the peso from 26 to the dollar to 100.[31]

Mexico would have to import its capital goods from the United States at a higher cost, and ballooning costs have a nasty result: cost-push inflation. In one year (1981–1982) inflation leaped from 26 percent to 100 percent.[32] As the economy went to pieces, the President discovered that banks were sending capital abroad. Enraged, in September of 1982 he nationalized the banks.[33]

The Mexican Revolution shot a final burst of fireworks into the political sky as the astonished nation discovered that the nationalized banks owned vast amounts of stock. Suddenly the Mexican state possessed 35 percent of industry. The public sector of the economy had become larger than ever, and the panic-striken elites screamed in terror about invading socialism.[34]

During the 1970s the rich industrial countries had quietly been cutting back on oil consumption, discovering their own sources in Alaska and the North Sea, inventing energy-conserving technology, and secretly building up huge reserves. They suddenly stopped buying oil. The Organization of Petroleum Exporting Countries was caught flat-footed, for its governments had become dependent on oil sales in order to pay their bills. With their income suddenly cut, they had to lower energy prices. In 1982, as oil prices went through the floor, the interest rates on Mexico's debt shot through the ceiling. The nation was faced with $10 billion of interest payments and little oil money. The northern powers had jerked Portillo's keystone from the cathedral, and the edifice crashed with a roar heard throughout Latin America.

Until his last year López Portillo had been a popular President. He clearly intended to hold the balance between capital and labor in the social pact of the Revolution. He was a charismatic orator who made speeches without notes and wrote his own poetry. Although most Mexicans could not understand his Hegelian dialectic, he projected a macho image of a strong and knowledgeable leader. But he ended his term standing in the ruins of a collapsed economy.

Later he would call himself "the last president of the Mexican Revolution."[35] And he would admit that in choosing as his successor Miguel de la Madrid, he made a mistake. But he excused himself by pointing out that as he ended his term, Mexico was sinking into a financial crisis and he selected Madrid as the candidate with the most experience in financial matters.[36] De la Madrid's work had been in banking and government finance. He had been a student of López Portillo, and seemed a trusted subordinate. He could recite the litanies of the revolutionary ideology with ease, and believed in it with part of his mind. But his heart lay elsewhere. In the 1980s Mexico's debt left the new President struggling in the claws of the International Monetary Fund. When the winds of doctrine began to blow in a neoliberal direction, he finally changed course to keep from going under.

4

The Revolution Betrayed

In 1982 President López Portillo ended his term, taking a hit from the oil boom that boomeranged. When the frustrated President discovered that banks were sending huge amounts of capital abroad, he nationalized the banking system. This act infuriated the business class.[1]

After a nine-month populist presidential campaign, President Miguel de la Madrid took office in December 1982 and found the economy falling into an abyss: capital fleeing abroad, no investment, no growth, no jobs. Inflation was soaring into the skies: Mexico had to buy tools, parts, technology, materials, whole factories from the United States with López Portillo's devalued pesos. Costs rose, and so did prices. Prices pushing into the clouds panicked the government as inflation began to feed upon itself, later reaching 150 percent a year.[2]

The economic wizards at the International Monetary Fund and the Banco de México advised incoming President De la Madrid to raise interest rates in order to cut investment and make businesses contract; they urged him to shrink the money supply so that consumers would have less in their pockets to spend; they asked him to stop government spending on public works and to hold wages down to survival level. To control inflation, millions of Mexicans would become a horde of ragged people with empty pockets, looking for work while goods on shelves rotted until prices fell. Those are the tools of orthodox economic theory.

With immoderate zeal the President used those tools to slash what was left of the economy to bits.[3] Soon wages were so far under the debris that it took an archaeologist to find them. But the unions did not revolt. Mexico's corporate state stood fast: the 83-year-old labor boss Fidel Velázquez, who ran the workers' movement from an office containing six secretaries with computers, remained loyal to *el Presidente* and there were no strikes.

During the first three years of his term Miguel de la Madrid discreetly let it be known that he was only temporarily ignoring the Constitution and the goals of the Mexican Revolution. He continued the Mexican diplomatic offensive to end Washington's low-intensity war against Nicaragua and the Salvadoran guerrillas and in 1983 began to work with other governments for a peaceful diplomatic solution to the crisis in Central America.[4] Under the thumb of Washington's International Monetary Fund (IMF) and its belt-tightening program, he had temporarily caved into the IMF to get loans to pay the astronomical debt interest.

Though De la Madrid toned down his predecessor's roaring rhetoric to a hum, the business class remained hostile to the ruling Institutional Revolutionary Party. The big money punished the PRI government for its flickering antibusiness ideology by keeping the money abroad: tens of billions of dollars in flight capital put down roots in greener pastures.

Vanishing investment, no economic growth, only population growth hurling a million new young people onto the job market every year. When the upraised arms pleading for work grew in numbers, their hands clenched into shaking fists. De la Madrid begged the economic elite to bring back the money. It answered him with a snarl.

Finally *el Presidente* stopped the dribbling populist rhetoric completely. He moved toward reprivatizing the banking system by setting up a parallel bank. He held wages at starvation level. He implored big business to revive the economy—all in vain. The economic power wanted nothing less than an end to the government's 50-year program of populism and developmentalism. It required a surrender to international finance.

So in 1986 the President announced a new policy designed to appease the voracious corporate lion. Mexico would join the club of rich countries, the General Agreement on Tariffs and Trade (GATT).[5] During the next three years he lowered the impregnable tariff wall around the economy to less than 15 percent protection. He was under pressure from globalization and the free trade offensive of the multinationals; but he also argued forcibly that the 100 percent tariffs and the lack of foreign competition had made the economy an obsolete engine grinding out junk goods for a captive market. The time had come for an economy spewing out goods of world class.[6]

De la Madrid trimmed the bloated state economic sector, privatizing about a fifth of some 1,000 government enterprises.[7] He pointed out that the government could do without bicycle factories and soft drink plants. He argued persuasively that some government industries were run by lazy bureaucrats who were lining their pockets. Why not give the managerial expertise of corporate enterprise a chance to rev up production?

He hammered at the nepotism and cronyism of the federal bureaucracy: tens of thousands of relatives and their friends suddenly found themselves in the street, where they could no longer strangle economic activity with red tape.[8]

He faithfully paid tens of billions of dollars in interest on the public debt to U.S. financial centers: refusal to do so would bring political isolation in the Western world. He also bowed to the International Monetary Fund's anti-inflationary policies by keeping wages at starvation levels. He devalued the peso, and so devalued himself.[9]

All in vain: the corporate lion switched its tail and roared, THAT'S NOT ENOUGH.[10] For Miguel de la Madrid had not officially repudiated the ideology of the Mexican Revolution. True, the ideals of political sovereignty, economic independence, and social justice were no longer on his lips; the promises of land and freedom were no longer in his speeches. But were they not lodged in his heart? Had he not campaigned nine months for the presidency with populist promises? Had he not publicly said well into his term that the ideology of the Revolution was still valid? Had he not added progressive amendments to the Constitution?[11] Was not the agrarian, socialist *ejido* sector of the countryside intact? The State sector of the economy weakened, but alive and well, the foreign policy offensive in Central America in the 1980s a star on the PRI's "revolutionary" uniform?

De la Madrid chose as his successor Carlos Salinas de Gortari, his loyal economic czar, a Harvard man sporting a Ph.D. in economics. In 1988 the PRI oiled its mighty electoral machine and prepared to impose Salinas on a nation gasping for economic breath. In the campaign for the presidency he faced the scowling Cuauhtémoc Cárdenas, son of the legendary populist revolutionary President of the 1930s, Lázaro Cárdenas. The discontented Cuauhtémoc and other PRI populists had bolted the ruling party in 1987, in order to set up a countermovement determined to make government policy according to the ideology of the Mexican Revolution. The Communist intelligentsia rallied to his movement.

Salinas launched a seven-month campaign against the coalition of left parties, the National Democratic Front (FDN). This pragmatic economist more than once said that he was against free trade with the United States: the northern giant had an economy 35 times bigger than the Mexican pygmy's, and its cheaper and better goods would crush Mexican competition. But would Salinas's nationalism suffice to defeat Cuauhtémoc's populism at the polls?

In the election on July 6, 1988, the miserable population mobilized for a tremendous protest vote against the PRI's economic performance during the six years of snuggling up to the big money. An avalanche of votes poured in for Cuauhtémoc Cárdenas. What happened next was what many Mexicans knew would happen: an election fraud of world historical proportions. All the vote-counting computers mysteriously broke down for 48 hours, giving the PRI government time to arrange the count—50.4 percent for the PRI. Amid roars of laughter from political scientists at home and abroad, Salinas proclaimed himself the winner of the "election" with an absolute majority.[12]

The morose Cárdenas was not amused, and the opposition took to the streets with direct action: barricades, roadblocks, sit-ins, marches, demonstrations, protests, trashing in the streets. The PRI dictatorship easily beat them down. Dictatorship? Yes, a necessary condition for democracy is that there be some way to remove the people in office without shooting at them, and this condition was not yet present in Mexico. The armed movement that seized power in 1920 had continuously held office for 68 years—a world record. As the 88-year-old PRI labor boss Fidel Velázquez put it, "Bullets brought us to power, and only bullets will drive us from power."[13]

Cuauhtémoc Cárdenas was a poor speaker who lacked charisma. Few who voted for him and his Marxist backers had expected the PRI to allow him to win the count.

Carlos Salinas de Gortari took office on December 1, 1988. In 1989 President Salinas looked about for a policy that would end his country's economic ruin. He had come from a left-leaning family: on his mother's side Eli de Gortari was a leading Leninist; Carlos's inseparable brother Raúl had been a Maoist; and Carlos's father, Raúl Salinas Lozano, was a PRI populist who had served as economics minister under López Portillo. Salinas's close friend at Harvard had been John Womack, the biographer of Zapata. When Salinas baptized his presidential airplane *el Emiliano Zapata*, the Mexican left held its breath. Would Salinas turn left and try to revive the ideals of the Mexican Revolution? They were still in the Constitution, and violation of those principles meant disobedience to the highest law of the land.

GALLOPING BACKWARDS INTO NEOLIBERALISM

The ideology of the Mexican Revolution was nothing less than the Constitution that everyone had been taught for a century to revere. It proclaimed that strategic areas of the economy should belong to the public sector; the need for a powerful interventionist State and democratic planning; the responsibility of the government to provide everyone with a job, a minimum wage adequate for the economic, social, and cultural needs of each family; price controls on basic goods; the eight-hour workday; legalization of unions and strikes; equal pay for equal work; compensation for accidents; Social Security; profit-sharing by workers in every business; the illegality of monopolies; the exclusion of the army from all internal police action; the right of each peasant to land distribution; the *ejido* as the semicommunal village owning land in common.[14] The *ejidos* combined a market economy with collective ownership.

Salinas, a pragmatist, simply went where the power was. He asked Mexican business interests to define their position: What do you want in exchange for bringing back flight capital, investing in Mexico, and reviving the flat economy? And the lion roared its answer: you must abandon the ideology of the Mexican Revolution! You must replace it with neoliberalism. A chorus of voices urged as a first step in this direction FREE TRADE WITH THE UNITED STATES. (Free trade would integrate the Mexican economy with that of the United States and make the coming retreat from nationalism hard to reverse.)[15]

The doctor in economics was converted.[16] Did his about-face come from rereading David Ricardo's theory of comparative advantage? Did it come from listening to the arguments of the Washington Consensus announced in 1989? Eastern socialism had collapsed, so there was no longer an alternative to the free market and to free trade. Korea and the Asian tigers had turned backward economies into export platforms; they did it with neoliberal policies, and Mexico might copy them. Whatever the force of these arguments, for pragmatic Salinas they were backed up by the realities of class power at home. And the arguments were coming from the big winner—Washington!

Salinas watched the rise of the new economic region, the North American Free Trade Agreement (NAFTA), and decided that after all it was better to be a tiny craft in the powerful northern squadron than an independent ship drifting through stormy waters alone.

Miguel de la Madrid had set up a parallel private bank, and Salinas finished the task by privatizing the banking system. De la Madrid had sold off about 20 percent of the public economic sector, but the coporate lion roared for more. During his term Salinas threw hundreds more into the champing jaws, including many with good bottom lines, and the gorged monster began to purr: tens of billions of dollars floated back to Mexico. Much of it was "hot money" going into the Mexican stock market; not creating new value, but only starting a speculative bubble bound to burst. Yet money did come back, and some of it was direct investment.[17]

Salinas openly abandoned the Mexican Revolution. He replaced its ideology with "social liberalism," a doctrine that mixed the theories of free market economics with populist demagogic phrases. In practice it meant attacking the welfare state while throwing scraps to the poor from a huge slush fund. *El Presidente* got billions by selling off the state industries at bargain prices.[18]

To stop the 1989 protests against his fraudulent election, Salinas had promised the reactionary Church hierarchy to take anticlericalism out of the Constitution. His amending scalpel soon carved that progressive muscle out of the sacred document. The Church could own property again, priests could vote, convents and seminaries were decriminalized. Salinas sent a representative to the Pope for the first time since Benito Juárez broke relations with the Vatican in 1859.

The encouraged Church seized the offensive: it demanded religious instruction in the schools, a TV station for itself, an end to information about safe sex, continued criminalization of abortion in a land where it is the main means of birth control for poor women. The intellectual community roared with laughter when the Church tried to convince Mexicans that condoms are dangerous, but demographers charting the population explosion scowled and health experts, worried about half a million carriers of the AIDS virus, were wringing their hands.

In the early 1990s the economic powerhouses—Japan, Germany, the United States—sank into recession, and transnational investors looked for somewhere else to put their money. They observed Salinas following neoliberal policies: he was getting corporatively controlled unions to raise production quality, investing in technological research, wiping out red tape that strangled exports and imports, buying computers for the Mexican bureaucracy, eliminating medieval holidays that meant taking off work on Thursday, not showing up on Friday, drinking on Saturday and Sunday, and recovering on Monday.

Salinas was trying to modernize a traditional society. He was tearing down what remained of the Mexican tariff wall, privatizing state industries, undermining the communal villages, keeping wages at starvation level, paying the exorbitant debt interest, and opening banking to international capital. Salinas's propaganda machine generated an image of Mexico as a modernizing nation and sold it in Europe and the United States. As he handed over his economy to foreign interests, the docile PRI obeyed him and the conservative National Action Party (PAN) yapped its approval. International investors decided to reward the neoliberal leader.

The Harvard Ph.D. did not join NAFTA just to bolster trade relations with the United States. Along with Mexico's entrance into the GATT in 1986 and the nation's joining the Organization for Economic Co-operation and Development, NAFTA was part of a strategy to raise Mexico from Third World to First World status. This strategy aimed to put Mexico back on the path of steady economic growth through financial stabilization and access to international capital markets.

Enough investment money arrived in Mexico to achieve a 3.5 per-cent annual rate of economic growth, and so to provide 350,000 of the 1 million new jobs needed each year to keep up with the exploding population.[19] Salinas's technocrats proudly pointed out that neoliberal policy was making progress: while the northern industrial states idled in a recession, Mexico sailed forward.

Since free trade with the United States began even before Salinas signed NAFTA in 1993, a flood of cheaper and better goods rushed in from the northern powerhouse. You could buy tomatoes and eggs from California in Mexican supermarkets, Jim Beam bourbon in bars, and Whirlpool washing machines in department stores. Huge sums flowed out of Mexico to pay for these goods and opened up a trade deficit: imports were much greater than exports. As money drained out of the country to pay for the imports, the money level in the banks and busi-nesses fell year after year.

Early on, Salinas appointed Arturo Warman, an agrarian sociologist who had published works defending poor peasants, as Secretary of Agrarian Reform in the cabinet—at a high salary. The big money con-verted Warman into the Secretary of Agrarian Counterreform. In 1991 he rewrote the sacred Article 27 of the Constitution, which for decades had proclaimed that every peasant had a right to a corn patch in a communal village but could not sell the land—only its products—on the market. In the original article the village "held" the land from the State. For 50 years the peasants had liked this agrarian market socialism.

Warman's proposed amendment declared that the land reform was over and that the right to a corn patch had ended. It declared that the village owned the land and that the peasants could sell it to one another and to corporations; the peasants had *dominium* over their plots.[20] The clear intent of the new law was to destroy the *ejido*, the communal village that tilled half of Mexico's cultivable land. It allowed corporations like Nestlé, General Foods, Campbell's and Del Monte to buy the land for agrobusiness and to drive the peasants into the cities, where there were already millions in belts of misery without water and services. This program of urbanizing ecodisaster was called "modernizing agriculture."

Agrobusiness was invited to sow the earth with miracle seeds, throw fertilizer on them, and then irrigate. (In the future such a food-for-export program, if really carried out, may bring salinization of the land, turning it into desert and causing more erosion.) Warman threw the *ejido* lands onto the market, and free trade began expelling the peasants from the market: as cheaper grain came in from the United States, the corn patch farmers could hardly compete.

Warman was an admirer of Zapata, and so was Salinas. As *el Presidente* zoomed through the skies in his presidential plane named after Zapata, the desperate peasants of the South joked that the Mexican Revolution had dismounted from its horse and climbed on an airplane. What they did not understand was that air travel is the fastest way to Washington.

Zapata rolled and tossed in his grave in Cuautla while the Zapatista Salinas handed Warman's amendment to the Senate in 1992 and the good men of the PRI dutifully ended the most sacred principle of the Revolution by stamping the amendment YES. The conservative PAN applauded.

We have seen how Salinas undermined two of the three pillars of the Mexican Revolution, the State enterprises and the *ejido* villages. How did he chop into the third pillar, the revolutionary nationalist foreign policy?

For decades in forums like the Organization of American States, Mexico had protested against Washington's military interventions in Guatemala (1954), in Cuba (1961), in the Dominican Republic (1965), in Chile (1973), in Central America (1980s), in Grenada (1983). When in 1989 President George Bush hurled the marines into Panama to seize President Manuel Noriega for his disloyalty to Washington, the uniformed killers murdered 15,000 people in the poor neighborhoods of El Chorillo and San Miguelito who were backing the President's military populism. The President of a sovereign nation was whisked away to prison in the United States, an unprecedented event in hemispheric history. Bush's ruthless agression was a violation of all international norms, of the Charter of the Organization of American States, of the UN Charter. A roar of protest went up from the Latin American governments, but Mexico was conspicuous by its silence.

Salinas refused to lead the continent in forming a Latin American debt cartel. And after the Iraqi invasion of Kuwait, he stepped up oil flows to the United States by 100,000 barrels a day. Then, as migrants and refugees from other countries fled through Mexico to seek jobs or asylum in the United States, Salinas had them arrested and deported. Since Lázaro Cárdenas, Mexico had been a haven for political refugees. But Salinas could hardly miss a chance to do Washington a favor by cutting down unwanted immigrants. And so it went for six years, while nationalists gnashed their teeth and cursed *el pelón* (old baldy).[21]

A MEXICAN *NOMENKLATURA*

In disgust the most fervent nationalists abandoned the ruling party, but in the tradition of Mexican presidentialism the plethora of weaker natures followed Salinas's assertive lead.

The middle and lower bureaucrats had no choice but to obey their masters. Their commanders were the top 700 bureaucrats in the political elite: secretaries and subsecretaries in the cabinet, and perhaps even the secretary of the secretary of the secretary; the top army brass at the Secretariat of National Defense and certain other generals; in the national Congress, the hundreds of senators and deputies; also the governors of states and their courtiers; the top diplomats in key countries; directors of big state enterprises like Petróleos Mexicanos and the Federal Electricity Commission; financial directors at the Banco de México and Nacional Financiera; administrators of government dependencies such as the Fondo de Cultura Económica, the Colosio Institute, or the gigantic National Autonomous University. And how could we forget the top labor bureaucrats of the government-controlled unions, such as the 95-year-old Fidel Velázquez? (Finally in 1998 the nonagenarian's command post was taken over by Leonardo Rodríguez Alcaine—a mere octogenarian.) With their big salaries these labor bosses made up a subordinate fraction of the political ruling class.

The upper 700 constituted the Mexican *nomenklatura*. The concept of *nomenklatura* was made world famous in 1980 by the Soviet sociologist Michael Vozlensky: it refers to top government bureaucrats who enjoy high salaries, special privileges, and secret perks. Courageous research by Pablo Gómez, published in *Los gastos secretos del presidente*, and studies by the Civic Association and other investigators has confirmed what was always suspected. The Mexican top 700 were not only receiving what for Mexico are astronomical salaries, many were also sucking up the economic surplus in hidden ways: splendid bonuses, juicy fringe benefits, big loans without interest, stock options, special bonds, travel expenses, dinners on the tab, cellular phones, limousines, chauffeurs, free gas, airplane tickets, family trips at government expense.[22]

On April 28, 1995, Demetri Sodi de la Tijera, a scholarly populist who bolted the PRI in 1994, revealed in *La Jornada* that the secretaries in the cabinet were getting $660,000 a year in salaries, bonuses, and secret payments. For Mexico's miserable salary scale, this was a great deal of money. How was it possible?[23]

As the investigation of Pablo Gómez later discovered, in 1996 the President had legally available in Section 23 of the federal budget no less than $4 billion to spend discretionally, and he was dedicating two-thirds of it to secretly boost the salaries of his "public servants" by means of big bonuses, special bonds, and other supplements. The Civic Alliance, a middle-sector reform movement, reported in *La Jornada* that its detective work had convinced it that this was only the tip of the iceberg.[24]

In 1997, the sociologist Julio Boltvinik reported in *La Jornada* that the federal budget expenses contain a clause authorizing the President to give any leftover monies to individuals as "reward for efficiency," such as the $90,000 bonus paid to the top bureaucrat Oscar Espinoza Villarreal.[25]

What had come to light was well advanced under former presidents. Europe's opening of information on secret monies revealed that Miguel de la Madrid put $2 billion in the Bank of Luxembourg in account number 27600800872.[26] The Mexican *nomenklatura* was paying itself much of this extra money—legally!

Raúl Salinas, who was a top bureaucrat in his brother Carlos's administration, is an example of the darker side of the *nomenklatura's* penchant for accumulating wealth. In 1988 Raúl began as an ordinary "public servant" and wound up in 1994 with at least $250 million in his personal fortune. He directed the National Company of People's Subsistence, the government agency that aided Mexico's poor with subsidized beans. When Raúl began, he was poor, but he aided his own poverty so well that he finished rich. When his brother left the presidency and fled into voluntary exile in Ireland, Raúl was arrested. Accused of several crimes, including "inexplicable enrichment," Raúl spent four years in a federal prison. Finally the former Maoist was sentenced to 27 years on charges of having ordered the murder of another "public servant."

Raúl's arrest made international headlines because the top 700 have usually stolen government money with impunity. Although it is rarely possible to present figures, the Mexican intellectual community is convinced that the money siphoned off from the public coffers has amounted to hundreds of millions of dollars a year. It is more than pilfering, it is "inexplicable enrichment."

The Mexican *nomenklatura* was also lining its pockets illegally. In the 1980s the U.S. Drug Enforcement Administration closed Florida and the islands to cocaine entry, so the narcotraffic shifted toward Mexico. During Miguel de la Madrid's administration (1982–1988), the general commanding the Mexican armed forces, the Attorney General, and the Secretary of the Interior were repeatedly accused of taking money from the drug lords. Secretary Bartlett, later the governor of Puebla, stays away from the United States because in California there is a warrant for his arrest. Under Salinas (1988–1994) much of Mexico's adminis-tration became a narcogovernment: the Harvard-trained economist al-lowed governors and generals to accept payoffs while Washington agreed to look the other way.[27]

Raúl Salinas salted away $132 million of drug money in Swiss banks: Switzerland's Justice Department has traced the origin of the money and announced the proofs.[28] With or without the consent of President Ernesto Zedillo (1994–2000), Mexico has now replaced Colombia as the number one narcocountry of the world. There are unpublished photographs of former governor Jorge Carrillo Olea walking arm in arm with capo Amado Carrillo, and *New York Times* reporters got a Pulitzer Prize for their exposé of Governor Manlio Beltrones. Mario Villanueva Madrid, the Governor of Quintana Roo, is wanted by Mexico's Federal Justice, and has gone into hiding.[29]

Mexico produces 50 percent of the marijuana consumed in the world and 70 percent of the heroin consumed in the United States, and is the main bridge for cocaine entry. Students of the narcotraffic agree that in Mexico it probably generates about $30 billion a year, some 10 per-cent of the Gross Domestic Product. Unconfirmed estimates of how much goes to pay off the Mexican police, generals, and governing fig-ures run into the billions.[30] Only key officials are in on the take, and there are honest professionals sprinkled throughout the administration, but Mexican sociologists sneer at the political system as "una cultura de corrupción."[31]

A few of Mexico's state bureaucrats managed to jack up their share of capital income (profits, dividends, interest, rent) until it rose above their professional salaries. How did they do that? By plumbing the State treasury, by taking kickbacks from corporate czars, by keeping the books of nationalized enterprises creatively, by pocketing payoffs from the narcotics trade, by investing on the basis of tips on stocks, by using inside knowledge of government projects, and by multiple direct investments of all this booty. But this occurred only at the pinnacle of power. Those who managed to draw more of their income from capital than from salary constituted a State bourgeoisie.

DINOSAURS AND TECHNOCRATS

Since the PRI's founding in 1929, its top stratum has changed dramatically. There has been a long evolution of the ruling party: from military men under Presidents Calles, Cárdenas, and Ávila Camacho through political professionals under Ruiz Cortines, López Mateos, and Díaz Ordaz to the first technocratic economists appearing under Echeverría, increasing under López Portillo, gaining the upper hand under De la Madrid, and reigning under Salinas. Eight out of ten newcomers to the cabinet elite between 1982 and 1988 were men with doctorates from Yale and Stanford, from Harvard and MIT, who had never run for elected office. Joseph Marie Córdoba Montoya, for example, was a French citizen who entered the government in 1985. Such men came into the National Palace with little political experience. In the Salinas years (1988–1994) the transformation to technocracy was completed. Córdoba, trained at Stanford, was finally given citizenship and became Salinas's director of the national security apparatus—a key post in the power elite. Córdoba symbolizes the elite's growing transnationalization.

In protest, honest populists, idealists, and nationalists streamed out of the PRI to join the new center-left opposition Party of the Democratic Revolution (PRD) led by Cuauhtémoc Cárdenas. They left behind the technocrats in the National Palace; they turned their backs on the PRI at the governor and municipal levels still staffed by dinosaurs from yesteryear, authoritarians like governors Roberto Madrazo in Tabasco, Manuel Bartlett in Puebla, the narcotrafficker Mario Villanueva Madrid in Quintana Roo, and Jorge Carrillo Olea and his gangster government in Morelos (his police chief was helping to kidnap the rich for fabulous ransoms until mass demonstrations finally forced Carillo's resignation). The dinosaurs were no longer united by the ideology of the Mexican Revolution, and the glue that held them together was their corruption. The booty of office kept them loyal to one another. The international community began referring to Mexico as "the new Sicily."

During the Salinas years, the President breakfasted weekly in Los Pinos with the Mexican Council of Businessmen, a group of 38 multimillionaires and billionaires with clout in the economy.[32] He carefully listened to their views and asked for their advice; they in turn had to listen to his occasional orders, such as demands for millions to finance the PRI. He even collected taxes from booming businesses that for decades had been showing the government account books in the red.

In those years, on PRI slates in by-elections businessmen appeared as candidates for office: the ruling party began openly sucking in the entrepreneurial elite. In the past the ruling party, whatever its name, had kept out business organizations such as the National Chamber of Commerce. Maintaining a difference between the populist party and business interests was one of the fundamental principles of the Mexican Revolution. With the partial "bourgeoisification" of the PRI, another piece of the ideological edifice crashed.

The conservative PAN threw open its door to businessmen and managers, and they ran for office, steadily winning municipal elections; by 1998 the PAN governed 6 of the 31 states and all the big cities of Mexico except the capital. Salinas proclaimed in public that the PRI considered the PAN a strategic ally. The PAN's charismatic bourgeois leader, Manuel Clouthier, had complained that the PRI was taking over the historic program of his conservative party: free trade, free enterprise, free market, free competition. In Congress many PAN representatives regularly voted for Salinas's neoliberal offensive. But besides its growing nucleus of technocrats, the PAN contained populists like Senator José Conchello, an economist who denounced free trade in widely read writings.[33]

A TECHNOCRATIC PRESIDENT

In the spring of 1994 the PRI switched on its powerful electoral engine, and soon its cylinders were booming behind Salinas's candidate for president: Luis Donaldo Colosio. The dashing young Colosio was a natural orator, but how could he praise to the miserable masses the neoliberal policies of De la Madrid, of Salinas, and of the PRI that were making the rich richer and the poor poorer?

The Mexico Resource Center in Austin, Texas, reports that in 1984 the richest fifth of Mexicans swallowed 48 percent of the national income pie, and by 1992 they were gobbling up 54 percent. The poorer fifth's share dropped from 5 percent to 4.3 percent.[34] And what happened after 1992? Mexico's National Institute of Statistics reported that in that year there were 13.6 million Mexicans in extreme poverty, and that when Carlos Salinas ended his reign in December 1994, there were 17 million in extreme poverty.

Suddenly in March 1994, PRI candidate Colosio began to sound like an old-time populist, and without bodyguards plunged into crowds to embrace the people. The intellectual community remembered how often in Mexico's political history an incoming President had kicked the previous president's policy in the teeth. Was Colosio going to turn left?

On March 23, as Colosio mixed into a crowd, a lone gunman killed him.

Salinas immediately picked as a successor a gray blur named Ernesto Zedillo, who bored Mexicans by reading his speeches. The narrow technocrat had never held elective office, but as the Secretary of Budget and Planning he had carried out Salinas's economic changes with neoliberal joy. An economist trained at Yale, he was a true believer.

In the 1994 presidential campaign Salinas and Zedillo pulled off a masterful manipulation of the Mexican people. The PRI got three times as much television coverage as the other parties together. Zedillo promised Mexicans the moon, promised to better the lot of every family, promised to create a million new jobs a year. He assured property owners and Mexican women—frightened by guerrillas and assassinations—that the tough old PRI would keep order. And that it has always been able to do.

Voters were impressed by the economy: after De la Madrid's period of zero growth, Salinas was getting more than 3 percent a year and creating 350,000 jobs for the million youth arriving annually on the labor force. (The neoliberal chickens were flapping toward Mexico but had not yet come home to roost.) Inflation was only 7 percent, the lowest since 1981, which Salinas achieved by keeping the peso seriously overvalued.[35] An overvalued peso meant that it would buy more outside Mexico. Thus the well-off could vacation in Colorado and go on shopping sprees in San Antonio; during the election year this cleverly created an illusion of prosperity. (The economy was a house of cards flashing with the red and green colors Mexicans love.) The stock market boomed like a snakehide drum, but mainly with hot money removable at the flip of a computer switch. Salinas boasted of $27 billion in the government kitty to fight off any run on the peso (money he got from selling off the State economic sector).[36]

In the August election the PRI used all its usual tricks. And the Mexicans really turned out to vote: an amazing 77 percent went to the polls. The opposition split, with 26 percent of votes going to the PAN's charismatic, macho leader, Diego Fernández de Cevallos, and 16 percent to the PRD's grim, honest Cuauhtémoc Cárdenas; the PRI coasted home with 50.18 percent. Of course, a lot of that absolute majority was won by dirty tricks, but millions really did vote for Zedillo. The PRI had done it again: the technocrat would be president.

NEOLIBERALISM AND ITS DISCONTENTS

Because of the dangerously overvalued peso, the trade deficit had opened like scissors, and threatened to cut Mexico's exports. Huge sums were flowing out of the country to pay for bargain imports. Mexican consumers were flying to New York to shop at Macy's. On the economic horizon the capped nimbus of DEVALUATION reared like a cobra and licked the financial markets with forked lightning. Foreigners' hot money fled the stock market in terror; and Mexican capital prepared to take off. The election was over and the time had come for devaluation.

In secret Washington begged Salinas to do it. His advisers told him, Do it now! September dragged by, October passed, but the wily Salinas hung tough. Billions were zooming out of Mexico, the rich were converting their pesos into dollars, a run on the peso began, Salinas secretly used $13 billion of reserves buying pesos no one else would.[37] November passed and Zedillo took over the presidency with a cabinet of neoliberal technocrats loyal to multinational agencies.

The insignificant president refused to devalue. There was a massive run on the peso. Zedillo's dollar reserves fell to $7 billion and were bleeding away at a billion a day. He finally devalued a mere 15 percent and dollar reserves dropped to $2 billion; the world money market took over and did the rest in spite of him: a devaluation of 50 percent.[38]

Because of the delay in devaluation, most of the capital had fled to more fertile fields. Since no investment means no growth, there would be no new jobs for the million hopeful youth that the population increase throws onto the labor market each year. As 1995 opened, the economy collapsed in the worst recession since 1932.

Buying machinery from the United States with devalued pesos raised costs and prices: inflation leaped to 50 percent. To control it, the President shoved the economy into the wringer and pressed away. During his campaign for the presidency he had promised that his neoliberal program would create a million new jobs a year. But in his first year the neoliberal wizard threw a million workers into the street in a country with no unemployment insurance.

In 1995 the rate of economic growth was a negative 6.2 percent, wiping out jobs gained under Salinas. As a million newly unemployed hit the streets, the usual new million job seekers joined them. But the wringer proved efficient: inflation dropped from 50 percent a year to 25 percent as 1996 opened. For the middle sectors, weary of inflation, the neoliberal policy was working again.[39]

With inflation anchored, Zedillo began to revive the economy, and in 1996 it climbed out of the abyss and reached the predevaluation level by 1997 with inflation at only 19 percent. During this agonizing climb in 1996, the usual new million youth arrived on the job market to find nothing. Neoliberal Zedillo continued selling off state industries.

As 1997 opened, Mexico had a debt soaring toward the clouds while Zedillo continued to faithfully funnel the billions of dollars of oil money to pay the yearly interest. The minimum wage held at $3 a day. In the schools teachers worked for pitiful wages and had little chalk, no money to fix a broken toilet or window, none to paint the scarred desks at year's end. In the countryside 100,000 people a year died of preventable diseases; most of the births occurred without medical attention. Two out of three economically active Mexicans found work only in the hell of the informal economy: street vendors, seasonal workers, domestic servants, shoeshiners, fire eaters, windshield cleaners, subway musicians, migrant laborers, fortune tellers, teenage prostitutes, seamstresses, messengers, women in illegal sweatships, unemployed teachers tutoring rich kids, unemployed lawyers steering Mexicans through the Kafkaesque bureaucracy—the list is endless.[40]

Armed social protest movements exploded in the Mexican countryside. In 1994 a guerrilla war broke out in the southern state of Chiapas, and in Guerrero and Oaxaca two years later. These were major insurgencies. In a dozen more states tiny bands of armed people began ambushing army patrols. In the cities, crime waves, bank robberies, and muggings frightened employed Mexicans as the illiterate, young, unemployed finally found something to do.

Such were the results of applying the neoliberal model: eliminating López Portillo's exchange controls, privatizing the national bank, deregulating the financial system, selling off 850 of the 1000 state industries at bargain prices, ripping down the tariff wall overnight, dropping government industrial policy, removing price controls on staples like tortillas, cutting back on free higher education, letting the rich escape taxes "so that they will invest in growth."

For neoliberalism 1997 was a good year. The formal economy recovered growthwise with a whopping 7 percent, and although a trade deficit opened in June, the neoliberal choir crooned that all was well. Some of the growth was mere reopening of idle plants, but after the devaluation thousands of export businesses appeared. And the already humming export of automobiles, textiles, computer equipment, electronics, auto parts, and food products surged ahead.

Another good year occurred in 1998. Mexico's export platform hurled millions of goods into the world economy. Growth held at 5 percent and created half of the million new jobs needed. Investors were impressed by the indicators. Growth continued at 3.7 in 1999 and 7 percent in 2000, but with the trade deficit steadily opening and the peso overvalued. This growth was a reflection of the booming U.S. economy. As the American economy slowed down in 2001, Mexico's dependent export sector began to slump.

What does the phrase "the economy is fine" mean? Does it mean that the tiny percentage working in export is employed and producing huge profits for foreign companies located in Mexico and that the marginalized millions are at least still alive? Back in 1971 General Emilio De Medici, the Brazilian dictator, surveyed the happy industrial managers exploiting his miserable people and then coined an immortal phrase: "The economy is doing well, but the people are doing badly."

In 1998 loans went bad and the banks ran out of money. In 1999 the neoliberal government handed out $100 billion of taxpayers' money to the bankers, and blocked an investigation of the collapse and of who had stolen what, when, how. Banks must follow rules, and neoliberal deregulation allowed both unwitting mistakes and sharp practices. While the opposition complains that it is "the biggest bank scandal in world history," the government pays huge interest on its staggering debt. With the bailout the debt rose again. President Zedillo inherited a debt of $130 billion, and with the bailout he added another $100 billion, to give Mexico the highest per-capita debt on earth.[41]

Mexican law declares that tax evasion is not a serious crime. Tax evasion runs at 40 percent: the superrich, who have most of the money, laugh at the collectors while the tiny, squeezed, desperate, helpless middle sectors pay through the nose.

NEOLIBERAL EXPORT SUCCESS

The United States absorbs 90 percent of Mexico's exports. In the period from 1995 to 2000 the American economy grew at an unprecedented average of more than 4.5 percent a year, and needed Mexican inputs.[42] Under NAFTA Mexican exports to the United States and Canada were worth $140 billion in the year 2000 (equivalent to a third of the 1998 GDP). Mexico's export platform passed Brazil's to become the most powerful in Latin America.[43] So the regime had reason to celebrate the success of its development policy. And there was no doubt that the upper 10 percent of income groups had prospered as never before.

What do neoliberal policies mean to most of the people? Mexico's economy is mainly one of small entrepreneurs. There are more than a million street vendors in Mexico City alone, and throughout the country the marginalized are hard at work selling things (and if they have nothing left to sell, they sell themselves). There are also millions of small businesses potentially more important to the economy: a host of family-owned firms and individual capitalists in services, artisanal production, tiny manufacturing or small construction companies. These puny producers are not connected to Big Business: the huge assembly plants along the northern border, the multinationals producing for the limited internal market, and the 300 gigantic semi-*maquila* export corporations.[44]

The 300 giants in such export industries as automobiles and textiles employ few Mexicans at low wages; the big companies import their inputs and export their products. Unlike northern Italy, where the export platform gets inputs and materials from small business, Mexico has big companies that don't pull the rest of the economy; and since the neoliberal hands-off-the-economy approach means hardly any industrial policy to connect the small entrepreneurs to the big companies, the export promotion drive leaves most Mexicans in permanent poverty.[45]

Mexico's small business culture is more like Mafia-ridden southern Italy than Turin or Milan, and the neoliberals see the little capitalists as incompetent. In a traditional society the small owners prefer to overstaff their management with know-nothing friends, relatives, and godfathers rather than with energetic graduates of the universities.[46]

The neoliberals hope that in the long run the export platform will suck everyone into the developed sector, as happened in Korea. But Korea's Confucian emphasis on education and discipline is missing in Catholic Mexico, where the government spends less of its GNP on education than the other big Latin American countries, and Mexicans are drinking and partying in the evenings instead of taking night courses. Korea prohibited unauthorized export of capital by making it a crime punishable by death, but Mexican superrich investors are helping the United States develop.

In 1999 the multinational giants produced 60 percent of the goods consumed inside Mexico. The corporate pyramids of organization in the country, both native and foreign, also made up the largest manufacturing exporters. One-third of the Gross Domestic Product was generated by the export sector. In this economic system both Max Weber and Karl Marx would find the dominant form of production in the community of giant corporations.[47]

In Mexico capitalism is widespread as small private enterprise, but the corporate giants of the new knowledge society have become the real productive power. Numberless stockholders own the corporations as collective property. Armies of directors, managers, experts, lawyers, technicians, marketers, and professionals of all kinds, together with bureaucratic administrators and professional technocrats in the government, rip off the economic surplus in high salaries.

Capitalism—especially present in myriad privately owned small businesses barely able to make ends meet—provides most of the real employment. But private enterprise is no longer the main force in the Mexican economy.

Of course, everyone "knows" that capitalism is universal, that it has triumphed in every nation on earth. They know it, just as in the 15th century everyone knew that the world was flat, in the 16th century everyone knew that the body contained four humors, in the 17th century that base metals could be transmuted into gold, in the 18th century that all species had remained unchanged forever, in the 19th century that matter was made up of hard little lumps, and in the 20th century that space was filled with ether.

In the election of 2000, for a third time the Left ran Cárdenas for the presidency. But the PAN launched the tall, handsome, macho, Catholic, charismatic Vicente Fox. Financed by the Monterrey millionaires and backed by the TV monopolies, this neoliberal Coca-Cola manager ran a brilliant populist campaign—he promised Mexicans to end poverty, to create jobs, to build schools, to help Indians, to aid small business, and to worship the Virgin.

In the elections, international observers curbed the PRI's dirty tricks and President Zedillo ordered his cabinet not to interfere. Desperate Mexicans voted against the PRI, and the PAN's great orator won. In December he took office and appointed a tough-minded neoliberal cabinet. At once the 18,000-foot volcano on the capital's skyline exploded. An old Zapatista peasant fleeing from the eruption believed that the ancient fire god living in the volcano's guts was angry because the government had abandoned its people.

WHAT HAPPENED TO THE REVOLUTION?

Until the PRI lost the presidency to the PAN, a dictatorship ruled Mexico. The dictatorship of the ruling party, from the presidential despot down through the state governors, a servile Congress, city mayors, the managers of state enterprises, and union bureaucrats, was veiled by a democratic Constitution and periodic elections. But the official party of the Revolution did not rule alone—it had popular support.

Whenever the party's policies shifted rightward, the popular resistance flared up to warn it back toward populist politics. The popular resistance dating from the early 1940s fed the revolutionary nationalism of the 1910–1920 Revolution so that it stayed alive through most of the 20th century. Yet by 2000 its only support was outside the ruling circles. In that year Mexican TV began announcing the "end of the Revolution." Had the Mexican Revolution finally expired? The answer depends on how the Revolution is interpreted.

If we take the 1917 Constitution as the focal point, the Revolution was a multiclass movement expressing the interests of three antagonistic but allied social forces: a bourgeois-democratic current represented by Francisco Madero and Venustiano Carranza, a popular-democratic current of workers and peasants led by Pancho Villa and Emiliano Zapata, and an administrative-professional current led by the revolutionary generals. The bourgeois current wanted a liberal democracy. The popular current, under the influence of Ricardo Flores Magón and his journal *Regeneración*, wanted an egalitarian society. The professional current wanted to preserve the gains it had fought for, to institutionalize the reforms, and to maintain its newly won authority.

As long as the balance of interests remained and the social pact held up, the Revolution was an ongoing process. But the equilibrium of social forces was unstable, and tilted either to the political right (the bourgeois-democratic current) or to the political left (the popular-democratic current) until the administrative-professional current came under fire from both ends of the political spectrum.

The Revolution was defined by the social pact. Written into the Constitution of 1917, it aimed at destroying Mexico's traditional landowning society. It also aimed at reconciling the four classes opposed to that society: the bourgeoisie, the proletariat, the peasantry, and the administrative-professional class containing the revolutionary generals. The Constitution writers hailed from this fourth class. They were not people working for wages, they were drawing a salary: schoolteachers, journalists, engineers, civil servants, and army officers. (There was one general for every 200 soldiers.) To hang onto power and to expand their influence, the revolutionary generals supported by the rest of the professionals needed peace. The social pact aimed at harmonizing the interests of the other three classes under the leadership of the bureaucratic class; the pact pointed toward a balance of the struggling classes in the interest of each.

The bourgeoisie was protected by the Constitution articles guaranteeing individual rights, including the right to property. These guarantees were concentrated in the first 29 articles. In Articles 123 and 27 the Constitution assured a better life for the proletariat and peasants through profit-sharing, through the right to organize unions, through lawful strikes that aimed to restore the social equilibrium, through accident compensation, through a weekly day of rest, through the end of debt peonage and company stores, through the breakup of big landed estates, and through land to the tillers. And the administrative-professional elite also found support in Articles 27 and 123 securing a strong state with the right to intervene in the economy, to give property the forms dictated by public interest, and to curb the demands of both labor and capital. The government bureaucracy, growing ever larger, would use the Constitution to strengthen its hold on the economy and its power over other classes—through the despotic presidency.

Beginning in 1941, a new form of class struggle emerged, a contest not foreseen by the Marxist Left. It was not a traditional class struggle between peasants and landowners or between labor and capital. For decades it pitted the popular sectors against the administrative-professional class controlling the state. Finally, under the presidents governing from 1982 to 2000—De la Madrid, Salinas, and Zedillo—the popular sectors went down to defeat.

This defeat was a violation of the Constitution defined by the social pact. Rather than balancing class interests, the administrative-professionals gave preference to their own interests. In the next chapter we shall see that the professional class had replaced Mexico's bourgeoisie as the main beneficiary of the economic surplus. A silent revolution had happened, but one at loggerheads with the Revolution of 1910–1920.

For decades historians had been pronouncing the Revolution dead. As early as 1949 Jesús Silva Herzog, the former director of the School of Economics at the National University, believed that the revolutionary wave had reached its highest point at the end of 1938, remaining at its crest until 1941. The bourgeoisie blocked further rises, and the government's rhetoric soon changed. Then came the descent and revolutionary calm under Alemán. His administration was a decisive break with previous governments, marking "a new epoch in the history of Mexico." Foreign pressure had ended the Revolution.[48]

In 1960 the historian Daniel Cosío Villegas echoed Herzog's earlier thesis, noting that in economic matters the government was losing its grip, so much so that "the State is the prisoner of the private sector." If the State were to fight private enterprise, "the government would not win," but the government did not want to resist or challenge private initiative. As evidence Cosío Villegas observed that the huge increase in the size of public expenditures had yet to cause a rise in taxes, and that the goal of industrializing a backward country had obliged the government to create a favorable climate for the private sector. By that he meant "social and political stability, fixed wages, low taxes, easy credit." As a result 60 percent of the funds for industrial expansion came from private sources. It was a prohibitive price because it meant that "16 percent of Mexico's families receives 50 percent of the national income, and 46 percent receives only one seventh that amount."[49] In brief, the Revolution was betrayed when it gave up its goal of promoting the people's immediate interests for an abstract national interest to be fulfilled in the long run.

There were many other premature death certificates, but the Revolution was not yet dead. In the 1970s the democratic opening launched by President Echeverría, followed by the political reforms under López Portillo, aimed to salvage the Revolution. As in Gorbachev's perestroika, the reform got out of hand and threatened the power of the central bureaucracy and the official party. In the 1988 election, systematic fraud made the left-of-center winner lose the count; but the 2000 election menaced the PRI from the political right. In the 2000 election came the victory of the National Action Party backed by the multinationals. U.S. interests were at stake because of the threat to hemispheric democracy.

With the PAN in power, historians held a requiem Mass for the Revolution. The Revolution had died even before the elections at millennium's end. After Echeverría and López Portillo, the presidents whittled away at the social pact with neoliberal policies such as privatization and the signing of NAFTA—the official party betrayed the Revolution. Its closing of the social pact reflected a similar process in the United States, the chipping away at Roosevelt's New Deal that resulted in its burial by the Reagan administration.

THE FINAL FLOWERING OF MEXICAN NATIONALISM

For decades Mexico was the most nationalistic country in Latin America.[50] During its industrialization drive it required 51 percent ownership by national capital of all private and corporate businesses. The PRI government, even under Presidents like the corrupt Miguel Alemán, continually expanded the public sector. Zealous economic nationalists so wrapped the economy in tariffs that second-rate goods were produced for captive markets. But this favorable climate for private initiative also strengthened the native capitalists until they began questioning the existence of government-owned enterprise. Under Echeverría and López Portillo the government nationalized ever more industries, and finally even the banks. This final flare-up of Mexican nationalism burned brightly during the oil boom. With its collapse came the neoliberal retreat from nationalism under De la Madrid, Salinas, and Zedillo.

By 2000 the outcome of the Revolution no longer resembled its institutionalization in 1917. It was no longer the old multiclass phenomenon. The only thread of continuity was a bureaucratic class of salaried employees at the helm who served mainly their own interests and those of their class. They were no longer interested in representing mainly capital or labor.

The PRI and the PAN were no longer mortal enemies. Economic privileges and class privileges were no longer at stake in the elections of 2000, only political privileges. Whether the PRI or the PAN came out on top, the real winner would be the bureaucratic-professional-managerial class in charge of both the corporate sector and the public sector. Mexico's political system was finally converging on that of the United States, where the contesting parties were like Tweedledum and Tweedledee. The bird of prey has two wings—a left one and a right one.

The growing popular resistance after 1940 was partly responsible for the change. Under President Echeverría the first democratic opening was an answer to the student movement of 1968. He listened to the students' demands because some of them would become the future cadres of the ruling party. Thanks to pressures from these upcoming professionals, the system of presidential despotism would slowly corrode from within.

If we are right in thinking that the Revolution was betrayed by the ruling party and finally ended, does that mean that a counterrevolution triumphed? (That is the interpretation of the Mexican left.) Or does it mean that the privatizations signified a victory of capitalism over the latent socialism of the public sector? (That is the claim of the mass media.)

Paradoxically, the end of the Revolution was not a victory for Mexico's bourgeoisie. Yet the trashing of the social pact was not a defeat for the bureaucratic elites. It signified a metamorphosis—the trimming of their authoritarian shell for a modified democratic one.

The other forces of the Revolution have been swept aside: the popular sectors have yet to achieve a people's democracy; the bourgeois-democratic project survives in name only; and the social pact in the 1917 Constitution has been violated beyond repair. As Mexico enters the 21st century, a chorus of voices is calling for a new Constitution.

For decades, in the face of overwhelming power the revolutionary ideology held the nation upright, kept the presidents talking back, fired the engines of economic development, and inspired the political bureaucracy to resist business pressures both at home and abroad. But with the *nomenklatura's* abandonment of the nationalist and populist ideology in the 1980s and 1990s, the social pact and the Revolution were betrayed.

In January 1937, shortly after arriving as a political exile in Mexico, Leon Trotsky was greeted with the publication of the last book he completed before his assassination. *The Revolution Betrayed*, his political testament, grappled with the problem of an emerging bureaucratic or professional class—Trotsky called it a privileged stratum—that was gradually scuttling the Bolshevik Revolution and the workers' state.[51] His book may also be read as a commentary on the Mexican Revolution and its betrayal later in the century. For in both revolutions this new social class ignored by Marx and his followers would replace not only the business class; it would also replace the proletariat as the principal beneficiary of the economic surplus. The new order—in the common meaning of the terms—would be neither capitalist nor socialist.

What is this new postrevolutionary order? How did it creep in and undermine the Revolution?

5

The Revolution Undermined

In the theater of history, social revolutions may happen in slow motion, taking a century to push a dominant economic class into the background while inching another to center stage. Or the curtain may suddenly fall, only to rise on a new social arrangement: the old ruling classes pressed back into the scenery and new classes running the show. For most interpreters the Mexican Revolution was a rapid change of scene: in the agrarian reform of the 1930s the old landowning class disappeared, and by the early 1940s the native bourgoisie had clearly replaced it as the economic beneficiary of the new capitalist society. In the 1940s and 1950s, U.S. corporations in Mexico took even more of the economic surplus. The PRI government presided over this process, with the top bureaucracy taking a small slice of the surplus as high salaries. During the second half of the twentieth century, according to this standard interpretation, the country was ruled both politically and economically by the main fractions of the bourgeoisie: foreign, domestic, and State. (The State bourgeoisie or bureaucratic bourgeoisie is to be distinguished from the nonbourgeois component in government, the State bureaucracy. The State bureaucracy was presumably a junior partner of the bureaucratic bourgeoisie.)

In this widespread interpretation not only is the Mexican economy capitalist; the essence of the State is bourgeois. Capitalists run the State; and the bourgeoisie—both foreign and domestic—has no dangerous rivals. The Mexican Revolution was a bourgeois revolution, and the history of Mexico from 1910 to 2000 is the story of a steady triumph of capitalism.

In this portrait of the Revolution, history replaced a lazy landowner with a hard-boiled capitalist. Yet the portrait is a caricature. The Revolution did not end in the triumph of capitalism but in its agony. By 2000 a new class of decision-makers had displaced the capitalists as the main beneficiary of the economic surplus. The capitalists were skidding toward the sidelines of the economic game. There are arguments both against and for this new vision of Mexican social reality.

FREE TRADE VS. PROTECTIONISM

We first consider the arguments against our new view. Bill Weinberg is the correspondent on Mexico and Central America for *Native Americas*, the quarterly journal of Cornell University's American Indian Studies Program. We can sum up his description of the impact of NAFTA on Mexico's workers and peasants in a word: counterrevolution. As the term "neoliberalism" is used by the enemies of NAFTA throughout Latin America, it means a return to the laissez-faire policies of 19th-century liberal capitalism. That is why the opponents of NAFTA see neoliberalism as reactionary. By the time Mexican NAFTA architect Carlos Salinas captured the presidency through a fraudulent election in 1988, writes Weinberg, "it was clear that the technocratic coup was less a 'tilt' [in the social pact] than a permanent counterrevolution." Then, with the acceptance of NAFTA and the downsizing of the state's role in the economy, "the federal military and police apparatus crushed worker resistance . . . [leading to] the worst labor violence and repression in Mexico since the 1959 railworkers' strike."[1]

For a decade, with brilliant oratory Fidel Castro has thundered against neoliberalism. But he is not the only Latin American head of state to raise his voice against the neoliberal plague. The "spiritual son of Fidel Castro"—as France's *Le Monde* pictured Venezuela's populist president Hugo Chávez Frías—declared during his visit to Nicaragua in late November 2000 that "neoliberalism is the road to hell."

In Mexico Subcomandante Insurgente Marcos has repeatedly roared the same warning. "Globalization, neoliberalism as a global system," he wrote in a June 1997 communiqué of the Zapatista Army of National Liberation (EZLN), "should be understood as a new war of conquest for territories"—the prelude to World War IV on the heels of World War III (the Cold War). As Weinberg voices the American left's perception of this latest stage of imperialism, "Global capitalism is poised to deal the last remnants of the Mexican Revolution a *coup de grace*, finishing off the work started with the peso devaluation and the De la Madrid election in 1982"—a transformation of the corporate state into a globocorp state.[2]

In April 1996 Marcos and the EZLN held the First Intergalactic Encounter for Humanity and Against Neoliberalism in the Lacandon jungle. It was a monumental gathering of U.S. cybernauts, aging Latin American guerrillas, Mexico's indigenous peoples, and young European anarchists who recognized in Marcos a personification of their cause. The Intergalactic became the springboard for the International Network Against Neoliberalism, pledging cross-border resistance to free trade worldwide. In August 1997, the International Network sponsored the Second Intergalactic Encounter in Spain, the home of anarchist self-governing communes and collective farms during the Spanish Civil War (1936–1939). To the EZLN's earlier demands for ending the U. S. war on drugs, for legalizing soft drugs throughout the planet, and for channeling the monies for combating narcotrafficking into social programs, the Second Intergalactic Encounter added a call for resisting Euro-unification as a potential new imperialist bloc.[3]

From his hideaway in the Chiapas jungle, Marcos galvanized the new international movement of protest against the International Monetary Fund, the World Bank, the European Union, and the World Trade Organization—the global champions of neoliberalism. In 1999–2000 these organizations were slapped in the face by a series of direct actions: the trashing in Seattle, the march in Washington, the battle in Prague, and the demonstrations in Nice. In the front ranks of these direct actions were anarchist elements.

Marcos, who was born into a bourgeois family of literati, began his political life as a Marxist-Leninist. But since 1960 Leninist vanguards throughout Latin America have come to grief. By the time the EZLN opened fire in January 1994, revolutionary vanguards had everywhere ended in betrayal or near-betrayal. (Cuba was an exception.) Marxist-Leninists and Leninist-Marxists alike had softened into Social Democrats mouthing liberal slogans. The lesson of vanguardism? The seizure of power is not the way to bring about social liberation.

Marcos finally drew that conclusion. As he said in one of his early communiqués, "The result [of the revolution] will not be the triumph of a party organization, or alliance of organizations with their particular social programs, but rather the creation of a democratic space for resolving the confrontations between different public proposals . . . the requirement [being] that all projects must point the way to justice."[4]

In Marcos's letters and communiqués you will look in vain for Marxist ideology. In the 60,000 words in the first edited volume of his writings (ending in August 1994), the word "socialism" occurs only twice.

"Socialism is not rejected outright by Marcos, it just doesn't seem to matter much." Capitalism is rejected, and to a noteworthy extent so is the corresponding term.[5] The preferred term for Marcos's and the EZLN's Enemy Number One is "neoliberalism"—in other words, the new global order founded on free trade.

The masked Marcos is a practicing revolutionary, a master strategist rather than a theorist. If he had dug deeper into the anarchist tradition of Ricardo Flores Magón—cited in the same breath with Villa and Zapata as a forerunner of the EZLN—he would have discovered Mikhail Bakunin's critique of Marxist practice and theory. In 1872 the penniless Bakunin predicted that even if the struggle against capitalism were successful, it would not end the exploitation of man by man: "the aristocracy of labor, those who are the most cultured, who earn more and live more comfortably than all the other workers . . . would, if the Marxists had their way, constitute their *fourth governing class*." After the priestly First Estate, the aristocratic Second Estate, and the bourgeois Third Estate, the professional working class would have its turn at ruling as a Fourth Estate. The egalitarian Bakunin concluded that even if Marxists don't have their way, the rule of this New Class "could indeed happen if the great mass of the proletariat does not guard against it."[6]

As Bakunin developed this theoretical scenario—actualized in the course of the Mexican Revolution—the State "has always been the patrimony of some privileged class . . . [and] when all the other classes have exhausted themselves, the State then becomes the patrimony of the bureaucratic class." What will the rule of bureaupreneurs, professionals, state officials, technocrats, and masters of the liberal arts look like? Based on "an immense knowledge and many heads 'overflowing with brains' . . . [it] will be the reign of *scientific intelligence*, the most aristocratic, despotic, arrogant, and elitist of all regimes . . . [under] a new class, a new hierarchy of real and counterfeit scientists and scholars, and the world will be divided into a minority ruling in the name of knowledge, and an immense ignorant majority."[7] There we have an accurate description of the neoliberal syndrome that transcends both Marxist and neoclassical categories of economic analysis—the true image of Mexico in the year 2000.

What happened in Mexico at the end of the millennium was not a bourgeois counterrevolution, a revival of 19th-century liberal capitalism. What occurred was a revolution by this new class. Rather than being politically and economically regressive, it represented the march of progress, and in that sense was progressive. Once more history repeats itself: those who suffer are the people. Progress is on the side of the elites, not the know-nothings. The end of one revolution is the beginning of another, so far always to the benefit of a minority.

Here is the irony: if Marx were alive in the year 2000, he would have supported NAFTA against his dogmatic and would-be followers. In his September 1847 article "The Protectionists, the Free Traders and the Working Class," he recognized the dilemma of protectionism in industrially backward Germany: "If it wishes to protect industrial progress, then it at once sacrifices handicraft production [and] labor; if it wishes to protect labor [and handicraft production], then industrial progress is sacrificed." Free trade wipes out backward handicraft labor; tariffs protect it. In trying to enlist labor on their side, the protectionists say, "It is better to be exploited by one's fellow countrymen than by foreigners." But Marx questioned whether the workers would be satisfied with this pseudo solution, "which, it must be confessed, is indeed very patriotic." Of course, protective tariffs would preserve jobs and prevent the workers from being "thrown onto the street by foreign competition." Yes, "but the problem for the working class is not to preserve the present state of affairs." Workers demand a change for the better.[8]

At the Free Trade Congress in Brussels in September 1847, the celebrities of the international scientific community met to discuss the question whether free trade would benefit the world. Marx prepared a speech aimed at refuting the claim that it might also benefit humanity. He concluded by accepting all the advantages of free trade on economic grounds: "The powers of production will increase; the tax imposed upon the country by protective duties will disappear; all commodities will be sold at a cheaper price." Unquestionably, free trade would benefit the world economy, but it would not benefit the workers any more than protectionism. Instead, they would become worse off under free trade. But was Marx then against free trade? "No, we are for Free Trade, because by Free Trade all economic laws . . . will act upon a larger scale, upon a greater extent of territory, upon the territory of the whole earth . . . [from which] will result the struggle which will itself eventuate in the emancipation of the proletarians."[9]

In a follow-up speech, "The Question of Free Trade," delivered to the Democratic Association of Brussels in January 1848, Marx indicted both protectionism and free trade. But he continued to favor free trade. Generally speaking, "The Protection system is conservative, while the Free Trade system works destructively. It breaks up old nationalities [the indigenous peoples of Chiapas] and carries the antagonism of proletariat and bourgeoisie to the uttermost point [in the Mexican context, the antagonism of proletariat and bureaucrat-professionals]. In a word, the Free Trade System hastens the Social Revolution." In this respect, he concluded, "I am in favor of Free Trade."[10]

The case for free trade is as strong today as it was in Marx's time. The only significant change is that the capitalists he targeted are no longer its chief beneficiaries. In developing economies they are big losers. Bakunin's "many heads 'overflowing with brains' " have thrown the capitalists from the driver's seat and seized the throttle of the locomotive of history. Is NAFTA then counterrevolutionary? No, free trade is the engine of progress.

PROFESSIONALS DRIVE THE CORPORATIONS

"Capitalism" is a misused term. Capitalism no longer drives the Mexican economy. What kind of order has replaced it? The managers of the leading multinationals with headquarters in the United States used to be functionaries of the capitalists. But in most cases they have been transformed into an autonomous and self-perpetuating body of directors.[11] The so-called managerial revolution, little more than science fiction as first formulated in the 1940s, has now become reality.[12] The thesis of creeping managerialism—better still, creeping professionalism—is standard fare among economists in Britain and the United States. For three centuries these countries have led the world in economic theory because they have shown to the rest an image of their own future.

The transformations brought about by the scientific-technical revolution and by the large-scale use of computers have increased the demand for professional expertise. And these transformations have given rise to a new theory of so-called human capital to explain the astronomical salaries of professional workers. The salaries of professionals, according to this theory, conceal a form of revenue that is still capitalist. But that is stretching the meaning of the word "capitalist."

The process of social transformation is already visible within the corporation. One index of this transformation is the bureaucratization of management: the replacement of heirs and entrepreneurs by salaried and professional administrators. (The Rockefeller owners who clip coupons in the mosquitoless paradise of Hawaii don't run Standard Oil; the managers do.) Another index is the ratio of salaried professional workers to manual laborers, with its corresponding ratio of salaries to wages. (The president of Ford makes 300 times as much as a worker on the factory floor.) But the decisive index is the form in which the economic surplus is pumped out of the direct producers.

In the modern corporation the form of generating a surplus takes on a mixed capitalist and bureaucratic character. Are the capitalist shareholders actual owners of the business? No, they are like bond-holders, not really proprietors. They merely own an interest in the corporation. They don't possess it as their property: they can't dissolve the corporation, they can't sell off its assets, they can't manage it, they can't dictate its strategies, they can't move its headquarters to another city, they can't participate in negotiating labor contracts, they can't force the directors to pay huge dividends. They merely have a claim on corporate profits: if any shareholder is paid dividends, then all must be paid dividends. (Occasionally none are paid.) And this capitalist relation of distribution is based on a capitalist relation of production, the ownership of capital in the form of a legal claim on the corporation. A third party makes the producers create a surplus, and the shareholders merely have a title to some of it. This third party is the corporate bureaucracy.

The bureaucracy's relation to the producers is not based on the ownership of capital; it is based on professional expertise and the collective possession and control of the means of production, such as machinery and materials. But bureaucrats are not the owners of the corporation.

The bureaucracy has a claim on the workers' surplus, what is left after they have been paid. This part of the surplus takes the form of salaries for professional services. Professional services are based on the ownership of expertise—a fourth factor of production.

In the 19th century Adam Smith, David Ricardo, and Karl Marx wrote of three factors that enter into the production of material goods: land that includes natural resources, labor of a physical type, and capital such as tools and machines. Ownership of these three factors—land, labor, and capital—defined the main social classes of their time: land-owners, workers, and capitalists. In the 20th century a fourth factor of production appeared: expertise. Ownership of expertise defines the new class of professionals, managers, administrators, and bureaucrats.

What are the major changes in the corporation? How are they important for an understanding of Mexican social reality? The boards of directors of the top U. S. corporations with foreign subsidiaries are no longer made up of corporate capitalists receiving the bulk of their income from the ownership of capital. The boards of directors consist mainly of corporate bureaucrats rewarded for their professional know-how with salaries bordering on extortion, with fabulous expense accounts and juicy fringe benefits. (Sometimes stock options match the salaries of top executives, but the resulting dividends make up only a small fraction of their total compensation.)

These professional bureaucrats act as a team in the nominal interest of the corporation. The corporation's interest is a fetish the managers wave in front of the stockholders, a fetish that helps to conceal the bureaucrats' real interest. What is their real interest? Raising salaries, padding expense accounts, and achieving nonmonetary rewards not reportable to the tax collector. In professional decision-making the economic interests of capital, of functionless capitalists, of absentee shareholders play a minor role. A professional manager thinks of the shareholder the way a New Yorker remembers a parent in Peoria— only at Christmas.

Corporate professionals often operate their enterprises with borrowed capital. Does the fact that they are operating with other people's money make them functioning capitalists? No, those who both operate and own the means of production are capitalists. The giant corporation is a quasi-public trust that no one really owns in the sense of private property. And governments treat them that way. If a corporation the size of General Motors gets into trouble, governments enter the scene with special tariffs, import quotas, subsidies, state aid, bailouts, and public relief. Society cannot easily allow a giant corporation to fail.

The corporate bureaucrats are a self-perpetuating body controlling the giant enterprises. They are no longer functionaries of the big owners, no longer subordinates, clerks, underlings, and fat boys of top-hatted capitalists. They are no longer agents of the big money—they *are* the big money. They are no longer under the thumb of the shareholders; they are the shareholders' senior partners.

What is the work of a capitalist? The job of a capitalist is to pump out a surplus on behalf of propertied interests. The functionaries of capitalists can also do this work, and in doing it they personify the functions of a capitalist. But the professionals managing the great corporations are neither capitalists nor their functionaries.

In the 19th-century heyday of rising capitalism, and today in millions of tiny enterprises, owners manage a family business as private property: they can sell off the assets, blow them up, leave them to their heirs, close down the business, waste all the profit in riotous living, hire only their friends and relatives, do as they please with their property. They can reinvest their profits in the business in order to expand production. Such money is capital.

Today's corporations partially operate with money borrowed from banks and with funds raised in the stock market by issuing shares. These investment funds are not the corporation's capital; they are certainly not the capital of the corporate bureaucracy at the helm. The investment funds of the big corporations don't function as capital because the managers are not functionaries of the capitalists. The economic surplus generated with these funds is not a return based on ownership, but on operating the means of production.

If those who hire and those who fire are neither capitalists nor functionaries of capitalists, then workers paid wages are no longer Marx's wage-laborers. For him wage-labor was a function of the ownership of capital. The capitalists owned the means of production and the proletarians owned nothing but their bare hands, ready to work for a wage. The capitalist and the wage-worker were two sides of the same coin. They were trapped in capitalist relations of production, just as man and wife are bound in a marital relation. Remove the husband, and there is no longer a wife. Today capitalist relations of production no longer exist in the big corporations. So there is no longer a proletariat in the old sense.

Think of the corporation as a tiny mixed economy. There is a capitalist sector of shareholders and bondholders coexisting with a professional-bureaucratic sector. The professional sector generates an economic surplus on the basis of bureaucratic relations of production. Then this surplus may be shared with the functionless capitalist sector.

For the corporation to operate, professional salaries have to be paid, but interest and dividends don't have to be paid. Japanese corporations, for example, sometimes pay no dividends at year's end, because managers decide to reinvest the profits. U.S. managers usually pay some dividends, but only after they have taken care of themselves. Their amazing salaries are presented to the world as the costs of expertise. The part of the surplus taken in the form of these unnecessary and fictitious costs is often greater than the part paid out to capitalists.

With the replacement of capitalist by bureaucratic relations of production, the exploitation of labor in the modern corporation takes a bureaucratic form. The bloated salaries of administrative and professional bureaucrats are not a function of the ownership of capital. They are a function of science, of professional training, of expertise—a factor of production now on a level with the classical factors of land, labor, and physical capital. (Physical capital, such as machines, tools, factories, and computers is to be distinguished from money that buys these instruments of production.) In the United States, presidents of global corporations may pay themselves more than 300 times the paycheck of a manual laborer on a production line. They are exploiters.

The transformations within the corporation underlie the concept of a bureaucratic class defined by ownership of a fourth factor of production.[13] The professional elite that runs the corporations is the nucleus of the bureaucratic class. This productive fraction operates in the core of the class, but there are nonproductive fractions such as the political bureaucracy, the military bureaucracy, the educational bureaucracy, the media bureaucracy, and the labor bureaucracy.

In the past, leftist political scientists assumed that state bureaucrats belonged to the traditional classes or that they were a social stratum under the thumb of the economically dominant class. Today many Marxists still think of political bureaucrats as servants of the capitalists. But political bureaucrats are members of the New Class.

Does a state bourgeoisie that draws more of its income from capital than from high salary exist? Yes, but in government most bureaucrats make up the political fraction of the New Class, a class not just between but, unlike other intermediate classes, above capital and labor.

In both the United States and in Mexico, the State bourgeoisie is only a tiny component of the State bureaucracy, even at the level of the President's cabinet. Colin Powell, the U.S. Secretary of State, who runs the nation's foreign policy, is not a capitalist. Jorge Castañeda, Mexico's Secretary of Foreign Relations, is not a capitalist either.

A few PRI politicians turned themselves into capitalists, but far more numerous are the salaried administrators and related professional workers who have yet to amass enough from the spoils of office to become bourgeois. We can compare some of the bureaucrat millionaires to the socialist millionaires of Yugoslavia, but it may not be enough to make them capitalists. To qualify as State bourgeois, their millions must take the form of capital, and the bulk of their income must appear as profits of enterprise, dividends, and interest, or as rent from capital invested in real estate. That the millionaire bureaucrats wallow in wealth only shows that they have ripped off part of the surplus; it does not prove they are capitalists.

According to the conventional wisdom, the miserable and exploited Mexican workers slaving for $7 a day are facing a single class enemy: capitalists. But in fact they have two enemies. On the one hand, there are native capitalists big and small, and foreign shareholders of the multinationals. On the other hand, there are the professional bureaucrats running the giant corporations and the political professionals managing the Mexican state. Against the Mexican people these two classes combine, but they can also oppose each other. They enter into opposing alliances. For decades the bureaucratic mode of production has been slowly displacing the capitalist mode. The Mexican rip-off of the underclasses is not only capitalist exploitation.

THE ECLIPSE OF MEXICAN CAPITALISM

In the late 1930s and early 1940s, the Mexican Revolution issued in a capitalist economy by default. But what kind of capitalism?

According to Salvador Carmona Amorós, a brilliant PRI theoretician who edited the party's official organ, *La República*, the Mexican economy is more than a balanced mix of capitalist and socialist sectors. In 1974 Carmona's *La economía mexicana y el nacionalismo revolucionario* described the national revolutionary model as a "specific and unique road of development different from capitalism, socialism, and the transition from one to the other." Three squabbling groups were marching hand in hand toward the new society: the working class, the national bourgeoisie, and the national revolutionary bureaucracy (in the lead). (In urbanizing Mexico, Carmona ignored that invisible class, the peasants.) In this scenario, as the public sector encroaches on the private sector, the bourgeoisie slowly disappears. Thus the higher stage of the national-revolutionary model issues in Lázaro Cárdenas's workers' state: the professional bureaucracy is no longer a mere mediator in the conflict between capitalists and workers—it rules with a rod of iron. The bureaucratized Workers' State is usually called socialism.[14] (Carmona insists that socialism is unique. But it is not. It is not egalitarian, for it contains two core classes—workers and bureaucrats. Existing socialist societies, whether the former Soviet Union or contemporary Cuba, Vietnam, China, and North Korea, are also dominated by professional bureaucracies—just as surely as are the United States and Mexico.) In this chapter we shall see that Carmona's scenario for the future slowly materialized in an unexpected way.

Carmona's book is about the period from the gentle Ávila Camacho to the extroverted Echeverría. In this period the Mexican economy was certainly a form of capitalism. If we look at the role of the State and its encouragement of foreign investment on the part of U.S. corporations, the national revolutionary model was a euphemism for what Mexican economists called an advanced stage of corporate capitalism—"state monopoly capitalism."[15] State intervention, government subsidies for business, creation of new industries, takeover of failing ones, government financing of research and development, improvement of transportation and communication were relied on to keep Mexico's weak capitalism afloat in the stormy sea of world competition. State monopoly capitalism was the fusion of the state apparatus and the corporate sector—a marriage of official and manager. State monopoly capitalism nationalized failing businesses to preserve them and encouraged profitable enterprises with government aid.

This interpenetration of the public and private sectors, like Picasso's cubist faces, made it hard to see where one ended and the other began.[16] The State-owned oil monopoly PEMEX became so interlocked with foreign and domestic capital that many economists denied its public character. For example, during most of López Portillo's administration the director of PEMEX was the magnificently rich entrepreneur Jorge Díaz Serrano. His oil drilling company and petroleum-related interests were so tangled up with PEMEX that few could tell them apart: the distinction between public and private sectors seemed to vanish. This example of converging interests brings into focus the dual role many high-level state functionaries play.

Here are a few glaring examples of State aid to those who needed it least: fat government contracts, guaranteed purchases of intermediate goods, cheap energy from state utilities, and huge investments in air service, railways, roads, telephone and telegraph companies—all cutting the costs of capitalists and the supposedly capitalist corporations. Public health, education, and welfare also benefited the business community. The State provided free clinics, vocational schools, public housing, and basic foodstuffs that lowered the cost of labor power. The workers benefited, but so did the capitalists: the State bore the costs of maintaining and reproducing the labor force, and employers did not have to pay higher wages. Assuming that these were the only antagonistic classes, then almost every nationalization served business interests.

From World War II to the early 1970s, a useful label for the Mexican economy was "state monopoly capitalism." But since the late 1970s this concept has concealed Mexico's changed social reality. If there were only two classes struggling over the surplus, then this concept might still be applicable to Mexico. Yet that underlying premise is false. There were more than two great classes at loggerheads: the bourgeoisie, the proletariat, and the bureaucracy (both State and corporate). The professional bureaucrats in the public and corporate sectors were sharply divided from the people of property—the fattened bourgeoisie. Professionals and capitalists viewed one another with suspicion. In the struggle over the surplus, professionals were getting the upper hand.

While the sun of the professional elites was brightening, the moon of the private-sector bourgeoisie went into partial eclipse. Did the gradual eclipse of the bourgeoisie proceed through the public sector? Or did it advance through the corporate sector, especially the foreign corporate sector? Where did the professionals most increase their take?

From Lázaro Cárdenas to López Portillo it was in the public sector that professionals mainly raised their relative share of the surplus. Later, under De la Madrid, Salinas, and Zedillo, it was through privatization and the ascendancy of the corporations—especially the U.S. multinationals—that the professionals slurped up more of the surplus. To back up that claim, we dive into a dark pool of data but promise to surface with a few generalizations.

In 1960 José Luis Ceceña studied more than 2000 top enterprises. From his study emerges a picture of the relative strength of the foreign corporate sector compared to the domestic private and public sectors under López Mateos.[17] Of the 400 largest enterprises, accounting for 77 percent of the total revenue of the top 2040, those that were foreign-owned or foreign-controlled gobbled 54 percent. State enterprises took 25 percent and Mexico's native capitalists only 21 percent. Pablo González Casanova, the dean of Mexican sociologists, looked at the data and assumed (falsely) that the giant foreign corporations were capitalist like the small Mexican corporations; he then interpreted the data to mean that the combined share of foreign and domestic capital in the top 400 accounted for three-fourths of gross profits. In other words, the heavyweights left the government as a lightweight with barely one-fourth. From these data González Casanova concluded that private enterprise, both foreign and domestic, was the most powerful pressure group in Mexico. "Organized in confederations, chambers, associations, and clubs, it makes up the most unusual and vigorous combination of pressure groups the government must respond to."[18] González Casanova, the son of the general who crushed the Zapatista movement in 1916, had swung to the left in his political sympathies, and was worried by the increase in business power.

The defect of these figures? They don't reveal the percentages of foreign, State, and domestic private participation in revenues from the Mexican economy *as a whole*. For a larger sampling, we turn to Ricardo Cinta's 1965 study of Mexico's 938 biggest industrial firms.[19]

Although in 1965 foreigners controlled 48 percent of the assets of the top 50 firms, compared to 22 percent controlled by the State and 30 percent by Mexico's capitalists, in the 938 firms *taken as a whole*, foreign control amounted to only 27 percent, state control to barely 5 percent, and domestic private control to a whopping 68 percent. National capital was the largest sector after all.

The top 938 firms controlled only two-thirds of Mexico's total industrial assets. The more enterprises that are considered below this top level, the greater is the relative share of national capital. So it is a mistake to generalize on the basis of the data for the biggest corporations, even though the top enterprises hold sway in the economy. (We are showing the mistakes of the usual academic interpretations.)

The studies are fraught with difficulties. Comparisons are hard to make even for the same year, because some studies focus on the relative shares of corporate revenue (González Casanova), others on industrial assets (Cinta), and still others on industrial output. According to data included in *México 1982: Anuario económico*, the relative participation in total industrial production in 1970 was 35 percent for the multinationals, 5 for the state, and 60 percent for domestic private industry.[20]

(That is more like what we need. The figures provide a better index of participation in Mexican industry than the data from a study of only the top 290 industrial firms, where the percentages for the same year were 45.4 percent for the multinationals, 12.8 percent for the State, and 41.8 percent for national capital.)[21]

Up to 1970 Mexico's capitalists were munching the lion's share of the surplus.

What happened after 1970? The Mexican economy experienced a drastic change in the relative shares of the foreign, domestic private, and public sectors as a result of the populist turnabout in government policies in 1970 and the mushrooming of the public sector during the "tragic dozen" years ending with the nationalization of the banks in 1982. According to a report in *Excelsior* on June 18, 1983, the new wave of nationalizations had reduced the private sector's control to 30 percent, including both foreign and domestic capital, while raising the government's share to 70 percent—a remarkable increase over earlier figures. The conservative writer Luis Pazos wrote resentfully that in 1970 the public sector was responsible for 26 percent of Mexico's Gross Domestic Product, that this figure grew to 35 percent by the time Echeverría left office in 1976, and later escalated to 70 percent when López Portillo finished his term.[22] Pazos, a publicist for the private sector, was more than irritated. (His books have been promoted into best-sellers by the millionaires and their media, and he has become a rich man. The left complains that "he who pays the piper calls the tune," but this is not fair. Pazos is an honest man who believes in what he writes. He writes with a simple and engaging style for large numbers of people, while the academic left writes incomprehensible abstractions that rot on the shelves.)

But could the government's about-face have had such radical results for the Mexican economy? In view of the figures we cited for 1960, 1965, and 1970, these 1982 estimates appear to be exaggerated. Certainly, the rapacious plunder of the country by the multinationals is not evident in these data. And we should not forget to add the interest burden of servicing the total foreign debt of roughly $80 billion at the end of 1982. The *Anuario económico*, for example, disputes Pazos's figures for 1970 and 1976. According to its data about participation in the Gross Domestic Product, the share of the public sector was not 26 but 14 percent in 1970, and it rose to only 22 percent by 1980.[23]

On the premise that three-fourths of the Mexican economy in 1960 was in the hands of a foreign and domestic bourgeoisie with a decisive influence on both the executive and legislative branches of government, the leftist González Casanova concluded that the Mexican state continued to be bourgeois.[24] But on the premise that more than two-thirds of the Mexican economy in 1982 was owned or controlled by the public sector, the rightist Luis Pazos concluded that the country had already arrived at socialism.[25] The premises of both were mistaken. González Casanova wrongly believed that the foreign sector dominated by the multinationals was mainly capitalist. And Pazos assumed that heavy State ownership and control of the economy was a sufficient condition of socialism.

Only the bureaucratization of the social relations of production is enough for a transition to socialism—under the rule of the New Class.

Casanova and Pazos not only worked from wrong premises; their data also misrepresented Mexican economic reality. González Casanova exaggerated the bourgeoisie's rip-off of Mexico's workers. And Pazos called the Mexican bureaucracy *una clase dorada*—a golden class—a term the left always used to sneer at the bourgeoisie. (When the left throws mud, Pazos throws it right back—and he is an excellent propagandist.)

The State bureaucracy, claimed Pazos, along with its extortionate salaries and systematic looting, had led the Mexican people into bondage to the international bankers. For Pazos it was not Mexico's private sector, both foreign and domestic, that was sucking the blood of the nation: "The funds that leave Mexico because of interest payments on the public sector's foreign debt are about 10 times what foreign enterprises repatriate in the form of profits."[26]

Remember that in 1970 the share of national capital in total industrial output was nearly twice the share of the multinationals. There is no doubt about it: the 1982 nationalization of the Mexican banks cut deeply into the share of domestic private capital because López Portillo nationalized only Mexican properties. So the result of the expropriation was a change in the relative shares of domestic and foreign capital. Home capital lost ground. What does this tell us about the Mexican rip-off? That native capitalists, not the multinationals, were pocketing the lion's share of the economic surplus until the 1982 bank nationalizations evened the score—temporarily.

Yet the rash of privatizations beginning in 1986 did not restore the status quo and shore up the native capitalists. Privatizations benefited the multinationals: these giants "overflowing with brains" could buy up failing state enterprises and make them profitable. As profits rose, so did professional salaries.

The conventional wisdom has always complained that the multinationals had been siphoning off the surplus as dividends and interest.

What nationalist economists overlooked was that part of the surplus was concealed in a percentage of professional salaries. That percentage was the difference between the real and fictitious costs of expertise: know-how has to be paid, but the astronomical pay of the multi-national managers was ridiculous. Professional salaries in the multi-nationals were much higher than those in the private sector. So in the matter of relative shares, privatization slowly undermined the comparative advantage of the bourgeoisie.

Contrary to the media, privatization is not in the interests of private enterprise. The word "privatization" is a misnomer. The process of selling off state enterprises that end up in the corporate sector is not "privatization"—it is "corporatization."[27] So blame the politicians, the mass media, and the influence of Marxist ideology for confusing people.

The subversive role of the multinationals loosened the capitalist noose in the United States. Therefore, we can guess that Mexico's privatizations—beefing up the multinational sector—have cut down the size of the capitalists' slice of the surplus. The more developed country shows the less developed an image of its own future.

Anyhow, Mexico's capitalists have to share the spoils, and today the people must contend with more than one exploiting class—they struggle with two.

THE BURGEONING KNOWLEDGE FACTORIES

Privatization fattened the corporate sector. This sector, with state-of-the-art technologies and batteries of computers, demands much more expertise than the capitalist sector. Capitalists can't keep up with the new professionalism, especially the myriad small businesses that provide employment for the boss's friends and relatives. The capitalist sector is slowly bleeding to death.

With the increasing demand for professional expertise has come the burgeoning of Mexico's institutions of higher learning. In 1950 the largest and most important knowledge factory—the National Autonomous University (UNAM)—was located in downtown Mexico City. A haven for exiles from the Spanish Civil War, many of its professors were Marxists, anarchists, and socialists from the Republic.[28] But in 1952 President Alemán built a gigantic campus for the university on the lava flow south of the capital. The university grew, but the move was also political: Spanish refugees could no longer drop by and teach a class or two; radical students were quarantined on the city's outskirts, too far away for their demonstrations against the PRI's right turn to take effect. (Even so, a decade later the student left was a power in the

National University. There were more than 50 socialist organizations on the University City campus, and Marxist works sold like hot tamales on the downtown sidewalks.)

El Colegio de México, founded by Spanish refugees who built for it the best social science library on the Latin American continent, was turned into a brilliant thinktank by Mexico's leading economist, Victor Urquidi. At last the Mexican government could draw on experts when it needed advice in formulating policies. The government also created the National Polytechnic Institute to train engineers and scientists.

In the early 1970s Echeverría made a bid to win back the students seething over the Tlatelolco massacre. In response to the increasing demand for professionals to man the economy and the state sector, he established the Metropolitan Autonomous University and the National Schools of Professional Studies on campuses in the four corners of the capital. He strengthened the UNAM, where students hoping for careers in government went after studying at the National Preparatory School underneath the revolutionary murals of Orozco.

After two decades of galloping capitalism, the business community was stronger than ever. It countered the populist Echeverría's moves by setting up private universities. Opus Dei, whose members are laypersons of the Catholic Church and a few priests with worldly intentions, established the Institute for Top Company Managers and CEOs (IPADE) and got big money to back it up. The IPADE awards the equivalent of an MBA. The Legionnaires of Christ, even more reactionary than Opus Dei, sponsored the Anahuac University in Mexico City.

The LaSalle University, a stronghold of the reactionary Catholic and semifascist *Sinarquista* movement, also made its debut. An outgrowth of the earlier *Cristero* movement, the *Sinarquistas* are adept at street fighting, and many a federal university student head has cracked under their blows. Another private university, the Technological Autonomous Institute of Mexico, appeared about the same time—it has two campuses in the capital. These private institutions charge high tuition and are also financed by business interests. When the older Iberoamerican University of the Jesuits went over to liberation theology, it lost funding and modified its stance in order to survive.

The Technological Institute of Advanced Studies in Monterrey expanded, and by 2000 had 29 campuses scattered throughout Mexico. Mexico City College moved to Puebla to become the University of the Americas—the language of the classrooms is English. Graduates of these private institutions got jobs in private and corporate business, while graduates of the federally funded universities worked mainly in the public sector.

The private institutions teach microeconomics and business administration, advertising, marketing, and commercial TV from a technocratic, neoliberal standpoint. They have money, libraries, and top salaries for professors. Their academic standards are the highest in Mexico, with tough discipline and rigorous grading—just the opposite of the public universities. Sociology and history are also taught, but with little interest in politically sensitive issues.

Echeverría's administration hired the first technocrats, López Portillo's hired more, and in De la Madrid's term Ph.D.s sparkled in the cabinet. Under Salinas everyone at the cabinet level had a doctorate from Harvard, Yale, Princeton, MIT, Chicago, or Stanford. Technocrats from Mexico's private institutions filled the remaining positions, hired because the social and economic evolution of Mexican society required their expertise.

For decades the turnover among Mexico's top political elites has been among the fastest in the world. Fifteen years of government service and then out. Only 20 percent of the top governing figures under Echeverría remained under López Portillo, and only 10 percent of them remained under De la Madrid. The demand for expertise in top government circles continues to grow.

The graduates of Mexico's knowledge factories, whether in business or in government, receive handsome rewards. Although the ratio of professionals to minimum-wage earners is several times greater in the United States than in Mexico, the corresponding differentials in pay are several times greater in Mexico than in the United States. In 1999 the salary of a full-time university professor without a Ph.D. at the National University was 216,000 pesos, corresponding to what in the United States would be the salary of an assistant professor with a Ph.D. at a top university, around $48,000. The annual minimum wage in Mexico ($37.90 pesos per day for 365 days a year) came to 13,834 pesos compared to the U.S. minimum wage ($41.20 per day for 250 days) of $10,300 a year. What does this tell us? Roughly, that the ratio of professional academic salaries to minimum wages was more than 15:1 in Mexico; in the United States it was less than 5:1. (Mexican law obliges employers to pay their underpaid workers on rest days and holidays, whereas U.S. workers are paid only for the days they actually work— 365 less 104 weekends and 11 holidays equals 250 working days. Although Mexican workers are paid for 115 days more than U.S. workers, they are still worse off relative to the professional elites.) If we take the pay of second-class professors in Mexico and assistant professors in the United States as a rough index of professional salaries in both countries, then it certainly looks as if the professional elites in Mexico were better off than those in the United States relative to those President Fox calls earners of one, two, and three minimum wages.

PROFESSIONAL IDEOLOGIES

Besides giving professional education, Mexico's knowledge factories formulate and spread an ideology for their graduating *licenciados*. (This is the title that certifies a professional, so important nowadays that Mexicans without a degree often call themselves *licenciado* anyway.) The division between federal and private education shows up in the professional biases: traditionally on the nationalist track in the National Preparatory School and the National University, students acquired the nationalist-populist ideology of the Mexican Revolution; on the technocratic track in the private universities students learned neoliberal ideology. From Alemán through López Portillo the nationalist ideology held sway, thanks in part to its influence in the public universities. (Earlier the revolutionary generals acquired it on the field of battle against the old order.) The neoliberal ideology that replaced it flourished under De la Madrid, Salinas, and Zedillo with the private universities competing successfully with federally funded education.

De la Madrid was the transitional figure. By the middle of his administration, the technocratic elites were edging out their nationalist rivals. In 1985 the nationalist economist Jesús Silva Herzog resigned from the cabinet in disgust, while Harvard-trained Carlos Salinas followed De la Madrid's turn toward neoliberalism. In 1988 Cuauhtémoc Cárdenas bolted from the PRI and took with him the nationalist top leadership that still clung to the ideology of the Mexican Revolution and its social pact. The populists who stayed behind either shut up or switched to neoliberal ideology. Salinas made the switch. When he started out under De la Madrid, he was a left-wing nationalist, but ended as a neoliberal lapdog even before he became president.

During the first three years under De la Madrid there was no talk of the Mexican Revolution and its ideology, except for occasional announcements that it had not been abandoned: it seemed that it would be revived when the government escaped the grasp of the International Monetary Fund and the flight capital came home. (In 1983 De la Madrid financed the setting up of *La Jornada* on the grounds, said he, that Mexico needed a strong left newspaper.) But the IMF did not let go of Mexico's jugular and the flight capital stayed out. So in 1985, halfway through his term, he became the first president to espouse the neoliberal ideology. In the political minicrisis that followed, three members of his cabinet resigned in protest over the right turn. Salinas stuck with De la Madrid.

Salinas tried to fly a new official ideology labeled "social liberalism," but it never got off the ground. The intellectual community laughed at his effort to square the circle, the technocrats ignored it, and the workers and peasants loyal to the PRI hated it—they preferred populism and nationalism.

What is neoliberal ideology? It is the ideology of private competitive enterprise revived under conditions that no longer favor private enterprise. Contemporary economic conditions favor corporate enterprise.

According to neoliberalism, free trade is the driving force of the world economy, and leads to increasing prosperity for all. Free enterprise and the free market are efficient, and will bring growth and welfare in the long run. Capitalism is the end of history. South Korea raised itself from economic lower depths to become an export platform with free market economics, and is the model for developing countries. All statism and planning tend to ruin economies, just as they ruined the Eastern bloc. Liberal electoral democracy is the political expression of this economic program, and the United States is the model for the world. So say the corporate elites.

This professional ideology is now hegemonic (though not in all the Mexican federal universities). If there is a total collapse of the world economy, neoliberalism will not outlast it. But right now the ideology rides in the whirlwind and directs the storm.

There has been an ideological change paralleling the shift in the balance of power. Not only did the capitalists lose out under Echeverría and the next presidents; so did the national revolutionary sector of the professional class. At the turn of the century most professionals with jobs in government or the economy sided with the technocrats.

NAFTA is a logical outcome of corporate professional ideology. In his presidential address on January 29, 1991, NAFTA's chief architect, George Bush, praised it as a pillar in his coming "New World Order." (The multinational professional elites were delighted.) The United States was a superpower with global interests in the information age and an economy dependent on overseas trade and a stable world order. So the chronic instability in the Third World had become a major concern in governmental circles. To cope with the new problems of terrorism and leftist insurgency financed by the narcotics trade, the Pentagon would have to police the world as an agent of the U.S. government and its allies in the International Monetary Fund, the World Bank, and the World Trade Organization.

The inflow of foreign investments that aimed at modernizing the economy hit the indigenous peoples of Mexico hard. They were not the only losers. A report by the Citizens Trade Campaign, *The Failed*

Experiment: NAFTA at Three Years, claimed that free trade had not only driven 8 million Mexicans into poverty while eliminating some 2 million jobs; it had also bankrupted 28,000 businesses in the private sector. As reported on June 27, 1997, in the Mexico City daily *The News*, this was the flip side of Mexico's economy that was doing well while the people were doing badly. A professional ideology was behind it.

No one likes to see millions of Mexican workers jobless and already poor peasants reduced to misery. But let the responsibility for the NAFTA tragedy be laid at the right door. For the most part, capitalists were not to blame. The people who floated this new state of affairs were U.S. technocrats, university-educated and salaried professionals committed to state-of-the-art technology and cost-cutting on a global scale—in other words, competitiveness and efficiency. The wizards at the IMF and World Bank were backed by millions of middle-level professionals who shared the same ideal of progress. In the long run, we are told, it is economic performance that counts. Yes, and in the long run we all die—and go to heaven.

What confuses most observers is that neoliberal ideology claims to defend capitalism. Thus the ideology disguises the real interests of the New Class and helps corporate business professionals to keep the support of the small business capitalists it is ruining. The outstanding Mexican historian, Francisco López Cámara, wrote a study of the social and economic history of Mexico in the 1840s. He showed that a developed bourgeoisie did not yet exist and that there was at most an incipient capitalist sector. But the Revolution of Ayutla in 1854 and the movement of the Reform that followed, down to the triumph of Benito Juárez in 1867, made do with bourgeois ideology—land reform and political democracy, Adam Smith and the Republic. There was no bourgeois revolution: the liberal fraction of the landowning class waged a civil war to expropriate the clerical fraction of the same class. But the whole bloody process took place with bourgeois liberal ideology as a disguise.

There are dozens of such examples from world history. When a historical movement gets going, it takes its ideology where it can grab it, whether it really fits the facts or not. This is what has been happening in Mexico. The corporate fraction of the professional class needs an ideology, so it takes what is available and interprets that to its own advantage. As when in the 1850s semifeudal landowners seized upon a capitalist ideology, so now the technocrats seize upon a capitalist ideology, even though they are not capitalists. And what happens? Everywhere leftist scholars are misled by the ideology and fail to see what is actually happening in the socioeconomic process.

The nationalist scholars denounce neoliberalism as defending capitalism, and so play into the hands of their enemies, who need this ideological disguise. As the giant corporations ruin hundreds of thousands of small capitalist businesses in Latin America, they call for their support: "We are capitalists, just as you are, vote for our *políticos*." For example, in the 1990s tequila became fashionable in the United States. Tequila factories doubled their demand for the cactus-juice input, just as droughts and plagues cut the supply of blue agave in half. Mexican small producers of tequila found the price of agave shooting upward. But the price for the giant tequila firm José Cuervo, owned mainly by a British conglomerate, stayed low: the monster corporation had control of many agave plantations. It began to undersell the little tequila capitalists. The neoliberal government did not intervene to regulate the agave market, and many little producers went broke.

Is this the free play of supply and demand determining price in Adam Smith's capitalism? And yet, in the election of 2000, hundreds of thousands of small entrepreneurs voted for the neoliberal Fox "because he is an ally of the capitalists."

Meanwhile, the professoriate, the journalists, the artists, the independent writers of the Mexican left nominally committed to a nationalist and populist ideology are going to seed. While they spend their time writing poetry, publishing novels, and devoting themselves to literature and art, one out of three Mexican children suffers from anemia due to malnutrition. (While governor of Guanajuato, Vicente Fox complained that nine out of ten children in his state suffered from malnutrition.)

The populists and nationalists who followed Cuauhtémoc out of the PRI spend much of their leisure time and energy not on class politics, but defending feminism, ecology, human rights, sexual liberation, and indigenous cultures, and attacking machismo, racism, Eurocentrism—just like "progressives" in the United States. How much does the social question in its traditional sense—the existence of hunger amid plenty—really concern them?

Many Mexican leftists find analyses of labor and the economy boring. The leftist daily, *La Jornada*, knows the taste of its readers: the newspaper has big supplements on gay rights and women's issues. It devotes almost a third of the paper to movie reviews, entertainment, TV, literature, the arts, and philosophy.

Before De la Madrid's switch to neoliberalism, a sampling of student opinion at the National School of Professional Studies at Aragón in Mexico City showed a lively interest in the social question. In the year 2000, there was a significant change. The fact that a majority of students in Mexico City went for Fox against the PRI's pseudo nationalist Francisco Labastida and the national-populist Cuauhtémoc Cárdenas tells a lot about the new generation of upcoming professionals brainwashed with neoliberal views through the press, TV, and the ruling party. Even some students in the federal universities are making the switch to neoliberalism.

For this new generation, socialist ideology has become old-fashioned and politically regressive. Such ideology focuses on remedying inequalities in distribution instead of improving economic performance. While the popular classes agonize on the neoliberal cross, Mexico's youth attend the latest movie or gape at their favorite TV show. As in the United States, instant gratification is fast becoming the norm. In 1998 students at Aragón were greeting one another with the English words "It's all right!"—the title of the hit song on TV. But for 70 million marginalized Mexicans the correct answer was It's all wrong!

A HISTORICAL REVIEW

Carlyle complained that economics was "the dismal science."[29] Karl Marx noted that it was a necessary evil, but he hated it and dubbed it *Scheisse* (shit)—one of his favorite words. With Marx and other historical sociologists, we find that not the schemes and machinations of political parties is fundamental in historical change but rather economic evolution. Nowadays, economists machine-gun us with statistics. It would be preferable not to end this book in this way, but you are going to be spattered with statistical "shit."

First, a historical review. Between 1910 and 1917 a combined bourgeois revolution under the idealistic Madero and the calculating Carranza, and a proletarian-peasant revolution under the cruel Villa and the incorruptible Zapata swept across northern and central Mexico. In February 1917 the new Constitution gave hope to the masses thirsty for social justice. So most of Mexico calmed down (although the fires of agrarian revolt raged on in Zapata's Morelos). With Obregón's coup against Carranza in 1920, Mexico's new political order took shape, and a political-military bureaucracy tightened its grip on the state and the economy.

For the next 20 years there was an uneasy truce between the bureaucracy at the political helm and Mexico's emerging native capitalists. The bureaucracy carried out a series of agrarian reforms that finished off landlord rule over a semifeudal system; nascent Mexican business filled the vacuum. Until 1940 the State bureaucrats and allied professionals held the reins of political power, but from 1940 to the middle 1970s they struggled with the threat of rising bourgeois counterrevolution.

A comeback of the legacy of the naive Madero and the realistic Carranza would blow away the postbourgeois bureaucratic State. With it would disappear the stalemate between the capitalist class and the political bureaucracy. The unstable equilibrium between capitalists in control of the economy and professionals in control of the State—how long could it last? One or the other, it seemed, would eventually swallow the government and the economy. Would the victor be Mexico's bourgeoisie?

In the 1970s, to hold off the bourgeois counterrevolution, the ruling PRI went on the offensive. It revived the revolutionary nationalism of the 1920s and 1930s. The bourgeoisie suffered a setback that business leaders called the "tragic dozen," the 12-year reign of the talkative Echeverría and the pocket-lining López Portillo. These were the years of the oil boom: billions of megabucks from Petróleos Mexicanos heated up the economy and financed populist programs.

The boom ended in bust, and for a decade the government floundered about in the debris of debts and devaluations. The Presidents retreated before the encouraged bourgeoisie and finally caved in to pressure from business interests. Under De la Madrid, Salinas, and Zedillo, privatizations contributed to wrecking the social pact. Revolutionary nationalism sank, the *políticos* abandoned ship and floated away on the frail raft of neoliberalism. Was this the end of bureaucratic aspirations for running the economy—and the ship of State?

Like the news media, political analysts stay on the surface of history, focusing on men of power and targeting vested interests. But gaping at the actions of government celebrities hardly reveals the deeper political currents or the ebb and flow of economic evolution. Historical actors gratify their own interest, wrote Hegel, but "something else results from the actions of men than what they intend and achieve, something else than what they know or want . . . which was not in the consciousness of the actors."[30] The voyage into the future is only partly guided by deliberate intentions, for society is pushed about by winds and currents beyond human control. In analyzing human actions, historical sociologists talk of the logic of unintended results.

At the 20th century's end, the erosion of bureaucratic power seemed to be confirmed. Both the Mexican press and political analysts believed that the institutionalized revolution had run its course. They pointed to the handwriting on the wall: the 1988 split in the ruling party, the mounting PRI losses at the polls, the downsizing of the public sector, and the triumph of the private sector. Was this the bourgeois counter-revolution that had threatened during the 1950s and the 1960s? Was it finally arriving?

From the beginning the Mexican Revolution had been Janus-faced: a bureaucratic political revolution moving toward more public ownership and a capitalist economic revolution aiming at privatization. But by the middle 1970s privatization was no longer at odds with pushing capitalists from control of the economy.

The political left did not grasp this fact, and the right also missed it. While the ideologists relaxed in their certainties, history passed them by. For the consolidation of capitalism in the government and the economy was only apparent; it was the bureaucratic current in the Revolution that was emerging victorious.

Consider the appearances: in his last year in office President López Portillo was forced to devalue the peso; next the neoliberal De la Madrid privatized a fifth of the State enterprises; and during the Salinas years the "bourgeois" PAN put ever more representatives into municipal, state, and federal government; it helped to roll the ball of privatization forward while it huffed and puffed neoliberal ideology. But by supporting privatization, this party of conservatives was unconsciously serving bureaucratic and professional interests.

Most of humanity is satisfied with appearances, but things are not as they appear. For Mexico today is not a capitalist order with a bourgeois state. It is a postcapitalist system. In this system professional workers collectively sit in the driver's seat of the economy and gulp down the bulk of the economic surplus. The capitalists ride in the back and nibble a smaller portion; every year they grow more dependent on the professionals' expertise.

But isn't privatization the fashion? Don't governments throughout Latin America rush to outdo one another in turning over public industries to corporations? Privatization by the bureaucracy implies that business interests are calling the tune. Yes, but which business interests? Those of Mexico's middling entrepreneurs or those of professionals working for big corporations? The corporate giants play first fiddle in the economy. Are the corporations really run by capitalists? Aren't they run by an elite of professionals sharing common interests with those in the ruling PRI—by bureaupreneurs instead of entrepreneurs?

WAGES OUTSTRIP PROFITS

Now we turn to the statistical "shit." The *Estadísticas históricas de México*, published by the National Institute of Statistics, Geography, and Information in 1999, contains the data for understanding the Mexican economic formation and for answering the burning question Who gets what, how, when?

Our source uses the old category of wage earners. It is as old as Karl Marx. In his time, factories were small. In 1868 the largest factory in England had only 300 workers and was co-owned by Marx's sidekick Friedrich Engels. In Manchester, he handled accounts of the textile mill as a partner of Erman and Engels. A few clerks and foremen helped him, and to these simple managers Engels paid wages. In the category of the "proletariat" Marx combined both kinds of wage earners: the mass of sweating manual workers and the tiny group of professional managers.

Armed with this category of proletarian wage earners, we return to the closing decades of the 20th century, in order to find out who sits on the economic throne. We start with the old category of wage earners but will soon go beyond it. First, we need to know something about these proletarians' wages; we need information concerning the wage-profit ratio.

By "wages" we mean current wages, deferred wages, and transfers of all kinds—all this under the heading of employee compensation. By "profit" we mean investment income: capitalist profits, stock dividends, bond interest, and rent from real estate—the income of both owner-managers and absentee capitalists who do nothing but clip coupons and live off rents.

If wages and profits are equal, the wage-profit ratio is 100 percent—wages and profits are at parity. If the ratio is more than parity, then wage earners collectively get more than the capitalists; but if the ratio is less than parity, the social strata receiving capital income will be on top.

Our statistical guide is volume 1 of *Mexico's Historical Statistics*, and the ammunition is found in tables 5.16.1–5.16.5.[31]

1963. President Adolfo López Mateos, the eloquent populist who fascinated macho Mexico with his romantic exploits from 1958 to 1964, neared the end of his term in 1963 after an affair with the 18-year-old beauty queen of Monterrey. In that year this most popular President since Cárdenas presided over a wage-profit ratio that stood at 170 percent.

1968. President Gustavo Díaz Ordaz had a face like Frankenstein, and his policy of repressing dissent was even uglier. This *Presidente* was right of center, and he was responsible in 1968 for the terrible massacre of the students at Tlatelolco. In that year the wage-profit ratio slumped to 130 percent.

1977. President Luis Echeverría was left of center. He continually quoted Lázaro Cárdenas in his populist speeches and spouted even more nationalist rhetoric, although he hardly matched the great agrarianist in his actions. In 1977 the wage-profit ratio zoomed to a record-breaking 300 percent.

1983. President De la Madrid had no political experience; his work had been in banking and government finance. He was an admirer of 19th-century liberalism, and he privatized industries, pulverized wages, and forgot the nationalist rhetoric. In Los Pinos—the Mexican "White House"—he spent the afternoons bending his elbow. Under this rightist in 1983 the ratio fell to 240 percent.

1994. President Carlos Salinas de Gortari was a man of the "left" who turned so far to the right that he fell off the PRI's tightrope suspended between rich and poor. If Díaz Ordaz had governed like a lion, Salinas was a fox. His careful selection of information for the public was a model of opinion manipulation. The neoliberal Salinas privatized hundreds more of the state enterprises in order to please business interests, but what a surprise: the ratio recovered by rising to 270 percent in 1994.

Mexico's wage earners were almost as well off under the neoliberal Salinas as they were under the left-leaning Echeverría. Under Salinas they were far better off than they were in 1963 under the handsome populist López Mateos, an agrarianist who gave out much land to the new peasants thrown up by the population explosion.

Under the corrupt Salinas the public sector was disappearing in the fires of privatization, yet wage earners were still slurping up the bulk of the national income. But which wage earners? Surely not the desperate workers in fields and factories.

Marx's proletariat of wage earners is called the "working class." But is it really one class? After more than a century of socioeconomic evolution, we see that wage earners divide into two classes with clashing interests: the exploited proletariat paid less than the average wage, and an exploiting salariat of professional employees sitting in privileged offices with desks (or bureaus, which makes them bureaucrats).

So the pregnant question is not, Do wage earners munch more of the surplus than the capitalists? The deciding question is whether those who devour the most belong to this new class of bureaucrats.

If capital income tops what professionals collectively pocket as employee compensation, then the Mexican economy must still be capitalist. But if bureaucrats gulp down more of the surplus than the capitalists, then the evolving economy has crossed the threshold to a postcapitalist order. We are going to argue that it crossed that threshold in the 1970s.

PROFESSIONALS TAKE THE LION'S SHARE

What remains is to find out the size of the bureaucratic surplus, its slice of the wage pie. The *Historical Statistics* can guide us down the road toward an answer.[32]

From 1950 to 1958 the percentage of households with less than the average income remained steady at 80 percent, but from 1963 to 1983 it leveled off at 70 percent. The long-range tendency has been for the percentage to fall. So we may reasonably infer that after 1983, it either continued at the same level or fell even lower. For lack of other data we take the most conservative estimate and assume that it remained at roughly the same level until 1994. In brief, the percentage of households with less than the average income was 70 percent.[33]

What interests us next are the privileged wage earners, those getting more than the average household income. How does the bureaucratic rip-off, professionals snapping up surplus wages, compare with capitalist exploitation? We begin our journey in the early 1960s.

1963. Mexico was entering a turbulent decade with ever more student protest marches. In April 1961, at the entrance to the Zócalo, some first tasted tear gas. But while they made news, what was happening in the invisible social structure? How were wages distributed? The professional share of household income stood at 36.7 percent. Since capital income was 35.6 percent of household income, the professional surplus barely led the field by 1.1 percentage points.[34] The threshold had been crossed, but would the new order that had crept in unnoticed be able to hang on?

1968. This was the year of the student revolts in Paris, in Beijing, in New York, in Belgrade, and in Mexico City. In the Mexican capital the student movement issued in the Tlatelolco massacre. In that fateful year the professional share of household income fell to 32 percent. Although the share of capital income fell to 33.5 percent of household income, it was again ahead— but only by 1.5 percentage points.[35]

1977. In Mexico in the 1970s, the student movement had taken to armed struggle. But while these storm clouds in the political sky made headlines, the real revolution was occurring unnoticed in the depths of the economic structure. The professional share of household income had soared to 42 percent, leaving capitalists trailing behind with a meager 23.4 percent.[36] Echeverría's policy of beefing up the public sector had loosened the economic hold of people of property.

1983. In Mexico the revolutionary left had gone underground in the form of the People's Union: Claudestine Worker Revolutionary Party (PROCUP). The professional share had fallen to 30.8 percent of household income, while profits remained steady at 23.6 percent.[37]

1994. In this year the Zapatista guerrillas seized the central highland towns of Chiapas. Inspired by their example, the underground PROCUP surfaced in several states as the Revolutionary Popular Army. The professional share remained roughly steady at 29.6 percent, while profits collapsed to 17.7 percent.[38]

To sum up: from 1968 to 1994 the professional-bureaucratic share of household income, buffeted by the winds of historical change, did not consolidate its advantage over capital income until 1977, roughly a decade after the comparable consolidation of postcapitalist society in the United States.[39]

In its compilations the *Historical Statistics* introduced a new category in 1983, a column showing nonmonetary income.[40] Nonmonetary income is a hangover from the hacienda system that endured for centuries with company stores paying Mexicans in kind. Payment in kind became institutionalized in the cultural system and escalated during the 1980s and 1990s. Examples from 2000: factories often pay part of their wages in shoes or shirts, farmers pass out to their laborers bags of corn, peasants give sacks of tomatoes to helpers building a fence, the government bestows free beans upon poor people, the state gives bureaucrats gasoline allowances, universities hand out to professors chits redeemable for books, businesses give their office workers food stamps redeemable in supermarkets (such food chits are nontaxable income). Top government figures and corporation managers have free limousines.

In 1983 nonmonetary income was a whopping 18 percent, and in 1994 a staggering 25 percent of household income. As a general category it is impossible to tell how much of it helps to supplement ordinary wages and how much is siphoned off by professionals. But one thing is sure: it is not readily available to capitalists.

That means that our comparative figures for professional and capitalist shares of household income in 1983 and 1994 need to be revised upward for the class of professionals. Instead of 7 percentage points ahead of capital income in 1983 and 12 percentage points in 1994, they were probably closer to the 19 percentage points in 1977—before the category of nonmonetary income was introduced.[41]

These observations are consistent with our conclusion. In the 1970s Mexico passed through an economic revolution, the professional-bureaucratic completion of the bureaucratic political revolution of the 1920s.

IMPERIALIST PERESTROIKA

How does U.S. imperialism—the main enemy targeted by the revolutionary nationalist current in Mexico—fit into this picture? Mexico City's grim Churubusco Convent houses the Museum of the

Interventions, where schoolchildren wander among cannons, maps, martyrs, photographs, flags, and lists of the 270 military attacks suffered since Independence. In 1848 Mexico lost almost half its territory to the United States, and in 1862 France invaded to seize the rest. Years of guerrilla warfare finally forced the Foreign Legion to withdraw.

On the heels of French dynastic imperialism followed capitalist imperialism; during the Díaz dictatorship from 1884 to 1910, U.S. business investments in land, mines, railways, oil, and banks outnumbered those of all European powers together. For Mexico, the nationalistic Haya de la Torre saw this monopolistic penetration as the first stage of capitalism. For the northern giants, Lenin saw this imperialist penetration as the highest stage of capitalism.[42] Mexico is so rich in natural resources that everyone has come to loot it: few countries have suffered so many blows from foreign powers.

True, 19th-century imperialism had rooted up weeds of feudalism and kicked along modernization, but imperialism was a vampire letting the blood of the underclasses and sucking up value. The Revolution of 1910–1940 throttled the vampire by seizing properties and canceling oil rights of the hated gringos. Mexican patriots wanted more than political sovereignty; their Revolution also aimed at economic independence.

In the decades after World War II the nationalizing thrust weakened and imperialism returned. But was it the same imperialism? No. It was neither the first stage of capitalism in Mexico nor the highest stage in the United States. The monster had assumed a new form: as the age of brainpower dawned in the Knowledge Society, the neoliberal economic policies peaking in NAFTA meant for both recolonized Mexico and U.S. imperialism a postcapitalist order.

Today, the multinationals are again playing a progressive role. Instead of eroding semifeudal institutions and propping up local business, they are subverting domestic capitalism and strengthening the grip of corporate bureaucrats over local governments. Imperialism is no longer decidedly capitalist; it is the herald of a new bureaucratic mode of production. With help from State bureaucrats, the multinationals are slowly forcing this mode on the underdeveloped countries. Until recently, the only version of this new bureaucratic mode of production was the "real socialism" of the Eastern bloc.

The multinationals are not an exclusively nor even a dominantly bourgeois penetration of the Mexican economy. Economic imperialism degrades many Mexican middling capitalists to the status of a dependent bourgeoisie—a junior associate of the multinationals. (This sort of dependency is not the same as dependency on foreign capital.) Imperialism takes more out of the Mexican economy than it puts in, but it also contributes to a change of economic and class structure. In brief, the main beneficiaries of the Mexican Revolution are no longer capitalists, but the government of bureaucrats and the millions of Mexico's professionals in league with the corporate bureaucracies of the multinationals.

The Mexican left is lost in a labyrinth of 19th-centry theoretical concepts. A new thread of Ariadne can lead it into the 21st century to analyze the emerging bureaucratic society and to find strategies for improving the lot of the underclasses. In the march of history, throughout Latin America micro enterprises and small capitalist businesses are falling by the wayside. There are hundreds of thousands of these minnows swimming in the sea of competition, and they disappear in the wake of the multinational whales.

In Mexico's evolution toward a new economic order, imperialism changed from a reactionary to a revolutionary force. This astonishing metamorphosis needs explanation.

First, after the final spurt of nationalizations under Presidents Echeverría and López Portillo, U.S.-trained presidents applied neoliberal policies that ruined tens of thousands of small and middling Mexican capitalists: much of the national bourgeoisie could not compete with the invading multinational giants. That caused a big drop in capital income for Mexicans—the profit column in Mexico's statistics on national income tells the tearful tale.

Next, the high-tech companies that cornered Mexico's national bourgeoisie needed so much professional and technical expertise that the aggregate salaries of their Mexican employees ballooned. The graduates of the Monterrey Technological Institute's many branches no longer had to take jobs in the United States: daughter companies of U.S.-based multinationals offered them positions in their native land. Not only did these multinational affiliates pay better salaries; they often paid higher wages for manual workers than native-owned business. Along with the relative decline of capital income there was a relative increase in both wages and professional salaries.

Finally, Marxist political economists mislead us in defining the bulk of U.S.-based foreign investment and multinational corporations as capitalist. For professional managers control the corporations, and salaried professional workers reap the bulk of the returns in the form of surplus wages.

Here is the big secret: the surplus siphoned off by professional salaries in Mexico exceeds the part taking the form of capital income. In 1926 John Maynard Keynes pointed out in a pathbreaking article in the

New Republic that giant corporations don't belong to the private sector; they belong to a quasi-public sector that has much in common with state corporations. Noting the "tendency of big enterprise to socialize itself," he added that the "battle of Socialism against individual private profit is being won in detail hour by hour," if not in the form of State socialism, then in the form of the "semi-socialism . . . [of] semi-autonomous corporations."[43] That is where the big salaries abound—in quasi-socialist rather than capitalist enterprises.

Can we really insert the word "socialist" into this description of the emerging society? Marxists have always said that socialism is a matter of nationalization and public ownership of the means of production. But socialism is concerned with class. And we have seen that there is a fourth great class overlooked by Marx and his disciples, the class that rules the roost in Mexico. So it should not surprise us that the socialization of the Mexican economy during the 1980s and 1990s rode up the escalator, even though the nationalized sector fell down the stairs.

The imperialist share of capital income does not figure in Mexico's national income. This means that privatization of the country's public industries into the hands of foreign interests does not alter the shares in the Gross National Product. (Such privatization to foreigners only changes the share in the Gross Domestic Product.)

IMPERIALIST RIP-OFF

Imperialism is Janus-faced. We have examined one of its faces; in what follows we examine the other. To understand how the imperialist rip-off operates, we begin with the basic concepts. As defined in the *Statistical Abstract of the United States*, published yearly by the Bureau of the Census, the Gross Domestic Product is the "total output of goods and services produced by labor and property located in the United States, valued at market prices." We can also define it as a sum of expenditures: personal consumption, private investment, government compensation, state investment, and net exports of goods in relation to imports.[44]

The definition is tricky, because so much of the economy is related to the world economy. Governments borrow money abroad to invest in their economy or to pay bills, but this money has a price: yearly interest payments. Companies import materials for production, export goods and services, borrow money abroad, invest overseas, transfer technology, repatriate profits, move factories offshore and home again, pay taxes now here and now there. In the United States one out of six giant corporations has a foreigner sitting on its board of directors. A hotshot MBA speaks English, Spanish, and French.

How much of production is really national? How much is foreign? The Gross National Product (GNP) is the difference between the Gross Domestic Product (GDP) and the net returns from income transfers to and from the rest of the world. This means that the GNP may be more or it may be less than the GDP.

The GNP/GDP ratio is a measure of economic imperialism. If it is more than parity—over 100 percent—we have a country that takes more than it gives. To be sure, it is not a so-called favorable balance of trade in physical goods, services and other invisibles that constitute the crucial variable in defining economic imperialism; it is the favorable balance of income from private and corporate investments (interest, dividends, etc.) and of a government's foreign credits relative to debt and debt interest. When a country has a positive balance in these payments, it may be considered imperialist.

In 1950 the economies of Japan, Germany, and Russia were in ruins, while the United States was intact. From 1950 to 1955 the ratio of returning income to investment outflow was over 200 percent for the United States. While the American people thought of Uncle Sam as a kindly old gentleman caring for humanity, the rest of the world saw him as an imperialist monster.

Between 1955 and 1960 the ratio fell from 253 percent to 139 percent. It rebounded to 162 percent in 1963, but in the long run it kept on falling. Some three decades later the U.S. ratio was only a bit more than parity.[45]

Where does Mexico rank in the international rip-offs? As a sample we take the first year of the legal existence of NAFTA. In 1994 Japan topped the heap of imperial powers with a GNP/GDP ratio of 178 percent, followed by Switzerland with an enviable ratio of 160 percent. Germany, France, Italy, and the United Kingdom also exceeded parity, but at much lower levels. Countries in southern Europe performed below parity and were therefore economically colonized. Portugal's GNP was 71 percent of its GDP; Greece's was 66 percent. At the bottom of the heap was Turkey with a 40 percent ratio.[46]

Next to Turkey, Mexico puffed along with a GNP/GDP ratio of 54 percent. Its GNP was barely $363 billion, while its GDP stood at $673 billion.

In 1995 Mexico plummeted below Turkey, landing in last place. Mexico's GNP tumbled to $237 billion, and its GDP rose to $698 billion. Its GNP/GDP ratio hit a low of 34 percent. Mexico had broken all records in its race to the bottom.[47]

(Although South Korea's GDP was below Mexico's, the Asian tiger still outperformed the tropical republic. Korea's GDP fell short of Mexico's by $133 billion, but its GNP of $425 billion topped Mexico's by $188 billion. So its overall performance was better.)

With a 34 percent ratio, Mexico neared the end of the 20th century as it had entered it—a prey of imperialist looters. During the 1990s its leaders once more handed their country to the northern powerhouse for pillage and plunder. In 1990, before NAFTA appeared on the horizon, Mexico's GNP/GDP ratio stood at 66 percent, but by 1995 was only half as much.[48]

The first big downturn happened in 1993—the year of Salinas's triumphant ratification of NAFTA—when the ratio collapsed to 55 percent. Mexico soon became the nation with the highest amount of foreign investment among the developing countries.

Europe's Organization for Economic Cooperation and Development signed up Mexico as a member of the club of rich countries, and Salinas chortled that the nation had joined the First World. But the riches have yet to reach millions of peasants in villages connected only by burro trains or to help marginalized hordes in urban misery or to feed the children of starving workers or to relieve small capitalists with homes threatened by bank foreclosures.

The *Estadísticas históricas de México* is not the only reliable source for understanding the transformation of the Mexican economy. The annually updated *Anuario económico de los Estados Unidos Mexicanos* provides more data about Mexico's rank. Income transfers received from and paid to the rest of the world tell a revealing story. In 1988 net losses amounted to some 5 billion pesos; the losses peaked in 1994 at more than 98 billion. Although they dropped to around 10 billion in 1995, they began climbing upward again to more than 13 billion in 1996.[49] And they have continued to climb.

U.S. bureaucratic imperialism bites deeper into its victim with loans. In the late 1980s only Brazil and India had a larger public debt than Mexico. From 1990 to 1994 Mexico ranked first in debt service payments. In 1994 the unhappy land coughed up $11.7 billion of interest.[50] Today the public sector, the Banco de México, private enterprise, and commercial banks have a net external debt of $146 billion—the highest per capita debt on earth.

On September 1, 1999, Mexicans turned on the televised State of the Union message (*Informe*). President Zedillo, tense and rigid, read the message and was his usual boring self. Disgusted Mexicans quickly turned off their sets and went for a drink, only to find that the government had cleverly closed the bars and liquor stores for the day. Next day economists rummaged through the dry statistics annexed to the presidential *Informe* and found something that sent them racing for their PCs. Their discovery made headlines: in the decade of the 1990s payments of debt amortization and interest leaving the country amounted to $445 billion. (The calculation made before year's end is the official one.) In the neoliberal decade the northern giant had sucked out almost half a trillion megabucks!

The Secretariat of the Economy and the Banco de México have published figures showing that between 1989 and 1999, for every dollar of direct foreign investment entering Mexico, five dollars of external debt amortization left the country—and those dollars did not include the payment of debt interest.

According to the UN Economic Commission on Latin America, in the 1990s the money Mexico scrounged up to amortize its external debt (not counting interest payments) was 55 percent of Latin America's total external debt of $700 billion. The U. S. company store lashes all its Latin American peons, but Mexico has the bloodiest back.

Although these payments slashed into the national income, there are no data showing that they held back the increasing ratio of professional salaries to capital income in the GNP. The growing victimization of Mexico by foreign interests reveals that the economy is dependent. But it is not capitalist dependency; Mexico has passed beyond capitalism.

Imperialist perestroika has dragged it forward, a restructuring that has whittled away Mexican capitalism under conditions of bureaucratic dependency on the new global economy. In the world economy, brainpower drives the knowledge societies; the United States, Japan, and Germany have led the global system into the Information Age.

MEXICO'S POSTCAPITALIST SOCIETY

Our data indicate that during the 1970s Mexico crossed the threshold to a new postcapitalist economic order. Almost all economies are mixed. The only way to classify them is to find the basic ingredient in each. So to describe Mexico as a mainly feudal economy before the Revolution of 1910 is not to deny its capitalist component; and to describe the capitalist order that arose in the 1930s is not to deny its quasi-feudal residues. In describing the economic order since the 1970s as postcapitalist, we recognize hangovers of capitalism in the system.

Mexico has been privileged to join the United States, Britain, France, Germany, and Japan in the new world order of postcapitalist societies.[51] The former Soviet Union was the first to achieve this status, followed by the countries of Eastern Europe, North Korea, China,

Vietnam, Cuba, Guinea-Bissau, Angola, and Mozambique. The Cold War was a struggle between capitalism and socialism, between propertied interests and the new professional-bureaucratic class. The major Western powers were also at loggerheads with the major Eastern powers over political and ideological differences. But the major Western powers ended up in the same camp economically as they, too, crossed the threshold to postcapitalist society. The struggle between capitalism and socialism has become a dead issue. Even the former countries of the Soviet bloc and China have succumbed to neoliberal ideology.

With the Cold War over, the diversity among postcapitalist societies is increasingly taken for granted. The old disputes have faded into history, but new struggles are emerging over the benefits of professionalism. In some countries, such as the United States, there has been a dramatic rise in living standards for the elites but the underclasses have yet to catch up. Other countries, like Russia after the demise of the Soviet Union, have gone into reverse gear and are experiencing a decline in living standards for most of the people. With the arrival of neoliberalism this has also happened to Mexico.

The only common denominator of the professional societies is the dominance of the New Class and "the decline of the industrial working class, the backbone of the traditional class struggle."[52] But there is growing resistance to the new order from those victimized by neoliberal policies.

What happened to the Mexican Revolution's proletarian current, the workers and peasants struggling for social justice? That current still swirls about among the indigenous tribes in the southern state of Chiapas, led by their Zapatista Army of National Liberation, and among the indigenous peoples of Oaxaca and Guerrero, led by their Revolutionary Popular Army. But not in Mexico, or in any other country, is an exploited proletariat the vanguard of a new world order. A republic of experts is the reality; a republic of equals, the dream. Yet no one can stop people from dreaming.

The signing of NAFTA provoked a resurgence of guerrilla warfare in Mexico. So in 1994 the Mexican government began importing armored vehicles and crowd-control weapons from the United States. The neoliberal regime also bought cut-rate Russian war materiel to use against the guerrillas. In September 1996 the Revolutionary Popular Army unleashed a wave of violence; in Acapulco there were bomb threats against U.S. businesses by unknown radical elements. President Zedillo answered these attacks by boosting the army's troop strength 15 percent, at a cost of $2 billion. During the economic downturn that was a lot of money spent on repression. In the same period U.S. military sales to Mexico increased sixfold; Washington even handed Zedillo 50,000 free carbines.[53]

Neoliberal policies deepened Mexico's problem of growing unemployment, and crime waves swept the country. Mexican troops began replacing civilian police in enforcing law and order. New bodies of armed men appeared, such as the Preventive Federal Police, dressed in boots and black uniforms. There are 50,000 armed men in this paramilitary force; their roadblocks and checkpoints dot the nation. As Mexicans drive about the Republic, they nervously eye the new "Gestapo." The prison system also expanded, imitating the state-of-the-art federal prisons in the United States, the nation with the highest proportion of prisoners to population on earth—a first for neoliberal America, model for the world!

Counterinsurgency and the war against crime are expensive. Neoliberals tell us that their policies are cost-effective, but the price of domestic peace is rising, and on balance may make neoliberalism cost-defective. In 1999 the forces of repression cost the nation 12 percent of its GDP.[54] Most of the taxes pressed out of the middle social layers are spent on repression.

As society becomes more unequal, as unemployment and marginalization mount in Mexico and health standards deteriorate, the social costs of caring for the criminal, the uprooted, the homeless, and the sick may finally force the government to abandon its neoliberal ideology. The growing greed of professionals for an ever bigger slice of the economic pie and its surplus may boomerang. That is why a few of the enlightened elements of the professional class are warning against neoliberalism.

The neoliberal conception of free trade as a global panacea may be short-lived. The economic savings it brings are already undercut by the social costs; in the long run neoliberal policy could be too expensive to maintain. Progressive today, it may become reactionary tomorrow. Meanwhile, this policy is destabilizing Mexican society. The neoliberal wizards, with their Internet and computers commanding the genies of military authority and police power, have conjured up demons out of control.

Notes

CHAPTER 1

1. Quoted in James D. Cockcroft, *Neighbors in Turmoil: Latin America* (New York: Harper & Row, 1989), 76.

2. Michael C. Meyer and William L. Sherman, *The Course of Mexican History* (New York: Oxford University Press,1987), 211. Strictly speaking, Cortez did not conquer "Mexico" but Middle America, for Mexico came into being only later. But we follow Meyer and Sherman and common usage in referring to "Mexico" for the sake of clarity.

3. The underclasses in Europe were not in school either, but Spanish colonial law prevented Indians and mestizos from studying to be lawyers, doctors, or teachers. Andrés Lira and Luis Muro, "El siglo de integración," in *Historia general de México*, vol. 2 (Mexico City: Secretaría de Educación Pública, 1981), 163.

4. Manuel López Gallo, *Economía y política en la historia de México*, 3rd rev. ed. (Mexico City: El Caballito, 1988), 46.

5. Díaz controlled the country directly or indirectly during this period. For a short time (1880–1884) he had puppet Manuel González in the presidency.

6. Hans Jürgen Harrer, *Die Revolution in Mexico* (Cologne: Pahl-Rugenstein, 1973), 84, 86, 88.

7. John Kenneth Turner, *México bárbaro* (Mexico City: Costa Amic, 1974), 96, 99. This is the traditional view of the figures. "Over one-half of all rural Mexicans lived and worked on the haciendas by 1910," say Meyer and Sherman in *The Course of Mexican History*, 458. But the number of peons ac-

tually trapped by debts was less. Also there were perhaps 2 million share-croppers. For a more detailed discussion of the difficulties in calculating the figures, see the discussion in Friedrich Katz, *La servidumbre agraria en México en la época porfiriana* (Mexico City: Era, 1976), 33–42.

8. Villa, born in 1878, was a bandit from 1894 to 1910. Because there are few documents and many legends about his early years, this period of his life is controversial. For the interpretation of him as a Robin Hood, see Friedrich Katz, *Pancho Villa*, vol. 1, trans. Paloma Villegas (Mexico City: Era, 1998), 21–22.

9. Turner, *México bárbaro*, 96, 99.

10. Ibid., 27; Harrer, *Die Revolution in Mexico*, 90.

11. Meyer and Sherman, *The Course of Mexican History*, 458.

12. Harrer, *Die Revolution in Mexico*, 57, 61.

13. American historians such as Ramón Eduardo Ruíz, *The Great Rebellion: Mexico 1905–1924* (New York: Norton, 1980), and James D. Cockcroft, *Intellectual Precursors of the Mexican Revolution* (Austin: University of Texas Press, 1968); Argentines such as Adolfo Gilly, *La revolución interrumpida* (Mexico City: Ediciones Era: 1994); and Mexicans such as Sergio de la Peña, *La formación del capitalismo en México* (Mexico City: Siglo XXI, 1982) argue that Mexico was capitalist during the Porfiriato and that the most frightful social explosion the Western Hemisphere has ever seen (1910–1940) was nothing but a failed rebellion against the bourgeoisie. Have these Marxist writers understood Marx? In his chapter on labor power in volume 1 of *Capital*, Marx says that a necessary condition for capitalist production is the presence of wage laborers who are free to work for wages, and in a note he remarks that the Mexican peon was not free (and of course scrip from a company store is hardly a wage). See Karl Marx, *Das Kapital: Kritik der politischen Ökonomie*, vol. 1, in *Marx-Engels Werke*, vol. 23 (Berlin: Dietz, 1965), 181, 182, 184. There is a tendency among Marxists to interpret Juárez's *Reforma* as a bourgeois liberal revolution because of its liberal ideology, and the Porfiriato as capitalist. But the *Reforma* was a war of the liberal fraction of the landowning class to expropriate the property of the clerical fraction of the same class, not a social revolution involving the transfer of economic power from one class to another. See the fundamental study of the *Reforma* by Francisco López Cámara, *La estructura económica y social de México en la época de la Reforma* (Mexico City: Siglo XXI, 1967). "Not until 1834 was a competitive labor market established in England; hence, industrial capitalism as a social system cannot be said to have existed before that date," writes Karl Polanyi in *The Great Transformation* (Boston: Beacon, 1960 [1944], 83. Mexico was at least 100 years behind England's development. In his two-page chapter 22 in *Wirtschaftsgeschichte: Abriss der universalen Sozial- und Wirtschaftsgeschichte* (Berlin: Duncker and Humboldt, 1981), Max Weber gives a brilliant exposition of "The Meaning of Capitalism" that also excludes its dominance during the Porfiriato.

14. Karl Marx, one of the great students of social revolutions, claimed that this was true for all the important revolutions down to his time. Karl Marx, *Die Revolution in China und in Europa*, in *Marx-Engels Werke*, vol. 9, 101.

15. Quoted in Donald Hodges and Ross Gandy, *Mexico 1910–1976: Reform or Revolution?* (London: Zed Press, 1979), 10.

16. Doroteo Arango took the pseudonym Francisco Villa, but we refer to him as he is known to world history in song and story, as Pancho Villa.

17. Quoted in Meyer and Sherman, *The Course of Mexican History*, 502.

18. Friedrich Engels, letter to Karl Marx of September 26, 1851, in *Marx-Engels Werke*, vol. 27, 353.

19. Alan Knight, *The Mexican Revolution*, vol. 1 (London: Cambridge University Press, 1986), 218.

20. Harrer, *Die Revolution in Mexico*, 69.

21. John Womack, *Emiliano Zapata et la révolution mexicaine*, tr. Fredéric Illouz (Paris: Maspero, 1976), 123.

22. Ibid., 181.

23. Ibid., 185.

24. Meyer and Sherman, *The Course of Mexican History*, 520.

25. Friedrich Engels, *Revolution und Konterrevolution in Deutschland*, in *Marx-Engels Werke*, vol. 8, 36.

26. Díaz called his rubber-stamp Senate "the herd of tame horses." Lesley Byrd Simpson, *Many Mexicos* (Berkeley: University of California Press, 1952), 263.

27. John Reed, *Insurgent Mexico* (New York: International Publishers, 1969), 211.

28. Turner, *México bárbaro*, 269.

29. Womack, *Emiliano Zapata et la révolution mexicaine*, 218.

30. Karl Marx, *Der achtzente Brumaire des Louis Bonaparte*, in *Marx-Engels Werke*, vol. 8, 115.

31. Meyer and Sherman, *The Course of Mexican History*, 542.

32. Corinthians 9:22.

33. "Aristocracies do not endure. For whatever reasons, it is undeniable that at the end of a certain time they disappear," writes the historical sociologist Vilfredo Pareto. Aristocratic elites finally become decadent: "Revolutions happen either because of the clogging of the circulation (renewal) of the select class or for some other reason there accumulate in the upper strata decadent elements that no longer have the instincts capable of maintaining them in power." In revolutions, idealists peel off the decadent upper strata to join ambitious rebels in the middle strata who mobilize the masses against the aristocratic elite: "Generally, in revolutions the individuals of the lower strata are captained by individuals of the upper strata, because in the upper layers are found the intellectual qualities for directing the battle, while they lack the instincts that are supplied by the individuals of the lower ones." The instincts supplied by the lower ones are resentment and the courage to fight and die for the revolution. Vilfredo Pareto, *Trattato di sociologia generale* (Florence: Barbera, 1916), 2053, 2057, 2058.

34. "In the twentieth century a new era opened. Marxist movements encountered revolutionary peasants in Russia and China, peasants that craved

land. These peasants backed proletarian revolutions. . . . Marxist-Leninists have found that under the guidance of a communist party even an illiterate peasantry can bring off a revolution." D. Ross Gandy, *Marx and History* (Austin: University of Texas Press, 1979), 164, 165. Marxists are aware that military elites can also lead revolutions, as in Turkey (1918) and Ethiopia (1974), or religious elites, as in Iran (1979). But they look to workers and peasants to do the fighting and dying. Marxists have failed to understand Weber's prophecy that the 20th century would not see the dictatorship of the proletariat but rather *die Diktatur der Bürokratie.*

35. Chalmers Johnson, *Revolution and the Social System* (Stanford, Calif.: Hoover Institution on War, Revolution and Peace, 1964), 10.

CHAPTER 2

1. Karl Polanyi, *The Great Transformation* (Boston: Beacon, 1960 [1944]), 247, 251.

2. Edwin Lieuwin, *Arms and Politics in Latin America* (New York: Praeger, 1960), 110.

3. H.B. Parkes, *A History of Mexico* (Boston: Houghton Mifflin, 1960), 382.

4. Michael C. Meyer and William L. Sherman, *The Course of Mexican History* (New York: Oxford University Press, 1987), 639.

5. Quoted in Ralph Roeder, *Juarez and His Mexico* (New York: Viking, 1947), 584.

6. No priest can refuse the sacraments to any Catholic who asks for them. To do so is against canon law and makes a mockery of Catholic theology.

7. Anatoli Shulgovski, *México en la encrucijada de su historia*, tr. Armando Martínez Verdugo (Mexico City: Cultura Popular, 1972), 94.

8. Hans-Rudolf Horn, *Mexico: Revolution und Verfassung* (Hamburg: Übersee Verlag, 1969), 58.

9. Ricardo J. Zevada, *Calles el presidente* (Mexico City: Nuestro Tiempo, 1971), 99.

10. Jean Meyer, *La Cristiada* (Mexico City: Siglo XXI, 1973), 182, 209, 255–257.

11. Jorge Basurto, *Cárdenas y el poder sindical* (Mexico City: Era, 1983), 27, 42.

12. Quoted in Shulgovski, *México en la encrucijada de su historia*, 86.

13. Frank Tannenbaum, *Mexico: The Struggle for Peace and Bread* (New York: Knopf, 1950), 146–147.

14. Frank Brandenburg, *The Making of Modern Mexico* (Englewood Cliffs, N.J.: Prentice-Hall, 1964), 22.

15. John of Salisbury, *Policraticus*, in *The Great Political Theories*, ed. Michael Curtis (New York: Avon, 1961), 161–163. John warns that if the tax collector in the body's stomach takes too much, the intestines become clogged and there is a sickening constipation.

16. Meyer and Sherman, *The Course of Mexican History*, 583.

17. T.R. Fehrenbach, *Fire and Blood: A History of Mexico* (New York: Bonanza, 1985), 567.

18. Jorge Basurto, *El proletariado industrial en México (1850–1830)* (Mexico City: Universidad Nacional Autónoma de México, 1975), 248.

19. See Zevada, *Calles el presidente*, 153; and Vicente Lombardo Toledano, *La libertad sindical en México, 1926* (Mexico City: UOM, 1974), 116–117.

20. Basurto, *El proletariado industrial en México*, 257–258.

21. Daniel Moreno, *Los partidos políticos del México contemporáneo* (Mexico City: Costa Amic, 1979), 115–116. Emphasis added.

22. *Programa de acción del Partido Nacional Revolucionario (January 29, 1929)*, in Moreno, *Los partidos políticos del México contemporáneo*, 397–398. Emphasis added.

23. See Enrique Krauze's video, *Lázaro Cárdenas: Entre el pueblo y el poder* (Mexico City: Editorial Clio, 1998). Krauze is one of Mexico's outstanding historians.

24. Partido de la Revolución Mexicana, *Pacto constitutivo, declaración de principios, programa y estatutos*, quoted in Tsvi Medin, *Ideología y praxis de Lázaro Cárdenas* (Mexico City: Siglo XXI, 1972), 106–107.

25. The classic work is by Robert Michels, *Political Parties: A Sociological Study of the Oligarchical Tendencies of Modern Democracy*, tr. Eden Paul and Cedar Paul (New York: Free Press, 1962 [1915]).

CHAPTER 3

1. Enrique Krauze, *Mexico: Biography of Power*, tr. Hank Heifetz (New York: Harper & Row, 1997), 506.

2. Donald C. Hodges, *Mexican Anarchism After the Revolution* (Austin: University of Texas Press, 1995), 39, 56–57, 66.

3. Krauze, *Mexico: Biography of Power*, 491.

4. Ramón Eduardo Ruiz, *Triumphs and Tragedy: A History of the Mexican People* (New York: Norton, 1992), 426.

5. Michael C. Meyer and William L. Sherman, *The Course of Mexican History* (New York: Oxford University Press, 1987), 644.

6. Mónico Rodríguez, Interview at his workshop in Chiconcuac, Morelos, January 10–11, 1978.

7. Juan de Dios Vargas Sánchez (in collaboration with Donald Clark Hodges), "La resistencia popular en México, 1940–1976" (professional thesis, Universidad Nacional Autónoma de México, 1986), 62. Also see Aurora Loyo Brambilia, *El movimiento magisterial de 1958 en México* (Mexico City: Era, 1979), 52.

8. Niccolo Machiavelli, *The Prince* (New York: Collier, 1910), 61.

9. Meyer and Sherman, *The Course of Mexican History*, 652.

10. Barry Carr, *Marxism and Communism in Twentieth Century Mexico* (Lincoln: University of Nebraska Press, 1992), 230.

11. David Barkin, *Distorted Development: Mexico in the World Economy* (Boulder, Colo.: Westview, 1990), 81.

12. Meyer and Sherman, *The Course of Mexican History*, 655.

13. Speech by Díaz Ordaz to the U.S. Congress on October 27, 1967. Quoted in Roberto Blanco Moheno, *Si Zapata y Villa levantarán la cabeza: Díaz Ordaz, Echeverría, López Portillo* (Mexico City: Bruguera, 1982), 150.

14. Alicia Girón, *Cincuenta años de deuda externa* (Mexico City: Universidad Nacional Autónoma de México, 1991), 51–53, 244.

15. José Agustín, *Tragicomedia mexicana*, vol. 1, 2nd ed. (Mexico City: Editorial Planeta, 1998), 139.

16. José Gil Olmos, "En los 70, casi mil 500 muertos por la guerra sucia en México," *La Jornada*, October 24 and 26, 2000.

17. Bertrand de la Grange, *Marcos, la genial impostura* (Mexico City: Aguilar and Taurus, 1997), 444–447.

18. *La Jornada*, June 18, 1999, 1–4. General Marcelino Barragán, Secretary of National Defense, found out what really happened at Tlatelolco and left the truth in documents entrusted to his children. These have finally been made public. *La Jornada* tells all. There is a more extensive account in Julio Sherer and Carlos Monsivais, *Parte de guerra: Tlatelolco 1968* (Mexico City: Aguilar and Taurus, 1999).

19. Carr, *Marxism and Communism in Twentieth Century Mexico*, 256.

20. Interview with Enrique González Pedrero, quoted in *Como México no hay dos*, ed. Gerardo Dávila and Manlio Tirado (Mexico City: Nuestro Tiempo, 1971), 131, 132, 134.

21. Krauze, *Mexico: Biography of Power*, 741.

22. Carr, *Marxism and Communism in Twentieth Century Mexico*, 270–271.

23. Girón, *Cincuenta años de deuda externa*, 244.

24. Héctor Aguilar Camín and Lorenzo Meyer, *A la sombra de la revolución mexicana* (Mexico City: Cal y Arena, 1989), 243.

25. Agustín, *Tragicomedia mexicana*, vol. 2, 2nd ed., 171.

26. Manuel Pastor, Jr., "Globalization, Sovereignty, and Policy Choice: Lessons from the Mexico Peso Crisis," in *States and Sovereignty in the Global Economy*, ed. David A. Smith, Dorothy J. Salinger, and Steven C. Topik (New York: Routledge, 1999), 217.

27. Meyer and Sherman, *The Course of Mexican History*, 697.

28. Ibid., 680.

29. Girón, *Cincuenta años de deuda externa*, 244

30. Nora Lustig, *Mexico: the Remaking of an Economy* (Washington, D.C.: The Brookings Institution, 1991), 20–21.

31. Ibid., 24–25.

32. Pastor, "Globalization, Sovereignty, and Policy Choice," 217.

33. Miguel Basañez, *El pulso de los sexenios: 29 años de crisis en México* (Mexico City: Siglo XXI, 1990), 76–80.

34. Arturo Ortiz Wagdymar, *Política económica de México 1982–1995: Los sexenios neoliberales* (Mexico City: Nuestro Tiempo, 1995), 43–48.

35. Quoted by Luis Javier Garrido in "La Revolución mexicana: Sólo una memoria," *Proceso* no. 1255 (November 19, 2000): 67.

36. José López Portillo, "Con De la Madrid me equivoqué," *¡Siempre!* no. 2475 (November 23, 2000): 9.

CHAPTER 4

1. Nora Lustig, *Mexico: The Remaking of an Economy* (Washington, D.C.: Brookings Institutions, 1991), 25.

2. Ibid., 61.

3. Manuel Pastor, Jr., "Globalization, Sovereignty, and Policy Choice," in *States and Sovereignty in the Global Economy*, David A. Smith, Dorothy J. Salinger, and Steven C. Topik (New York: Routledge, 1999), 217; and Arturo Guillén, Eugenia Correa, and Gregorio Vidal, *La deuda eterna: Grillete de la nación* (Mexico City: Nuestro Tiempo, 1989), 65.

4. James D. Cockcroft, *Neighbors in Turmoil* (New York: Harper & Row, 1989), 97–98.

5. Arturo Ortiz Wadgymar, *Política económica de México 1982–1995* (Mexico City: Neustro Tiempo, 1995), 64–66.

6. Robert J. Alexander, "The Import Substitution Strategy of Economic Development," in *Latin America's Economic Development: Institutionalist and Structuralist Perspectives*, ed. James Dietz and James Street, (Boulder, Colo.: Lynne Rienner, 1987), 120–122, 125–126.

7. Dieter Boris, *Mexico im Umbruch: Modellfall einer gescheiterten Entwicklungsstrategie* (Darmstadt: Wissenschaftliche Buch Gesellschaft, 1996), 66.

8. Ortiz Wagdymar, *Política económica de México 1982–1995*, 72.

9. Alicia Girón, *Cincuenta años de deuda externa* (Mexico City: UNAM, 1991), 114–115.

10. Jorge Castañeda and Robert Pastor, *Límites de la amistad* (Mexico City: Joaquín Mortiz, 1989), 295.

11. Article 123 declares: "Every person has a right to dignified and socially useful work; so that jobs and the social organization of work will be promoted . . . the general minimum wages should be sufficient to satisfy the normal needs of a family head, in the cultural, social and material order." *Constitución política de los Estados Unidos Mexicanos* (Mexico City: Mexicanos Unidos, 1999), 133–134.

12. "There is no doubt about the fraud, it has been well documented many times," says Lorenzo Meyer, one of Mexico's leading historians, in a video, *EPR, retorno a las armas* (Mexico City: Canal 6 de Julio, 1996).

13. Scott Sherman, "Mexican Elections," *FEED* Internet magazine, July 7, 2000, p. 1 (http://www.feedmagazine.com).

14. *Constitución política de los Estados Unidos Mexicanos*, Articles 25, 26, 27, 28, 123, and 129.

15. Pastor, "Globalization, Sovereignty, and Policy Choice," 212–213.

16. Jorge Castañeda, *La casa por la ventana* (Mexico City: Cal y Arena, 1993), 245–246.

17. Boris, *Mexico im Umbruch*, 66–67; and Michael Tangeman, *Mexico at the*

Crossroads: Politics, the Church and the Poor (Maryknoll, N.Y.: Orbis Books, 1995), 76.

18. Ortiz Wagdymar, *Política económica de México 1982–1995*, 154–156.

19. Economic growth was 3.5 percent in 1989, 4.3 percent in 1990, 3.9 percent in 1991, 2.8 percent in 1992. Pastor, "Globalization, Sovereignty, and Policy Choice," 217.

20. Philip L. Russell, *Mexico Under Salinas* (Austin, Tex.: Mexico Resource Center, 1994), 196.

21. Tom Barry, *Mexico: A Country Guide* (Albuquerque, N.M.: Interhemispheric Education Resource Center, 1992), 72–74.

22. Michael Voslensky, *La nomenklatura: Los privilegiados en la U.R.S.S.*, 2nd ed., tr. Mario Morales (Barcelona: Argos Vergara, 1981), 17–26; and Pablo Gómez, *Los gastos secretos del presidente* (Mexico City: Grijalbo, 1996).

23. Demetri Sodi de la Tijera, "Enriquecimiento inexplicable," *La Jornada* (Mexico City), April 28, 1995.

24. Alianza Cívica, "Aumentan en dos años 328 porciento el ingreso del presidente," *La Jornada*, June 12, 1996.

25. Julio Boltvinik, "Vivir fuera del presupuesto," *La Jornada*, December 12, 1997.

26. José Ureña, "Clase Política," *La Jornada*, Mexico City, July 21, 1996.

27. Miguel Badillo, "Sobornó a Carlos Salinas de Gortari el cartel de Cali," *La Jornada*, June 8, 1998.

28. "Recibe Raúl Salinas narcodinero, Suiza," *Reforma* (Mexico City), July 17, 1998.

29. "Desplazan los narcos mexicanos y colombianos a los asiáticos de Estados Unidos," *La Jornada*, June 3, 1998.

30. Peter H. Smith, "Drug Trafficking in Mexico," in *Coming Together? Mexico–U.S. Relations*, eds. Barry Bosworth and Nora Lustig (Washington, D.C.: Brookings Institution, 1997), 128, 129, 137.

31. Marcos Kaplan, "Vive Latinoamérica una expansión de las narco-economías," *La Jornada*, March 6, 1998.

32. The 38 businessmen who make up the national private enterprises elite of elites "control 70 industrial, commercial, financial and service groups that operate in Mexico with a decisive incidence on the economic and political plane." Carlos Fernández Vega, "Concentración y poder. La élite del empresariado mexicano (primera parte)," *Perfil de la jornada* (Mexico City), April 1, 1991.

33. See, for example, Conchello's article "Nova pax americana," in *El Financiero* (Mexico City), August 21, 1996, in which he attacks the United States as an imperialist country. Recently a trailer truck ran over Conchello's Volkswagen Beatle and the driver vanished, a standard way of eliminating conservative populists. Elimination of threats within the strategic ally were done discreetly, whereas PRD militants were gunned down openly.

34. Philip Russell, *Supplement to Mexico Under Salinas* (Austin, Tex.: Mexico Resource Center, 1995), 57.

35. "Inflation fell from the aforementioned level of 159.2 percent in 1988 to 7.1 percent in 1994. . . . The use of the exchange rate as an anchor led to an increasingly overvalued peso." Pastor, "Globalization, Sovereignty, and Policy Choice," 212.

36. Michael Veseth, *Selling Globalization: The Myth of the Global Economy* (Boulder, Colo.: Lynne Rienner, 1998), 76–80; and Russell, *Supplement to Mexico Under Salinas*, 44.

37. David Márquez Ayala, "Indicadores macroeconómicos," *La Jornada*, July 17, 2000. In the first trimester of 1994 imports were valued at 21.6 percent of GDP, whereas exports were only 17 percent of GDP. The trade deficit was draining Mexico of its money and had to be corrected by a devaluation that would make imports expensive again.

38. Russell, *Supplement to Mexico Under Salinas*, p. 44.

39. Ibid., 59.

40. Roberto González Amador, "25 millones en el subempleo," *La Jornada*, July 12, 1996.

41. Roberto González Amador, "Han salido 445,000,000,000 de dólares en 10 años para pagar deuda externa," *La Jornada*, September 5, 1999.

42. León Bendesky, "Crecimiento económico," *La Jornada*, December 18, 2000.

43. Márquez Ayala in "Indicadores macroeconómicos" tells us that in the first trimester of 2000 the exports were 33.4 percent of GDP while imports were 34.3 percent.

44. Leonel Corona Treviño, "Introducción," in *Pequeña y mediana empresa: Del diagnóstico a las políticas*, ed. Leonel Corona Treviño (Mexico City: Universidad Nacional Autónoma de México, 1997), 8.

45. Juan Castaings Teillery, "Política industrial y equilibrio externo," in *Economía y democracia: Una propuesta alternativa*, ed. Ifigenia Martínez (Mexico City: Grijalbo, 1995), 309–312.

46. Antonio Maza Pereda, "Reflexión sobre las causas de mortandad de la micro y pequeña empresa," in Corona Treviño, *Pequeña y mediana empresa*, 85–113.

47. How do you determine the dominant form of production in an economic system? Max Weber: "If we imagine this form of production taken away the whole economic system must collapse." *General Economic History*, tr. Frank Knight (New York: Collier, 1961 [1920]), 207. Marx identifies the mode of production in which the bulk of the economic surplus is produced as defining the economic system. Karl Marx, *Capital* (Moscow: Foreign Languages Publishing House, 1961), vol. I, 217; vol. 3, 772, 855.

48. Jesús Silva Herzog, "La Revolución mexicana es ya un hecho histórico," in *¿Ha muerto la Revolución Mexicana?*, 2nd ed., ed. Stanley R. Ross (Mexico City: Premia, 1978), 117–119.

49. Daniel Cosío Villegas, "La Revolución mexicana, entonces y ahora," in Ross, *¿Ha muerto la Revolución mexicana?*,125, 130–133.

50. John Mason Hart, *Revolutionary Mexico: The Coming and Process of the*

Mexican Revolution (Berkeley: University of California Press, 1987), 18; and Gary Gereffi and Peter Evans, "Transnational Corporations, Dependent Development, and State Policy in the Semiperiphery," in Dietz and Street, *Latin America's Economic Development*, 171–175.

51. Leon Trotsky, *The Revolution Betrayed*, tr. Max Eastman (New York: Merit, 1960 [1937]), 234–256.

CHAPTER 5

1. Bill Weinberg, *Homage to Chiapas: The New Indigenous Struggles in Mexico* (London: Verso, 2000), 63, 64, 87,

2. Jorge Salaverry, "O Chávez o Hayek," *Diario Las Américas* (Miami), December 1, 2000, 6A; and Weinberg, *Homage to Chiapas*, 190, 191.

3. Weinberg, *Homage to Chiapas*, 161, 162, 385.

4. Subcomandante Marcos, "Communiqué of January 20, 1994," in *Shadows of Tender Fury: The Letters and Communiqués of Subcomandante Marcos and the Zapatista Army of National Liberation*, tr. Frank Bardacke, Leslie López, and the Watsonville, California, Human Rights Committee (New York: Monthly Review Press, 1995), 85.

5. Frank Bardacke, "Dear SUP, Much Obliged: An Afterword," in *Shadows of Tender Fury*, 36, 259.

6. Mikhail Bakunin, "The International and Karl Marx," in *Bakunin on Anarchy*, ed. and tr. Sam Dolgoff (New York: Knopf, 1972), 294.

7. Ibid., 318, 319.

8. Karl Marx, "The Protectionists, the Free Traders and the Working Class," in Karl Marx and Friedrich Engels, *Collected Works*, 46 vols. (New York: International Publishers, 1975–1992), vol. 6, 280.

9. "Speech of Dr. Marx on Protection, Free Trade, and the Working Classes," appended to Friedrich Engels, "The Free Trade Congress at Brussels" (September 1847), in *Collected Works*, vol. 6, 290.

10. Karl Marx, "Speech on the Question of Free Trade," in *Collected Works*, vol. 6, 465.

11. In Adolf Berle and Gardiner Means's sample year of 1929, ownership control of the 200 largest nonfinancial corporations was barely 55 percent. Starting with their data, Larner's research shows that by 1963 ownership control had slipped to 16.5 percent, while management's share had mushroomed to 83.5 percent. In his study of income and stock ownership of 94 top executives in large industrial corporations in 1962–1963, Larner estimates that the median value of dividends from management-owned stock in the employing corporation was $23,605, compared to the median value of salary and bonuses of $158,221. Robert J. Larner, *Management Control and the Large Corporation* (New York: Dunellen, 1970).

12. James Burnham, *The Managerial Revolution* (New York: John Day, 1941).

13. See the arguments for a bureaucratic class in Donald Hodges, *The Bureaucratization of Socialism* (Amherst: University of Massachusetts Press, 1981).

14. Salvador Carmona Amorós, *La economía mexicana y el nacionalismo revolucionario* (Mexico City: El Caballito, 1974), 14–15, 107–114, 126–136.

15. See, for example, Alonso Aguilar and Jorge Carrión, *La burguesía, la oligarquía, y el estado* (Mexico City: Nuestro Tiempo, 1972), 107–108, 170–172, 181–182.

16. Fernando Carmona, "Estado y capitalismo en México," in *El Estado Mexicano,* ed. Jorge Alonzo (Mexico City: Nueva Imagen, 1982), 35, 41.

17. See the interpretation of Ceceña's data by Pablo González Casanova, *La democracia en México* (Mexico City: Era, 1967), 52–54.

18. Ibid., 53.

19. David Barkin, "Mexico's Albatross: The United States Economy," *Latin American Perspectives* 2, no. 2 (Summer 1975): table III.

20. *México 1982: Anuario económico* (Mexico City: Somos, 1982), 201, table 4.

21. Ibid., 213, table 14.

22. Luis Pazos, *La estatización de la banca* (Mexico City: Diana, 1982), 69–70.

23. *México 1982: Anuario económico,* 176, 197.

24. Pablo González Casanova, *La democracia en México,* (Mexico City: Era, 1964), 53, 160–162.

25. Pazos, *La estatización de la banca,* 62.

26. Ibid., 87.

27. Donald Clark Hodges, *Class Politics in the Information Age* (Champaign: University of Illinois Press, 2000), 5, 187.

28. Roderic A. Camp, *Intellectuals and the State in Twentieth-Century Mexico* (Austin: University of Texas Press, 1985), 140.

29. Thomas Carlyle, quoted by Robert Heilbroner in his *The Worldly Philosophers,* 6th ed. (New York: Simon and Schuster, 1986), 78.

30. From the Introduction to G. W. F. Hegel's *The Philosophy of History,* tr. Carl J. Friedrich, in *The Philosophy of Hegel* (New York: Random House, 1954), 16–17.

31. *Estadísticas históricas de México,* 4th ed., vol. 1 (Mexico City: Instituto Nacional de Estadística, Geografía e Informática, 1999), tables 5.16.1—5.16.5.

32. In Mexican statistical abstracts, as in those in the United States, the professional share of employee compensation and the corresponding share of the surplus can be determined only with considerable difficulty. Profits, dividends, interest, and rent—the surplus in excess of capital costs of income from mere ownership—are exposed for everyone to see. What is not evident is the professional surplus over and above the costs of education prorated and recovered over the life span of professional careers. Our job is to unravel, first, the professional salaries concealed under the heading of total wages; and second, the corresponding share of the total surplus. To do so, we rely on the auxiliary assumptions used in calculating the professional surplus in the United States. We assume, first, that the annual wage surplus consists of total employee compensation in excess of the costs of subsistence plus the costs of professional education prorated annually over a lifetime of professional

work; second, that professional salaries represent a minimum of 60 percent of the total wage surplus, a conservative estimate that leaves 40 percent to ordinary workers earning more than the minimum wage. See Donald C. Hodges, *America's New Economic Order* (Aldershot, U.K.: Avebury, 1996), 53–58, 66–67.

33. *Estadísticas históricas de México*, Table 5.13. In estimating comparative shares of the surplus, we assume that professional income from expertise and capital income from ownership show up in the statistical tables as average and above-average household incomes.

34. Ibid., table 5.16.1

35. Ibid., table 5.16.2

36. Ibid., table 5.16.4

37. Ibid., table 5.16.5 (*primera parte*).

38. Ibid., table 5.16.5 (*conclusión*).

39. Hodges, *America's New Economic Order*, 59, 67.

40. *Estadísticas históricas de México*, table 5.16.5 (*conclusión*).

41. If capitalists are treated like everybody else by including their costs of subsistence as a deduction from their surplus, then the annual professional shares of the economic surplus will be comparatively larger, and Mexico will have crossed the threshold to postcapitalist society several years earlier than the foregoing figures would suggest.

42. Victor Raúl Haya de la Torre, *El antimperialismo y el APRA*, 2nd ed. (Santiago de Chile: Ercilla, 1936); and V. I. Lenin, *Imperialism: The Highest State of Capitalism* (New York: International Publishers, 1938).

43. John Maynard Keynes, "Laissez-Faire and Communism," in *Great Political Thinkers: Plato to the Present*, 4th. ed. (Fort Worth, Tex.: Holt, Rinehart and Winston, 1979), 680.

44. *Statistical Abstract of the United States: 1996* (Washington, D.C.: U.S. Bureau of the Census, 1996), 439–440; tables 685, 688, 691.

45. The figures are from Paul A. Baran and Paul Sweezy, *Monopoly Capital: An Essay on the American Economic and Social Order* (New York: Monthly Review Press, 1966), Table 2; and *Statistical Abstract of the United States: 1996*, table 691.

46. *Statistical Abstract of the United States: 1996*, tables 1334–1335.

47. Ibid.

48. *Statistical Abstract of the United States: 1998* (Washington, D.C.: U.S. Bureau of the Census, 1998), tables 1354–1355.

49. *Anuario estadístico de los Estados Unidos Mexicanos: 1997* (Mexico City: Instituto Nacional de Estadística, Geografía e Informática, 1998), table 10.2

50. *Statistical Abstract of the United States: 1996*, table 1373.

51. That the United States has been joined by Britain, France, Germany, and Japan at the core of a global professional society is the thesis of Harold Perkin's *The Third Revolution: Professional Elites in the Modern World* (London: Routledge, 1996), 6–27. For a critical discussion of the principal theories of postcapitalist society, see Hodges, *Class Politics in the Information Age*, 20–54, 123–151.

52. Perkin, *The Third Revolution*, 179.

53. Weinberg, *Homage to Chiapas*, 283, 353, 358.

54. David Zúñiga, "La inseguridad cuesta al país 12 porciento del producto interno bruto," *La Jornada* (Mexico City), January 18, 2001.

Selected Bibliography

Aguilar Camin, Hector, and Lorenzo Meyer. *A la sombra de la Revolución mexicana*. Mexico City: Cal y Arena, 1989.

Agustín, José. *Tragicomedia mexicana: La vida en México 1940–1994*. 3 vols., 2nd ed. Mexico City: Editorial Planeta, 1998.

Brandenburg, Frank. *The Making of Modern Mexico*. Englewood Cliffs, N.J.: Prentice-Hall, 1964.

Cárdenas, Lázaro. *Ideario político*. Ed. Leonel Durán. Mexico City: Ediciones Era, 1996.

Cline, Howard F. *Mexico: Revolution to Evolution, 1940 to 1960*. London: Oxford University Press, 1962.

Cockcroft, James. *Mexico's Hope: An Encounter with Politics and History*. New York: Monthly Review Press, 1998.

Córdova, Arnaldo. *La ideología de la Revolución mexicana: La formación del nuevo régimen*. Mexico City: Ediciones Era, 1973; 21st ed., 1997.

Gilly, Adolfo. *La revolución interrumpida*. Mexico City: Ediciones Era, 1994.

Hamilton, Nora, and Timothy Harding, eds. *Modern Mexico: State, Economy, and Social Conflict*. Beverly Hills, Calif.: Sage, 1986.

Hammet, Brian. *A Concise History of Mexico*. London: Cambridge University Press, 1999.

Hansen, Roger. *The Politics of Mexican Development*. Baltimore: Johns Hopkins University Press, 1970.

Hart, John Mason. *Revolutionary Mexico: The Coming and Process of the Mexican Revolution*. Berkeley: University of California Press, 1987.

Heath, Jonathan. *Mexico and the Sexenio Curse: Presidential Successions and Economic Crises in Modern Mexico*. Washington, D.C.: CSIS Press, 1999.

Hernández Padilla, Salvador. *El magonismo: Historia de una pasión libertaria 1900–1922*. Mexico City: Ediciones Era, 1984.

Hodges, Donald C. *Mexican Anarchism After the Revolution*. Austin: University of Texas Press, 1995.

Hodges, Donald C., and Ross Gandy. *Mexico 1910–1982: Reform or Revolution?* 2nd ed. London: Zed, 1983.

Joseph, Gilbert M., ed. *Everyday Forms of State Formation: Revolution and the Negotiation of Rule in Modern Mexico*. Durham, N.C.: Duke University Press, 1994.

Kirkwood, Burton. *The History of Mexico*. Westport, Conn.: Greenwood, 2000.

Knight, Alan. *The Mexican Revolution*. 2 vols. London: Cambridge University Press, 1986.

Krauze, Enrique. *Biografía del poder: Caudillos de la Revolución mexicana (1910–1940)*. Mexico City: Tusquets Editores, 1997.

———. *La presidencia imperial: Ascenso y caída del sistema político mexicano (1940–1996)*. Mexico City: Tusquets Editores, 1997.

Lerner de Sheinbaum, Bertha, and Susana Ralsky de Cimet. *El poder de los presidentes: Alcances y perspectivas (1910–1973)*. Mexico City: Instituto Mexicano de Estudios Políticos, 1976.

Lieuwin, Edwin. *Arms and Politics in Latin America*. New York: Praeger, 1960.

López Gallo, Manuel. *Economía y política en la historia de México*. Mexico City: Grijalbo, 1967.

———. *La violencia en la historia de México*. Mexico City: Ediciones El Caballito, 1976.

Meyer, Michael C., and William L. Sherman. *The Course of Mexican History*. New York: Oxford University Press, 1987.

Ramírez Jacome, Gilberto, and Emilia Salim Cabrera. *La clase política mexicana*. Mexico City: EDAMEX, 1987.

Reed, John. *Insurgent Mexico*. New York: International Publishers, 1969.

Silva Herzog, Jesús. *Breve historia de la Revolución mexicana*. 2 vols. Mexico City: Fondo de Cultura Económica, 1995.

Tannenbaum, Frank. *Mexico: The Struggle for Peace and Bread*. New York: Knopf, 1950.

Terrazas, Silvestre. *El verdadero Pancho Villa*. Mexico City: Ediciones Era, 1985.

Turner, John Kenneth. *Barbarous Mexico*. Austin: University of Texas Press, 1969.

Valadés, José C. *Historia general de la Revolución mexicana*. 10 vols. Mexico City: Secretaría de Educación Pública, 1985.

Weinberg, Bill. *Homage to Chiapas: The New Indigenous Struggles in Mexico*. London: Verso, 2000.

Womack, John. *Zapata and the Mexican Revolution*. New York: Knopf, 1969.

Index

About the Authors

DONALD C. HODGES is a professor of philosophy and an affiliate professor of political science at Florida State University. The founder of *Social Theory and Practice,* he has served on the editorial boards of *Philosophy & Phenomenological Research* and *Latin American Perspectives* among others. He is the author of more than a dozen books on revolutions and revolutionary movements in Latin America, five of which have been translated into Spanish and published in Mexico.

ROSS GANDY is a professional philosopher and historian who has lived and taught in Mexico since 1970. During the 1970s he taught political philosophy at Ivan Illich's Centro de Documentacion Cultural (CIDOC) and, since 1981, has been professor of history and political science at Mexico's National University (UNAM).